GOD
and Sarah Pedlock

GOD
and Sarah Pedlock

BY
Stephen Longstreet

David McKay Company, Inc.

NEW YORK

Library of Congress Cataloging in Publication Data

Longstreet, Stephen, 1907–
    God and Sarah Pedlock.

    I. Title.
PZ3.L8662Gk [PS3523.0486]   813'.5'4   75-37714
ISBN 0-679-50482-6

TO

Dr. Morris Steinman
and
Henrietta Steinman

Whose views on the subject matter of this story,
and whose friendship of long standing, have sustained the research of this novel

Many daughters have done virtuously,
but thou excellest them all . . .

PROVERBS, XXXI, 29

THE PEDLOCK FAMILY

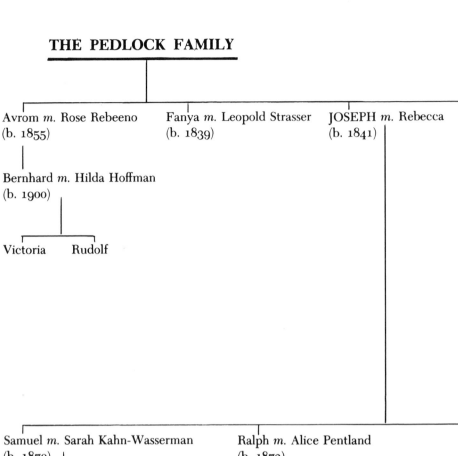

Avrom *m.* Rose Rebeeno
(b. 1855)

Fanya *m.* Leopold Strasser
(b. 1839)

JOSEPH *m.* Rebecca
(b. 1841)

Bernhard *m.* Hilda Hoffman
(b. 1900)

Victoria   Rudolf

Samuel *m.* Sarah Kahn-Wasserman
(b. 1870)

Ralph *m.* Alice Pentland
(b. 1873)

Albert
(b. 1891)

Morris
(b. 1892)
m. Alice
  Pearson

Harry
(b. 1893)

Nicole Perry
(b. 1905)

Peter Perry *m.* Lucy Gates
(b. 1907)

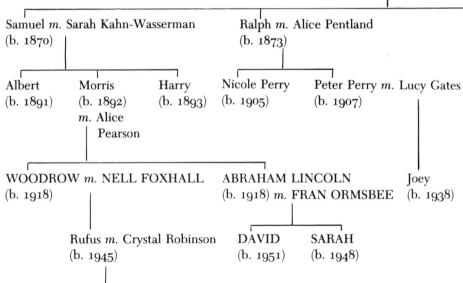

WOODROW *m.* NELL FOXHALL
(b. 1918)

ABRAHAM LINCOLN
(b. 1918) *m.* FRAN ORMSBEE

Joey
(b. 1938)

Rufus *m.* Crystal Robinson
(b. 1945)

DAVID
(b. 1951)

SARAH
(b. 1948)

Richard

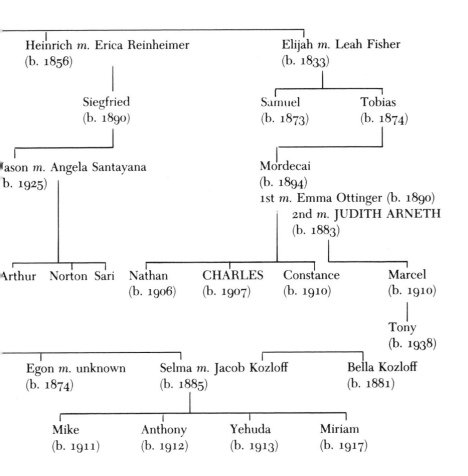

Heinrich *m.* Erica Reinheimer
(b. 1856)

Siegfried
(b. 1890)

ason *m.* Angela Santayana
b. 1925)

Arthur   Norton   Sari

Elijah *m.* Leah Fisher
(b. 1833)

Samuel   Tobias
(b. 1873)   (b. 1874)

Mordecai
(b. 1894)
1st *m.* Emma Ottinger (b. 1890)
2nd *m.* JUDITH ARNETH
(b. 1883)

Nathan   CHARLES   Constance   Marcel
(b. 1906)   (b. 1907)   (b. 1910)   (b. 1910)

Tony
(b. 1938)

Egon *m.* unknown   Selma *m.* Jacob Kozloff   Bella Kozloff
(b. 1874)   (b. 1885)   (b. 1881)

Mike   Anthony   Yehuda   Miriam
(b. 1911)   (b. 1912)   (b. 1913)   (b. 1917)

NAMES IN *CAPS* ARE
PEDLOCKS IN *GOD AND SARAH PEDLOCK*

BOOK ONE

The Girl

*In a world where the real never touches the ideal we act out
our times. We have no alternatives. The only pure love is the
eating of fruit.*

JACOB ELLENBOGEN
Waiting for the Messiah

.

CHAPTER

1

First you are very small and the color is old-rose and pink, and you are kept very warm. Sometimes you are wet, which amuses them. Later you are taken out in the English pram and people stop to poke their giant heads up under the hood and cry out, "What a beautiful baby. Whose big green eyes are those?" When you learn to put one foot in front of the other and stand uneasy as the room rolls, and don't fall plump down, people say, "What a charming little girl." And Daddy was warned against saying, "Goddamn sonofabitch," and "half-assed no good bastard" within ear range of her and baby brother, David.

That was what being Dedee Pedlock meant in Hawleytown on the Eastern Shore of Maryland. There was Daddy and there was Mamma, and David two years younger, with a wet thumb. And the big fat blackness of Tessie, who sometimes fed you greasy lamb stew and applesauce with the big kitchen spoon. Tessie had this music in her throat that came out thick and sometimes laughing. How marvelous, they said, when you were housebroken.

The room was dark when you slept, just a small night light behind a shade with a picture of Bambi on it. The yard, people didn't call it a garden on that street where the Pedlocks lived, was very green and rather unkempt, for Daddy was busy at the courthouse and Tessie's nephew, the handyman, was lazy; showed her and David there were toads in the old ash pit from the days all the fireplaces in the old house were in use, and there were hickory and oak chunks around for burning.

Aunt Kate smelled wonderfully good when she came in to kiss you goodnight, all dressed up, bare-armed and a spread of fine naked Ormsbee shoulders showing, going to the country club dance or Kinglet Roadhouse, or to the Barracloughs' fancy shindig across the neck of water, the lights all blazing up at the big white mansion, and the green and red pin-points of jeweled colors on the boat landing. The men Aunt Kate knew were important enough to be invited to the Barracloughs'. And Aunt Kate was, as Tessie put it, "No hure—jest a free-livin' girl."

Hawleytown was a good place to grow up in and Daddy was one of the assistant district attorneys, and sometimes there was a murder case good enough, so juicy, that even the *New York Times* sent down a reporter. But mostly it was cases of land conflict and barn burning, fishing rights and simple assault and battery. Women with black eyes, and men who had threatened somebody with a 12-gauge shotgun. Tessie attended the Christ Victorious Church, colored. Tessie said God knew all and punished. "He don't show favors—it's, 'Sinner, I point the finger at *you.*' "

When Dedee, she had been named Sarah, but everyone called her Dedee as a child—when she walked home past the courthouse from some birthday party for Jody Smith, or Nancy Wilkins or Bobbie Beninstock, there would be a half-dozen men with red faces, unshaven usually, in washed-out buttercup-colored denims lettered P—cutting grass and raking leaves in Court House Square by the cement Civil War soldier. Aunt Kate said they were prisoners because of "woman trouble, Dedee, short-term lawbreakers, drunks sobering up and working out their keep." Dedee would dream of the prisoners and wonder if

God had forgotten them. But then God was busy. There was the God in the Baptist, Lutheran and the Episcopalian (our) church. God was all gold and red with smoking incense and varnished jello-colored wounds in St. Mary's. Where people sometimes had ash on their foreheads and sometimes muttered "Black Protestant" if they were Irish from the kelp-collecting plant. And the Jews. Oh dear, the Jews. Their God Dedee knew from in the third grade, for Miss Sheaffer—penmanship and art—had this big brown picture on the wall of God floating on his long white beard and some clouds, all held up by what looked like ladies of the PTA, only Miss Sheaffer said they were angels and Michelangelo had made the picture. Dedee for some time wondered if Mr. Angelo had floated close while painting the picture, and seen God touch with a finger the naked man on the ground, with his thing showing. A thing like David had in the bath. A dingle, Tessie called it.

The Jews bothered Dedee. You see, Daddy's mother was a Pearson, and they were hell-fire preacher folk from way back, Deep Dip Baptist once. Mamma's people were Ormsbees, but Mamma was a Pedlock now. It was said to be a Jewish name, P–E–D–L–O–C–K, and that made Dedee think of percentages of Jewishness—like how much chocolate in a nut bar. In the sixth grade she had tried to get order—do it all out in pencil; Daddy was maybe part Jewish. As for the Ormsbees, all blond, and even bigots, Daddy said—that only made it more complex, so Dedee let it slide.

There were Pedlocks up north, certainly important people even if Daddy might, or might not, be related to them. There was the famous Fifth Avenue store PEDLOCK & SONS. EST. 1853. Even the matrons of Hawleytown when they got that far up among the Yankees in New York visited PEDLOCK & SONS. In some of the history books on American industry, there was mention of the great discoveries in the West of gold, silver and copper. A short paragraph was printed about Joseph Pedlock, who made the great Butte, Montana, copper discoveries, and invented the Pedlock Process for purifying the molten metal by blowing air under pressure through it. But Aunt Kate said, "Your father is mum on the subject. No relative as far as we know."

"Was he Jewish, Joseph Pedlock?"

Aunt Kate made some funny remark that she hadn't *looked*. Mamma had said, "Now, Kate, keep your bawdy ideas to yourself—little pitchers . . . Dedee, go play in the yard."

All Dedee knew was that little pitchers had big ears. It was a common expression used when the ladies had their bridge parties in the afternoon and some child wandered in. But how this matter of a pitcher's big ears applied to the Pedlocks, she couldn't guess.

She had met one of the Pedlocks from up north when she was seven, Judith Pedlock came to visit and stay a weekend with the Barracloughs, one whole weekend. It was old Mrs. Barraclough's birthday. This marvelous large Pedlock woman came over to Hawleytown in the Barraclough Rolls Royce. She had pink-gold hair, and dressed in very shiny pale-blue silk. Had come to have tea with Mamma and Aunt Kate.

"I was wondering, Pedlock isn't a common name, and they said up at the mansion, did I know you? And so I phoned, and here I am having tea."

"It's not a common name here, either," said Aunt Kate. "What a marvelous brooch, Mrs. Pedlock."

"Judith, not Mrs. P. just now. Yes, it's an original. Brancusi made it for me."

Mamma said, "My husband, Linc, is the only Pedlock on the Eastern Shore. His brother, Woodrow, lives in San Francisco. I think they have a son. That is all we know."

Daddy came home and was introduced and Judith said, "The Pedlock cheekbones—a Hungarian, or citizen of Vienna, in the woodpile someplace."

Daddy said, "Oh, hell—who knows," and watched Judith sip her tea. He asked for a martini, which Aunt Kate made, and Judith said, "Mix enough." Dedee was impressed by the size and the laughter of their guest, and Judith smiled at her and ruffled Dedee's hair so carefully dampened and curled by Tessie.

"What do you do to amuse yourself?"

Dedee said, "I don't. I practice."

"Piano," said Aunt Kate, starting on her second martini. "She plays very well."

Daddy sipped, relaxed. "Maybe she'll be a honky-tonk ivory tickler."

Mamma said, "Really, Linc. Dedee, you'll play the Chopin thing for Mrs.—Aunt Judith?"

"No."

"Good for you," said the large lady. "Damn if I wanted to recite or do a dance step when asked . . . A very natural child. If she ever needs a really great piano teacher, call me. Must roll—wonderful meeting you all. I'll keep in touch."

And she was gone, leaving a sharp scent of some heady perfume and an impression of a brisk way with words, a laugh deep in a plump throat. Best of all, she hadn't patted the top of Dedee's head as most visitors did on departing, and usually adding, "What a beautiful child."

Daddy whistled and said, "I like the old broad."

Aunt Kate finished off the martinis. "They say she's been a real high kicker in her youth, several L–O–V–E–R–S. Oh, a real high-stepping gal."

Daddy said, "I hope the Barracloughs don't start inviting us over to kiss their toes."

Dedee could spell better than most at her age, and L–O–V–E–R–S didn't puzzle her. There were bird lovers, and dog lovers and people in movies at the *Cameo* who held each other close and nibbled on each other's noses: That was being L–O–V–E–R–S too. Pretty silly and unsanitary, but you often saw such couples—when coming home from dancing school or the public library, some couple locked together in the yew hedges in the river park, or under a bug-luring porch light.

There was so much for a little girl in Hawleytown to do. School and piano practice. Miss Murdoch charged a dollar an hour, and the old Knabe in her parlor needed new felts and tuning. There were also the Brownies, which group of damp little girls Dedee attended for about six months, then some mother made a remark about Yids, and Aunt Kate took Dedee home and out of "the pissy drawers organization." There was a little garden where Dedee grew flowers, her own patch of hollyhocks, pansies and African violets. But nothing like the pictures on the packages came up, and what did, the bugs got. And she and David collected bugs in the cans with kerosene in them.

Most fun was Aunt Kate, who was Mamma's sister, and younger she claimed. Aunt Kate was a divorced woman ("an addled weekend at Yale"), which divorce seemed to cause some people to turn up the corners of their mouths. Aunt Kate was, however, very popular and always going out with charming men in very large cars and later, if she came home at all, Aunt Kate laughed a lot and told Mamma, "Damn it, Fran, it's the twentieth century. A bit of fun, a lot of laughs, a long time dead. A long, long time."

If you didn't stop her, Aunt Kate would sing late at night coming home, and in the morning she'd wake at noon, crying out, "Gawd, Dedee, I'm dying, dying Egypt dying, get me the powder."

Dedee was allowed to mix the powder, to go hissing in the two glasses with water. Aunt Kate would swallow, burp, and pat Dedee's shoulder, "Thank you, little friend. Life is a mixed basket of kittens, isn't it?"

Aunt Kate was lots of fun, unless you caught her pensive and frowning, sitting naked on the bed but for a slip—or alone on the big porch swing—waiting for the phone to ring. Sometimes it didn't ring and Aunt Kate would say, "They're all alike, all alike. Poor kid, you'll find out, we all find out."

"Kate," said Mamma, "spare us your philosophy of life."

Dedee was happy to announce, "The phone is ringing," before Aunt Kate could answer, "Oh, sheet," to her sister.

"Saved by the bell," said Aunt Kate. Mamma explained to Dedee, "Aunt Kate has had a very trying time. Life has not been kind to her."

CHAPTER

2

The summer Aunt Kate went out to California, Dedee missed her. There was this little theater group in San Francisco ("Ibsen, Shaw, Beckett, and Kaufman and Hart") that needed someone to watch the books and box office and talk to the prominent society people who were down as sponsors of the project. Aunt Kate was all excited. "Lord, to get out of all this buttoned-down respectability, and a place where they still call dinner, supper. Vistas opening up, Dedee. Vistas on the world!"

Daddy, as they stood in the Baltimore railroad station, smoked his pipe, smiled; he had had a hard three days in court; double murder on a commercial fishing boat, and a New York lawyer badgering Daddy, which was what Daddy wanted. The local jury could hardly wait to bring in a verdict against the damn Yankee shyster.

Daddy said to Aunt Kate at the train, "Now, Katherine, if things don't work out, wire and we'll send the fare."

"Fat chance . . . Dedee, you grow up fast and you can play the piano for me in the orchestra."

"I'd like that."

Everybody cried and Mamma blew her nose—all cried but Daddy in the Baltimore railroad station. Daddy, he said, as they ate soft-shell crabs in Millers, "I give it three months, Fran." It was in fact six months and Daddy had to send the room rent besides the fare.

Daddy always took a summer place for the family at the tip of the Eastern Shore, past Chincoteague, a shack on the bone-white beach, all the sky full of the palest silky blue and set off by white wheeling sea gulls going *gawk, gawk*—the smear of a black feather of smoke of some sea tramp making north on the Gulf Stream. The gold of dawn lacquered with soft pink . . . color . . . color . . . color . . . Dedee was painting watercolors for the first time. Daddy so big and laughing, and Dedee, she so thin and growing at nine. Mamma on long fine legs, very flushed from running over the white sandy beach and cast-up kelp, and Daddy catching her and they falling down in the sand in their bathing suits. Laughing and kicking. She and David, he at six, laughing and joining the fun, piling on. There was a pit dug on the beach and the hot stones with a covering of seaweed being brushed aside, and finding the lobsters scarlet as British soldiers, the soft-shell crabs hissing steam, the sweet corn . . . Country Gentleman corn, Daddy said—so hot to hold and butter and salt and pepper getting in your nose as you ate with teeth, the permanent set all in . . . chiggers in the blueberry patches, dragonflies over the tidal pools.

Later . . . one night loud voices and Daddy saying if he had a shotgun he'd blow their effen heads off . . . and a voice kind of lazy and even with a bit of laughing in it replying, "Now, now, you all listen here, Jew-boy. This yere beach is across the Virginia line and you don't belong yere . . . We don't want no Nigrahs and no sheenies on our beaches. Now we're just bein' neighborly and bein' it's jest a warnin', why yo' better pick yo'self someplace else to set down for yo'self and them little kikes . . ."

Mamma was crying and yelling on the screened porch, "You sons of bitches, poor white scum!" and Daddy was talking soft to her, "Now, Fran, now, Fran, they're full of cheap booze . . ." and Daddy talking loud, "I've got the sheriff on the phone, so you people better pull tail out of here . . ." Which was a lie as they had no phone in the beach shack . . . and all night she had shivered while David slept solidly, and Daddy had held her and said, "Dedee, Dedee, you don't want Mummy to see you're scared for her . . . darling . . . that's a good girl . . ."

They left the beach the next morning in the old Buick that never really worked well, something wrong in one of the cylinders, and came back to Hawleytown after dusk, the night canopied in a dark heat, crickets and frogs musical in cadence. The world wasn't at all as nice and fine as in the Books of Knowledge.

Nothing was ever the same after that summer. David lost all his baby teeth, and the new piano teacher, Mr. Muckell—$1.50 an hour—said she, Dedee, had a touch like no child he had ever seen.

At the Barraclough Grammar School on Bay Point Street, Miss Grimble taught music.

Sarah—not Dedee on the school lists—played the piano, and Miss Grimble said cheerfully, "Jews are naturally musical, some *special* essence in your people." Dedee was docile, perplexed and worried . . . As if she wore gypsy charms, had lice in her hair like the poor colored and people were nice about it . . . She went around in some incommunicable despair until Daddy got the truth out of her. "Now, Dedee, that's nonsense. Jews are just people who call the same God by another name than other people." Dedee asked, "They chop your thing off, don't they?" *"Thing?* Oh . . . when you're older, darling, we'll go into it." Dedee said, "Jews maybe are naturally musical. But Mamma isn't Jewish. The other Ormsbees go to the church . . ." Daddy jingled coins in a pocket. "Well, Dedee, don't let it bother you . . . Just grow up and play music well, and people will say, 'Dedee Pedlock plays like an angel.'" Only when she was twelve Dedee found all the wonderful old family pictures in the maple desk in the attic where she had gone to read with secret sinful shivers *Three Weeks* by Elinor Glyn. And on the back of grandma and grandpa's picture in blue ink was written *Harold Ornstein and Netta Ornstein—30th Wedding Anniversary*. Not Ormsbee—*Ornstein!* But she didn't ask Daddy or Mamma about *that* . . . It was a shameful thing to be a Jew, that was clear, a social disgrace. And you hid the fact if you could, like having six toes on each foot like Mamie Peris. You acted as if it didn't matter. But it did. Sarah gave up *Three Weeks* and found *The Well of Loneliness* about a girl named Stephen. Very confusing.

Was God a Jew? Her God, was He the big old man with yards of whiskers, living in a cloud and held up by attending pretty angels, and He still went around touching people with a finger to bring them to life? She had seen a picture of God naked with a compass measuring the world in the Art and Freehand Drawing room at the Edgar Allan Poe Junior High School, and William Blake, he wouldn't lie . . . She was playing in the school auditorium mornings at 8:30 for assembly, and going twice a week across Chesapeake Bay to Baltimore for piano lessons at the Beldenheimer Academy of Music . . . Cyrus Beldenheimer taught her himself . . . kept saying, "Ja, ja, keep the left hand from stuttering on the Haydn, and you still play the Rachmaninoff Preludes with too much spirit, ach, not enough care." Please, God, slow the world down . . .

Her fingers flew over the keys and she had this delirious sensation of turning herself inside out. There was nothing like music for giving you that choking feeling under the breastbone.

Actually, what Daddy wasn't too happy about was an invitation to go to Barraclough House. Dedee was thirteen then and the Barracloughs were giving what Aunt Kate called "a goddamn fete" for the yearly appeal for the Eastern Shore Historic Fund; something the Barracloughs had instigated and supported. It was a fund to make charming but dilapidated old houses into historic monuments, to set up bronze markers on salt-tide-marked turf and sand where some battle had been fought—and there were not too many of these sites on the Eastern Shore, so they were cherished. That year there was an old lighthouse at Point Mariner, to preserve a lonely, no longer needed light, to make it into a tourist attraction.

Dedee, listed as *Sarah Pedlock—Pianist* on the program of the trustees' annual meeting of the Historic Fund, would play two pieces for the Trustees; political figures, heads of Foundations, social folk, old family names, some of the best people, and some of the richest. "Not always the same thing," Daddy said; he didn't enjoy joining Mamma and Aunt Kate in escorting Dedee to Barraclough House.

Daddy, of course, had to agree to everything; he was in line for district attorney of Hawley County, now that old Mr. Hightower, the district attorney, the wise old coot, was really talking of stepping down. So, as the Barracloughs had political control of the party, and contributed to election funds, the nod of their heads at the mention of a name to run for public office was like a sure win. All the Pedlocks (but brother David), even Aunt Kate in a too-bold electric-blue dress, were in the big ballroom of Barraclough House, with a hundred people—trustees, officers and their mates—on folding chairs. On the walls were ancestors; what might have been a Copley painting of a forefather, Dedee was sure—and certainly a genuine Sargent of Elizabeth Barraclough when she was young with the century. Now rather old and rather boldly painted, she stood leaning on a gold-headed cane. Wrinkled and shrunken with time, she offered Dedee her hand, a hand surprisingly young and smooth, "My dear child, so good of you to come and play for us. How is your Aunt Judith? . . . Peter! *Peter!*"

A teen-ager in blue jacket, white buttons, yellowish flannel trousers—Dedee judged he was at least seventeen—too thin, neck too long, chin a bit spotted, topped by straw-colored hair, this youth pushed past some servants with trays and came over.

"Yes, Granny."

"This is Sarah Pedlock. She is going to play for us. Arrange the piano stool."

He was rather handsome, Dedee thought, but ungainly like a colt too long in the legs. He seemed to have trouble adjusting the piano stool, spinning it first the wrong way, until she took over.

"You go to school here?" he asked her as she took out her

music from a brown folder. His voice had changed, all but a few notes at the end of the sentence.

"Yes. You go to the Harbor School this side of the inlet?"

"No, worse luck. Prep school mostly."

His fingernails were chewed over, and for a boy he had a very active large Adam's apple. "Piano hard to play? I mean, to play well."

"I don't know. It isn't hard for me. You musical?"

"Heck, no, a stone ear. I write. Yes, I write."

Dedee said she had never met a writer before, and they both laughed.

Someone was striking metal to bring the ballroom to an attentive silence. Amos Barraclough was at Dedee's elbow. He was even older than his sister Elizabeth, a bit on the portly side with a bland face like a clock dial, a wisp of white moustache and not much hair left on top, but what was there was brushed forward.

"How grand of you, Miss Pedlock. My nephew been helping? Good boy, Peter. Helping?" He didn't wait for any answer. He turned to the people on the folding chairs, chairs which were to become uncomfortable. Dedee saw Aunt Kate up front, and Daddy and Mamma off to one side. The old man cleared his throat of what seemed soft pebbles. "We are here to aid in the preserving of our historic past on these shores—yes—and you all know what we are doing— yes—"

"Get on with it, Amos," said his sister.

"Yes, you all know our work. We have arranged some entertainment. To begin, we have this charming child, this dear girl, Sarah Pedlock, who will give us some splendid music." He peered at a card in his hand. "First, Chopin's Waltz in D flat, Opus 64, and a section of Debussy's *Au Clair de Lune* . . ."

The ballroom, French doors open, was filled with a briny summer breeze from the bay.

Dedee calmly seated herself, did not even flex her fingers. She said to the boy, "I'll nod my head—like this—then you turn the page." She was off, head well back, trim, full of grace and poise, perhaps too sure of herself. The old piano, a Steinway, was marvelous; she had not very often played on a concert grand. She was delighted with it and herself. Few noticed several wrong notes—and a misplayed bar. Actually, she played extremely well.

Later, after some ice cream, but refusing the Lady Baltimore cake as too sweet, Peter showed Dedee the old stables converted to a series of garages and patted the side of the yellow and dusty Dusenberg, and the Cunningham roadster—set on blocks, with no wheels. They walked down past the herb garden, and the boxwood hedges, some brush with green berries. They sat on a stone bench facing the sea. Its ripples caught in the afternoon sun were, Dedee thought, like scales of a moving fish. A dredge was busy clearing a channel and some gulls were fighting for tidbits across a mile of water where the cannery was smudging the sky. Peter lit a cigarette and coughed. "I smoke too much." He showed two faintly stained fingers. "I write poetry."

"Do you write a lot?" Dedee asked.

"It seems a lot. When I'm twenty-one, I'm going to publish. I have this trust my mother left me, and I'll have the money." He threw away the hardly smoked cigarette. "A slim volume."

"I read Emily Dickinson," said Dedee. "Well, not too much. 'The wounded deer leaps highest.' Elizabeth Browning, you like her?"

"Old-fashioned, very old hat, passé."

"I don't mind that."

It was not a brilliant conversation, not the kind Dedee expected from a poet. Peter Barraclough seemed given to sudden movements of arms and legs, and always appeared on the verge of saying something important, but never did. He didn't like Barraclough House, he admitted to Dedee as they stood on the beach by the stone boathouse, watching a sunset. He didn't like his Uncle Amos because—Peter didn't finish the reason. His grandmother was all right for an old lady, but she had destroyed his poems last year when she found them, and she said he was going to Harvard Law School, not muck around writing verse.

He was going to tell Dedee more when there was a "Yoohoo" from above in the rose garden, and there were

Aunt Kate, Daddy and Mamma. It was time to get back home. Peter asked if he could come and see her and talk some more "about the poets." Dedee said of course.

Peter Barraclough came across the inlet in a skiff with an outboard motor, came to the dock of the Rodman Construction Pier, at the foot of Cape Street. Dedee answered the bell and he said he was delivering some verse he had written about Dedee at the piano. He looked nearly neat in a brown sweater, blue linen trousers, hair all in disorder. Dedee was polite. They sat on the porch swing and Tessie brought out Coke-and-ice in julep glasses. He didn't ask Dedee to read the verse right there and then. When she remembered them before supper, she found six poems written out on crisp blue paper, with a fountain pen, very neat, and the first one began:

> There is ascending sound,
> The summer air vibrates,
> The ballroom catches
> What dead men
> Set to strings . . .

Very nice, she thought—a bit morbid. She read them all and put them away with letters and menus, a program of a Genêt play Aunt Kate had sent her during her stay in San Francisco.

Peter made many trips across the bay inlet that summer. He would come at least three times a week. They would have Cokes at Marvin's Drug Store on French Street, and after having done the Sea and Shore Museum, and not visited the fish-processing plant, they took to going off in the skiff and the outboard motor to the lonely shores with the armor of dead crabs under their bare feet. They trod on the air pods of tossed-up kelp and found sea life in rock ponds, waiting for the tide. They ate sandwiches which Tessie had wrapped for them in waxed paper, ate seated by the weathered wood and rusting bolts of some long-ago sea wreck. Peter ate as if starved, but remained thin.

He wrote love poems and his chin spots didn't bother her.

He was handsome in a shaggy way, but, yes, too thin. When he spoke of his uncle or his grandmother, he seemed ready to weep and he coughed as he smoked and said they wanted him to become a corporation lawyer. He was very unsure about kissing her, and Dedee didn't as yet have much breast to fondle. He didn't really take liberties the way the high school football jocks did. Dedee felt bold thinking of them as *jocks;* only the fast girls at school said words like that.

It was pleasant to lie on the warm yielding sand, the wind blowing through the vetch grass behind them, and watching distant clam diggers go slowly along, raking away by the rocks where the sea birds nested and had left white markings. Rocks that Peter said reminded him of the backbones of mountains being born, rising wet from the sea.

He said the same thing in a poem he wrote the day before he kissed her desperately—as if in some duty—when they parted, and he said something in French she couldn't make out. She was beginning to hope he might become ardent, even fresh.

Mamma didn't mind Peter taking her about, and Aunt Kate said a Barraclough was no different than any other male. "Just keep your legs crossed, and never go anyplace you can't walk home from."

Dedee was playing better than ever, amazingly well. In the fall she was going to go—Judith Pedlock had arranged payments—three times a week to Baltimore to study with Sandor Andrassy, who at sixteen had been the most talked of young pianist in Europe; at twenty-five he was burned out. At thirty-eight he took in a few pupils while, as Aunt Kate reported, his wife Julie ran a junk-filled store as an antique shop. Under the flat and studio where they lived, and Sandor taught piano in a tasseled smoking jacket of a faded burgundy color.

Peter in August, at eighteen, asked Dedee to marry him, to, as he put it, "save my soul." He didn't add a giggle. Dedee said she was going to be a concert pianist, and she didn't think artists should marry. She had been reading *Jean Christophe* and trying out Proust, fifty pages of *Du Côté de Chez Swann.* Dedee was fifteen, feeling vital, mysterious and pleasantly puzzled by life's patterns. She was very much adult, she assured herself, with a head of mink-colored hair. In the bathroom mirror very much a woman, slim, clear-skinned and with little Greek art breasts. Aunt Kate thought her a beauty, but too slim. "They like a bit of ass, you know. And while you don't need makeup, you just pinch your cheeks a bit, you know, when you really want to impress. A little pink-rose lipstick, give it a try. The lashes are long enough."

Peter began to send flowers, and he gave her a bracelet of old cameos on her fifteenth birthday. They went to a favorite beach with little blue crabs in the pools and grasshoppers in the shore grass. She hoped, as she thought to herself, "he would take me," as earnest young girls were always being taken in novels. She was young and she moved well, it wasn't just the dancing lessons. She was innocent, but was aware of that. She had all the romantic ideas of a bright girl who hadn't very often been away from Hawleytown or the Eastern Shore.

CHAPTER

3

The death of Peter Hastings Barraclough was always to remain an unresolved question in Hawleytown, all along the Eastern Shore and in those parts of Maryland where the Barracloughs were important, or of common interest. The official verdict was not suicide, though it hardly seemed possible that a boy going on eighteen would not know an old engraved Smith and Wesson presentation pistol was loaded: "Given by his comrades in arms to their commander of the 23rd Maryland Infantry, General Murdock B. Barraclough, from his brigade, April 19th, 1965."

If there was any note found by the body in the Barraclough boathouse, the coroner never reported it. The *Hawleytown Home News* announced, "Death by accident of a promising young member of this prominent local family."

What was never public knowledge was that the day before Peter Barraclough died, A. Lincoln Pedlock had come home at noon—raging mad, slamming the front door and facing his wife and daughter hooking a rug on the sun porch.

"That goddamn thief! He's not to be in the house again, *or* to see Dedee!"

"What are you saying, Linc? And such wild language."

"That bracelet he gave her! The bastard stole it from his grandmother. The insurance company sent us a list of Barraclough losses reported stolen. I recognized it."

Dedee asked, "That cameo bracelet?"

"Yes. You give it to me. And he's not to be here ever. Or see you, understand, Dedee? It's not just the stealing. I've just had a report on him."

"He's not happy," said Dedee, thinking of the scene on the lonely beach at Pilot Inlet two days before. She had slipped off her clothes and gone naked into the warm brackish water. Peter had turned his head away and she felt suddenly very tight-muscled, and very much ashamed. Amazing how her legs and belly turned pink with a blush of rejection. Later, when she had dressed, Peter had cried, his head on her lap, and said he was unworthy of respect *and* tainted, and the world was moving in on him and darkness, darkness was all he felt. But he would always love her, he said. She had been the only one who understood him, yes, understood, being herself an artist. She had been frightened, flattered, too—the ache and, yes, the pleasure of being needed.

Now Daddy was facing Mamma so earnestly: "He's been kicked out of two prep schools. And *don't* ask me why. A damn degenerate, and Dedee has been going off with him and we permitted it."

Mamma said firmly, "Linc, calm down. The Barracloughs aren't going to accuse him of stealing."

Dedee didn't say anything. She went up and got the bracelet. Amos Barraclough came himself to the house that evening, after Peter died, to pick it up. Dedee, sent to her room, listened through the old air vent in the wall that once sent up forced heated air from below, before they put in radiators. They must have been drinking—Daddy and Amos Barraclough—for she heard the click of glasses. Amos Barraclough's heavy voice was clear—not at all fuddy-duddy. "Well, Pedlock, it's not, I know, going any further with you, I'm sure of that. There's a freak in every family. We had the boy with this head-shrinking doctor in Boston for six months. Cost a fortune, not that that mattered. That last dirty bit of business at Groton—caught them at it. Maybe just a couple of nasty boys. I hear you've gotten hold of reports. We had hopes he'd change. I'm sure he hasn't harmed the girl. I'll not forget your understanding, Pedlock."

"Damn your understanding, sir. You should have warned us. But of course I'll destroy the reports."

"I understand your outrage, Pedlock. And discretion. Better all round."

It left a shaky feeling in Dedee, clinging in wonder (stomach churning) to a bedpost. All was not right with the world and clearly grown-ups had problems. And covered them up, did things that the young could not fully understand. After that, she was no longer a child, she felt. Aunt Kate called it "an experience." There was whispering at the high school and information—much of it wrong and nasty—passed around. She sensed there was an adult world, if not evil, at least not given to dreams and ideals that the school taught. Dedee, too, felt for the first time there was something fierce that lay in wait for all. As Aunt Kate, who seemed to understand it best, put it, "We all come, Dedee, to the day when the world gives us a swift kick in the pants. Well, yours was not a kick, just a slap."

Aunt Kate was very understanding and comforting. They went up to Washington, just the two of them, to see a musical comedy, and to hear Van Cliburn play Rachmaninoff's Piano Concerto #2. They went to a party at the British Embassy, and Dedee danced with a tall Englishman who had red tufts for a moustache with waxed ends, and was sorry to hear she was only fifteen. "Oh, hard cheese, dear girl." It was a very good weekend and she only thought of poor Peter when waking in the night, throat dry, to get a drink of water.

She told Mamma on her return from Washington, "I'd like to go to the temple on Boat Street. I mean, I want to have religion. Maybe it can explain what happened to Peter."

Mamma and she were canning tomatoes at the time. Mamma said, "We have a religion. We're members of Dr. Ambroise's Episcopalian Church on Rodman Road."

"Oh, that isn't real to me. It isn't—well—I don't know. Real. Maybe I want to be Jewish."

Mamma said, tapping the big spoon on the big pot, "Don't be a damn fool, Dedee. I'm not against Jews. It's just here in Hawleytown there is your father's position to think of, and the men who run politics, and the country club people who decide who gets elected."

"Ornstein," said Dedee, "is a Jewish name, and so is Pedlock."

Mamma put down her ladle and turned off the gas lower under the big bubbling pot full of cooking beef tomatoes. Mamma was smiling that firm smile of hers and brushing back the loose blond lock of hair on her damp forehead. Mamma, when you really figured her out, had a steel core and a solid way of being firm about certain things, when you got her down to the practical level of existence. She wasn't then the soft and admiring creature that met Daddy at the door with a kiss, or the proper matron who didn't like bad language, or acted the Pollyanna, which she wasn't, even if people who didn't know Fran Pedlock thought so.

"Now listen, my girl, and listen closely. Your father can be district attorney, and maybe governor of Maryland some day. Maybe more, who knows? But there are rules—oh, not written out—how you get places. Now about this church business—I don't care if we were fire eaters, Druids, Holy Rollers. But in this community you have to have, carry, the right flags. Understand? It doesn't matter what people gossip about. It's what we line up with. We can't join a Jewish temple, and we can't do anything that will, well . . ."

"Will keep us out of the country club?"

Mamma turned up the gas under the big pot.

"That may now seem snobbery to you, Dedee, and social climbing. You're old enough now to face the fact life isn't 'Black Beauty' and 'Cinderella.' It's the way the world exists, the way families are. Yes, sure I want to belong to the country club. I want us to be somebody."

"We are."

"The Barracloughs owe your father, us, something now . . . Let's finish canning these tomatoes."

That was Mamma unveiled. That was Mrs. A. Lincoln Pedlock with an eye on the main chance, ladling out big red tomatoes that Dedee felt looked like boiled human babies.

Dedee didn't bring up again her desires for a God she could feel close to. This matter of the Jews and belonging. She had tried to be friendly with Stacy Cohen, the daughter of Rabbi Jefferson Matthew Cohen of the Temple Oheb Sholomon, on Boat Street. But Stacy Cohen was fat and given to giggling and letting boys get her into the cloak rooms, and you could hear her laughter and her shrieks of protest at the liberties they took. Besides, Stacy sweated so at all times, and said "golly gee" too often.

Rabbi Cohen was a genial man, a mixer, who presided at the Catholic Church open house twice a year, went on interfaith picnics with Protestant ministers, played golf at the second-best country club in Port Wilard. And told very funny stories to the men in the locker rooms drinking Scotch. He practiced soothing the women of the congregation on the matters of sex habits of modern husbands, led the UJA fund drives, and at banquets pushed aside the shrimp cocktail.

The one time Dedee had tried to talk to Rabbi Cohen— when Stacy had a burst appendix, and came home to spend three weeks in bed—that time Dedee had come over to the rabbi's house with an album of the score of "Kiss Me, Kate" as a gift. She found the rabbi in the parlor of the Cape Cod house his congregation furnished him with, writing his sermon.

"Ah, my dear Dedee. How kind of you to come to see Stacy."

"She looks pale, but seems recovering."

"I tell the housekeeper: put her on a diet. Noshing is bad for body and complexion."

"Rabbi, I've been wondering, I mean, why are there so

many different versions of God? Every religion I read of thinks it has the only true one."

The rabbi sighed, put down his pen, set his fingertips together, held them against his lower lip. "Ah, my dear child, my dear child." (Nuts, thought Dedee, when the "dear child" routine comes on, the malarky, as Aunt Kate says, begins.)

"I mean, rabbi, I really am confused. You see, our family, it isn't exactly like any other family."

"Just believe with them there is a God, that we are His children, that there are concepts beyond our understanding —no matter how we have been given revelations, tablets, holy texts, it's all keeping faith. Faith, yes, faith." He closed his eyes, and pursed his lips. If he spoke from long practice, glibly, he was a good man, a family man, a man who worked for understanding, for an expanding of relationships between the creeds of Hawleytown, and he knew his small vanities, his seeking of popularity. But basically a man of principles—hardly a philosopher or much given to dogma. Dedee was unaware of any of this. As for Rabbi Cohen, a widower, young girls bothered him; even his daughter, the woman smell, the girl fat. They were people he could not comfortably react to; talk cheerfully to, as he did to Father O'Malley, or to the American Legion convention. He opened his eyes. "It's all, my dear child, just having faith. As Isaiah puts it, 'I will lay up stones with fair colors, and lay thy foundations with sapphires.' "

"Thank you, rabbi."

It was about this time that Dedee began to be called Sarah by some. Although the rare letter from Aunt Judith Pedlock addressed her as *Sari*. Aunt Judith was providing the funds for her musical education. Dedee was in her last year at high school, and the important thing was, even if still baffled from coming to an understanding of the godhead, she could go on with her preparing for a career as a pianist.

There would be three months with Sandor Andrassy, three times a week, to give her some sort of polish for going next fall to Juilliard or Curtis. Aunt Judith, still a remote figure to Dedee, would decide which was best for her. And

Aunt Judith knew her way around the best musical circles. Aunt Kate took Sarah to the first lesson in Baltimore with Sandor and left her to go shopping or, Sarah decided, maybe to meet a man. Sarah wasn't too sure which. Aunt Kate was thinking of going to New Orleans to take a course in cordon bleu cooking, and maybe open later an exclusive eating house on the Eastern Shore. It was always a danger sign when Aunt Kate wanted to travel to join some *outré* (her word) group.

Sandor Andrassy was by Baltimore standards "all Hungarian charm." He was in his late thirties, still retained those Magyar good looks, the stance of a hussar (actually Sarah was to discover his father had been a prosperous Budapest cattle dealer). Sandor carried a real sadness, a burning resentment that he, a child prodigy, had been rejected by critics as not lasting the route into full-fledged fame and greatness as an adult.

"Sarah, we shall begin the hard work. Brahms, Liszt, Fauré, some Scriabin. But first today I want to talk, only talk."

"Yes, sir." She sat in her best flowered dress, slim, delicate, sat as Mamma had taught her to sit, ankles crossed.

It was a good-sized studio, the ceiling a bit too low, and the marble mantel held busts of composers, a fleet of silver frames with pictures of high-bosomed women singers and men in the uniforms of the Austro-Hungarian Empire. Also photographs on the wall of whiskered performers at pianos, or holding violins. The oil painting of *The Death of Mozart* was rather ghastly, Sarah felt—but under dark varnish not too clear. And above it a sword with some sort of crest.

Sandor, in a worn maroon jacket with yellow braiding, talked well, and he spoke of art being all and life being tragic, and only the artist mattered. For only he, yoi istanem, or she, saw beyond the range of the ordinary mortal. Sarah believed all this, but nearly yawned. She had heard this *so* often. Hard work and talent and, one hoped, genius—Sandor insisted—could, would, produce a finished artist. It went on, talk which Sarah had already heard from other teachers and she hoped Aunt Judith got more for her money than this from the fascinating, hand gesturing, failed genius before her.

In three weeks Sandor was sure she was a great talent. Badly trained so far, full of faults, the fingering, the pedal touch would have to be done over. And the way she treated certain clusters of notes; he had his work cut out. Still, who could have gotten what she did out of Ravel's *Tzigane?*

Sandor would drink a cheap Tokay wine as he listened and taught and sometimes he got fuddled early and damned his wife, Julie, when she rattled the door to the studio if he dropped a vase or overturned a hat rack. He insisted he never be interrupted while giving lessons, and turned the big brass key in the door, shouting fearful oaths at his wife *"Haait!* . . . *Baszon az anyat,"* which fortunately Sarah did not understand.

If Sandor had too much of the wine, he would ruffle up his head of reddish brown hair into curls, like a Greek statue, Sarah thought, and he would lean against the marble mantel and look at the hussar's sword on the wall, and the photograph of his grandfather Geza shooting elk with Grand Duke Ferdinand, the one who got shot in Bosnia in Sarajevo and started the Great War, as Sandor told his pupil.

Sandor was an excellent teacher but lazy, and would talk of the great days of Franz Josef and of the great piano players of the past, of how an artist had to struggle and survive in vile cities like Baltimore, and whose damn shrew of a wife sold trash as antiques and rattled doorknobs. "So let us try the opening of the Mozart—the Concerto in F. Watch the left hand." She took to calling him Maestro.

He would come up behind Sarah as she played, and put his arm around her shoulder and mutter soft vowels in Hungarian. It delighted Sarah, and the secret corners of her body shivered and her nerve ends responded so she lost the sense of what she was playing. An ordinary drama was being played out between them. Only Sarah was unaware of how ordinary it was.

Sandor would kiss her neck and her shoulders and say

they would try Avshoolmov's "Chinese Themes and Rhythms" next time.

"Yes, Maestro."

She was fully committed to love with Sandor Andrassy by the fourth week of their working together. She pitied him his miserable existence, his few pupils, the sharpness of his wife, Julie, who smiled a crooked cold smile when Sarah passed her on the stairs, coming down from a lesson.

Sandor was drinking more of the cheap Tokay and playing old recordings a great deal on a fumed oak gramophone. There would be periods when he was truly a great teacher, when he drove Sarah and worked her solidly with Bach and Brahms—making her take the same few bars again and again, grabbing her wrists, positioning her fingers.

Sometimes, very rarely, he would unbutton his maroon jacket, sit down himself at one of his scarred but beautifully tuned pianos and play . . . It was only a dim echo of what he had once had while playing Brahms' Capriccio in B.

"That is what goes first, Sarah, the confidence. Then it's best to stop early and become a plumber, a veal butcher. Never go on after—after . . ." He left the sentence unfinished.

There were times when he'd sit and listen to Sarah play and he would rub his brow and stand under the sword and the pictures and nod. He was a true artist and a confused, unhappy man.

Sandor was the first human being who fully understood her gift, who said things to her as an artist that felt right. That was not just casual praise. They made, Sarah felt, a little kingdom of two, in which music, and her part in it, was perfectly understood between them. They were honest to their art, to each other, she felt, by being special and serious. She was unaware she was falling into an old trap. Sandor was not an evil man, but had set out to sexually dominate nearly every attractive female pupil. This game, drive, compulsion was the only prop to his vanity; seduction of some favorite pupil. Yet he was, had been so far, wary. Picking those from a distant town, who had no dangerous father or brothers in Baltimore. So far he had been careful to favor those of legal age. But this beautiful, grateful, as yet not fully awakened girl was breaking his resistance. She was, like himself, from the rare world of the true artists, those of major talent. Besides as his mother, Zita, had so well phrased it, when the old family cook had complained about the pregnancy of her fourteen-year-old daughter, accusing Uncle Béla Andrassy, "If they're big enough, they're old enough."

CHAPTER

4

Three days before she was to leave for Curtis, Sandor was rather nervous, locked in some desperate brusqueness. Not saying much, and she ran through what she was going to play as an entrance test at the school, including a bit of Tchaikovsky to cheer him up. That and a Chopin scherzo would be her school test; not that she needed a show piece. Aunt Judith was a patron of music schools; at least the Pedlock families were. Sarah said she could be admitted on her own merits. Sandor said, "Oh, my innocent. What do you know of the world?"

Sandor said nothing much after that pessimistic note. She sat at the piano head down, not affected by doubt. All bliss and wonder and, yes, expectation. There was now between her and the teacher an understanding without words. It was a good-bye, with an exaltation of thoughts of the future on her part. As for Sandor? As Aunt Kate had said, "What can you predict about Hungarians." (Of course, in another context.)

Sandor put a record on the gramophone; neither felt the irony of it being the beginning of *Don Giovanni*, the fabulous seducer. He came behind her and spun her around and holding her tightly, began to sob; most un-American, sobbing. She could feel his chest rise and fall, then his kissing her . . . She kissing back. She did not think herself shameless; she wanted to feel. She was intoxicated by the romantic bittersweet moment, perhaps too fully keyed by the situation from her reading. It was what she had experienced in books. So many times, women had been, in novels, gathered in. Now it was real and the music was rising in pitch, and he was carrying her to the red velvet sofa, was over her, the organdy dress was up and that other forked garment she had on was in his hands, he sliding it over stomach, thighs, calves and then he flung it like a captured banner over his shoulder. She was aware and yet, yet it was somewhat a dream—she was still very young and completely inexperienced, or understanding. It was all in a cloud without details, what followed as she sank back. From the beginning of the lessons she had felt nothing like this could happen, not just this way. And there was pain and there was thrust. And the rest? If not like in the novels, it was real.

Physical, oh, yes. A surging tide foaming in her blood, in her head, and his breathing strong, but irregular. The strain showing on his face, and also the puzzled look as if he was not sure he was doing that to this young and beautiful child. He was; and his expression changed to something she couldn't have described, being busy savoring sensation. So she closed her eyes and felt so much, so suddenly. Soon she began to cry out in plaintive pleasure and his hand was on her mouth, whispering, *"Sepe lonyah,"* which she supposed was Hungarian for something consoling, loving, *and* shut up. "Julie is near—and not so loud." Then, with a quiver in her thighs, a churning in her stomach, it was over.

For some time they were unaware of the doorknob rattling, a furious hand behind the action. The gramophone was turning in some smooth section of the score.

"Darling," Sarah said, "you are marvelously a man."

Sandor, tugging himself into order, covered his eyes with

an arm, and he choked a bit as he patted her cheek which was flushed skin warm to his touch. "Yes, yes."

He rose from the sofa and turned away, the sadness in his eyes causing her to wonder about how men felt about this thing of two-into-one.

"You're, you're not disappointed, Sandor?"

"Could I be?"

He went to the door and kicked it with the side of his foot; she noticed he had dropped out of his slippers. He growled in Hungarian and someone answered. It was Julie. A burst of words uttered in frustrated rage. Then they both heard the clatter of shoes going down the stairs, and the sound of what might have been a fall on the bottom step.

Sarah, aware of the disturbance, pulled down her dress, feeling moist. She walked, or floated rather, knees apart, to the little gilt table and poured out two glasses of ruby-colored wine. She knelt beside him and offered him one (the harem girl and the sultan—by Delacroix—Senior Year Art).

He took it and she said, "It wasn't wrong. Please don't think that."

"God knows," he said, taking a gulp of the wine.

For the first time since her ("deflowering?") she thought of the world beyond the studio, and for a moment, too, she thought of God. But not as Sandor had, as a mere questioning expression. Up there beyond Einstein's formula. He saw even a sparrow fall. How did He view her passing from virgin into woman on a dusty sofa? Shame came over her and she drank the wine, as she thought there might have been a witness and such a witness—and just a little wonder: God as a Peeping Tom? Sarah comforted Sandor by stroking his arm. She left soon after that, going swiftly down the stairs without touching the banister.

Julie was nowhere in sight, not even behind the small window of the antique shop. Sarah had her drawers and stockings stuffed into her music portfolio, and she dropped the stained garments into a trash basket by the bay ferry station, she running then to make the 5:10 boat. She stood on the upper deck by the rusted metal lifeboat as the ferry crossed to Hawleytown on the Eastern Shore. The captain looked down from the pilothouse—looked with pleasure at the young girl standing there, poised by the rail, and he thought of how many good things in life were now behind him.

Overhead there were blown-about clouds, like horsemen in battle, Sarah decided, and one huge cloud that was a tumbling figure of a giant. She felt dreadfully sorry for Sandor. She was going on, escaping into a larger, more colorful world. Poor Sandor would remain, drink more, shout oaths at his wife. And would there be other young girl students on the red velvet sofa to thump out its dust with whipping-about limbs? She did not regret that there would be. It would make Sandor's life a bit more vivid, bearable. If only she could bring him along with her to her new life; she was mature enough to know that was impossible.

That night she was very cheerful at dinner. The pain was dull and like a pleasant memory and it went away. After her bath, she saw herself in the full-length mirror and her body seemed unchanged; she liked the look of it. She must always remain slim, so finely colored. If only one's grace didn't fail with age—say at thirty. But age was something in another country, and wrinkles were for careless people. In her youth she musn't be too hard on the older generation. Sarah slept and dreamed of the giant figure in the sky seen from the top deck of the bay ferry.

The last time she saw Sandor, Sarah brought a gift of a pipe and a tin of John Cotton tobacco. Julie was not around. He said Julie had left him. But never mind, she would be back. "She has no place to go. She knows nobody—I'm all she has."

"I'm sorry for her," Sarah said and began to unbutton her dress. This sweet sad last time she insisted they be naked in parting. Images to imprint in her memory. Sandor asked, "Like something pressed in an album—a flower—a ribbon?" She said that if he understood her and what he meant to her, he would not talk that way. He said she was very young and did not know how hurt one could be. They undressed. It was again, she felt, a great outpouring of her love, of being alive, of being treated like this, as a woman.

Outside rain was falling and the sky was making thunder and flashing fire.

Then . . . She clearly saw God during that rainstorm in Baltimore. She squirming under Sandor. Yes, God printed on the studio ceiling just above the mantelpiece, over the bust of Wagner, the tattered score of Mozart's *Don Giovanni*, the family sword—God was fearsome and outraged; she copulating like this, a maiden of Judah with an uncircumcised barbarian. God's beard was long enough to sweep over the keyboard of the ancient Steinway with its yellow teeth, and He lifted up great Michelangelo arms. There was some kind of flashing light that destroyed lucidity. What He said must have been in Hebrew, and she had a frightened silly thought for a moment: He could do anything, so why didn't He speak English if He was warning, threatening her? She discovered she had beaten Sandor's back and chest with her fists, screaming to disentangle. "The Commandment! The Commandment . . . He's watching, He's watching! God is watching."

Poor Sandor, unaware of Jehovah's fury just over his head, was struggling to his feet, all exposed, his head cocked to one side, worried, wondering if he had driven the child mad. It took a half-hour to calm and dress her. The rain had stopped. For the last time she went down the stairs and went out into the wet day. For the first time she had touched the true unknown—and she was frightened.

That night she had a temperature of 102 and Doctor Kendall said it was most likely the flu. "Keep her warm, Mrs. Pedlock. Lots of hot tea, and don't let her up to practice for a few days."

She could not forget God's awesome, magisterial rage. Could she accept the idea that a flu brought fever, fever brought God to Sandor's studio, there to warn her? Was she a compulsive escapist from reality? It served—the flu theory—well enough for some time. She had read the lives of some of the female saints and the states of ecstasy in which feverish conditions close to hysteria were best for actual communication with God. But she was no female saint and He had showed no patrician benevolence . . . A hard God is the Hebrew God.

In a few days Sarah accepted the idea that her encounter with the godhead was all the result of a virus she had carried to her last love-making with Sandor. Busy with good-byes and packing, accepting, or at least nodding to advice given her, she recovered most of her sensations about herself and her relationship to the world. Almost all. She was afraid for some time to look at clouds.

Mamma took her to Philadelphia to a distant cousin's house where she would live—settle in for Curtis. Aunt Kate gave her some private advice. "Don't listen too much to what we tell you."

The life of a musical wunderkind—as has been proved by so many books written about them—seems to be a pattern, rather routine, consisting of hard work, years of practice among augmented and diminished chords. Sarah Pedlock at Curtis—Dedee no longer existed. Those formative years of training, practice, growing up from sixteen to nineteen when she gave her first major concert, were years of intense feeling—but to insist that was all, would give a false picture of her existence. She lived with the Wilmers, a pleasant enough family, a bit on the stuffy side, too solicitous—a father (accountant), a mother (social worker) and a son aged twelve (a collector of Dixieland jazz recordings). Too much television, few books, Chinese food in cartons brought in for Sunday dinners. It was a pleasant house, a bit hard to heat in winter; and that part of Delaware Avenue was not fashionable, but Sarah liked to stand in the bay window of her room after practicing on the old upright piano downstairs, looking out at the coal barges in clumsy strength unloading on the river, and turn away and wonder at the workload she was carrying. And what did shoe clerks and milkmen do with all their spare time?

She found school interesting, a bit given to attitudes that some might call snobbish. "Practical without being freakish," Mr. Kaufstein, one of the teachers, explained. Sarah studied harmony, and the compass of seven octaves and a minor third—even composing, with no idea she would ever want to write music. Most of all she lived at the piano with two teachers: Eli Kaufstein, a remarkable pianist, an expert on C.P.E. Bach—a teacher, who was never able to give solo concerts, as a certain terror came over him when on stage alone seated at a concert grand. And Albert Mishinoff, a cranky man with ulcer problems who, when not moody and given to spells of elation, danced around the studio and uttered birdlike cries. He was forgiven his bad periods as "that's the way Russians are. All out of Dostoevsky." Which was flattering, Mishinoff was born in Colorado to an Irish washerwoman and a Finnish lead miner. He was a music historian of some fame and the piano was his specialty; although he himself played badly, he was a remarkable teacher.

"To amount to anything in music," he told Sarah, "you have to be a specialist." She listened, observed—and played. She felt in herself a strength partly from delicacy and the grace of her body in tune with a mind educating itself. Also she had good hands, and her wrists, if slim, were strong. Socially she tried to remain in the background. She mixed with only about a dozen students, serious—too serious at times—known as "The Gang." But it was actually little beyond sharing two old cars, drinking sodas and beers, eating rather dreadful hamburgers in a favorite joint, The Music Rack—which had an old Babcock piano. Trooping together, they went to concerts, dance recitals with cut-rate student tickets. Or even for free to fill a failing house. Twice a year Sarah and The Gang were stage crowds, spear carriers or singing peasants with visiting opera companies.

The Wilmers, when the monthly check came for Sarah's board, would ask her how it was going, and she would say fine. She had breakfast at the house, and dinner with the Wilmers. As Aunt Judith paid the board bill on time and gave her spending money, all was well. Or rather Aunt Judith's bank did. About once a month—but not regularly— there would be postal cards from Maine, or Rome or Santa Barbara or Mexico City, signed Judith Pedlock. Often a picture postal card: *Sari: the work goes well I'm sure . . .* or *They need good musical concerts here. Keep practicing.* Never very informative messages or interesting personal comment. Sarah suspected Nora O'Hara, Aunt Judith's personal maid and traveling companion, actually wrote and mailed the letters and cards. Aunt Judith was a restless old lady as Sarah saw her—and like so many of the rich "Up North" Pedlocks, a traveler. Perhaps, Sarah thought, without reason, moving herself over the earth's surface. What was she hunting for? Sarah hoped she would know Judith Pedlock better, meet her often. But the old lady remained remote.

During her three years at school, Sarah never met Judith Pedlock. There were two phone calls from her home at Norton-on-Hudson; the first came the second year when Sarah won the Bellinton Award at a student audition, and another call after Sarah heard from Leon Solly, the concert talent agent, after Sarah's eighteenth birthday.

"I sent you Solly, because, Sari, he's the least greedy of all good concert managers. He's satisfied just with his commission and his name big on the posters. But you don't have to work with him, Sari, if you cannot like him. I don't tell young people what to do . . . Hello, is this a clear phone connection?"

"Yes. Thank you, Aunt Judith. For all you've done."

"You happy?" It sounded as if Aunt Judith had perhaps had a few brandies after dinner.

"I'm very busy."

"But happy? That's my question."

"Yes, I suppose I am."

"Suppose? Well, good luck, Sari."

She supposed she was happy. There had been no love affairs—no full sexual involvement. Even if some of the males at the school—students and teachers—had felt she was the school beauty and a hick from the sticks, but perhaps could be the great talent of the decade. But as one turned-away student put it, "She's cold tittie."

CHAPTER

5

Sarah was not at all emotionally cold, just she was somehow vaguely in fear of that fever-produced image of God in Sandor's studio, and also she wanted no entanglements while preparing for a career. That was her Daddy's practical side in her. She sublimated her emotional drives, her physical desires into hard work. Sometimes she wondered at music school life, the passion pit goings-on at the students' favorite movie house, where couples embraced, "took liberties," as one teacher put it, with each other. Even in extreme cases made love in second balconies. Music students were supposed to be more passionate than students in business school or law.

Sarah was liked. She did not change much in manner from what she had been as an Eastern Shore girl. She dressed neatly and well, but not in the extreme campus mode; the shaggy age of faded denim and careless disorder was already beginning to infect a few extremists. Sarah was no snob. She was rather shy with large groups, and she tried to favor some class wallflower, even the hardly sane misfit every class had. As they rarely responded, she saw there were reasons for their being rejects.

Her special friends were a dark intense girl from India, Jaki, who had a jewel set in her nose and who smoked thin black cigars. An older woman, Maude, a divorcée and a lapsed Catholic, who had two sons, teen-agers who ran a garage. Maude was a composer of music for children's radio programs, but wanted to write operas. Martin Hasek was a bit of an unwashed fingernail biter who was an organizer of string quartets and a master already at twenty-one of the cello. Hike English had a motorcycle and knew all of Gilbert and Sullivan by heart. The group ate together and went to avant-garde films en masse, "films of bare dirty feet mated in haystacks," she wrote Aunt Kate. Weekends with food in shoe boxes, and they in Maude's old Lincoln, went off to the Pennsylvania Dutch country, to taste of Aalsuppe and schmierkaese and country cider. They picnicked on only slightly polluted rivers and talked of music and composers and the gossip of famous concert masters.

It was fun, there were no entanglements with each other's emotions, but for Hike and Maude one autumn, and then Maude was found dead by sleeping pills when Hike went into the army. It shook Sarah up so much she dreamed of the giant cloud again.

Leon Solly turned up one Friday night and took her to dinner to one of the two Bookbinders. She was never sure which, as both eating places claimed to be the original.

Leon Solly was a short man—but not given to fat—with a bushy head of rust-colored hair going gray. He had a sharp little nose, silver-rimmed glasses, a voice with a rasp in it and a manner that hinted he knew the worst of everything, but held out hope.

"All right, you didn't know it, but I heard you play the Chopin this morning for Mishinoff. I don't have to be hit with a ton of rocks to know if what I'm merchandising is a smottah, or the real artist. Now, how do I bring you out, that's if you want old Shulmah as a manager and agent?"

She had expected a manager to be a cigar chomper, a fast-talking finger-snapping type. Leon Solly ("old Shulmah") had a New York accent and he smoked a cigarette oddly; holding it with his fingertips pointed up between a thumb and forefinger.

"My Aunt Judith felt you were the right person and—"

"Madam Pedlock, I've known her thirty years. That's why I'm here."

"I feel perhaps she was asking too much, Mr. Solly, of you. You don't take on students—I mean, your other clients . . ."

He held up a well cared for hand, showed mutton jade cuff links, to stop her continuing. "Between us, little lady, no lies. The whole truth is I fall down and worship anyone that has it *here.*" He wriggled his fingers, touched his waistcoat on the left side, "That's the whole *megillah.* I'm a victim of art. But to be practical, the truth is too many young artists just have talent. Talent? Who hasn't got it at nineteen or twenty? But at forty, fifty, that's the test. And then it's too late to become a post office worker or a millionaire. So I hate to encourage too much."

"You're doing my aunt a favor. I understand."

"Who says? Me. I'm doing Leon Solly a favor. You're playing at a student concert for some charity benefit in two days." He began to cut up his sea bass.

"Liszt and Debussy."

"I'll send down Matt Davis for an opinion. You understand, little lady, I can't handle you myself. How's your crab salad? I have the Russian ballet group. And they keep defecting—who's to blame them? Rashminyah and Chandler, modern dancers. Swenson, the Wagnerian tenor, all this season."

"Of course, if you don't—"

"Come, come, a little temper, please. Call me a momser. Play the prima donna. Ask why can't old Shulmah manage you himself, not some kocker on his staff."

Sarah laughed. "Sorry, I'm not temperamental."

"A bad sign you don't blow off steam; get mean, Sarah, get that nasty egotistical edge that a real artist must have.

Walk on people, trample them, kick anything that gets in your way." He was grinning as he sipped his cup of black coffee—yet she knew he was advising her, too.

"You don't think I'm hard enough?"

"Nobody is hard enough for a career on the concert stage. It's plain, simple murder. The demand of recording sessions, the lonely life of travel, hotel rooms smelling of afternoon *nafkas*, and trains, planes always the lousy timetables, and the sandpapering of critics."

"I think I can face it. I know I look soft, but I have, I feel, a core of purpose."

"You'll pardon frankness, but you're a beauty, so you got a man, a boychic? It's not I'm being nosy. Bedtime, believe me, makes more trouble for an artiste than sixteen drunken critics."

"No, there is nobody."

"Understand, Sarah, I'm no prude—I know the score. I say live a satisfactory personal life. It's normal and you need it, like food—some apple pie with cheese? It's good here. But I never knew a great talent, even a genius—oh, yes, I've known a few, handled them, wiped up after them—any great artist who was happy with just what people call love, love alone. No, I'm lying, here and there you find a couple—but in the main . . ." Leon Solly motioned to the waiter and made the gesture of writing on a slip of paper. "*L'addition* . . . We'll see what Davis thinks of your Debussy."

Sarah lay awake that night for some time and imagined herself on the concert stage, marvelously dressed, in white, seated, relaxed at the piano and the music was good and right as she played it. She dozed off, immersed in a sea of faces, people in evening clothes, applauding her, *but* there was no sound.

She went home for three days after school ended. Mamma and Daddy said she had grown, and Daddy said she had a Main Line accent. Which perhaps she had. She hadn't noticed. Aunt Kate said it was damn nice she had filled out a bit in the right places and always to wear pale clingy blue. They were all coming up to "Philly" to the students' charity concert. Sarah would have a whole half hour of solos on the program.

That evening Daddy was smiling at her, holding her hand, as she and he sat on the old porch swing. The fireflies were in the front bushes and the smell of burning leaves was nearby; the hoot of a dredger in the bay, the night sounds that always recalled for Sarah her once being very young and wondering if the hooting of the dredgers at dawn was the sound of the end of the world, as Tessie, the black cook, had once told her.

Daddy asked, "Dedee, is everything going well?"

It was strange to be called by her childhood name—she'd been Sarah now for so long. She leaned against her father and he patted her cheek and she kissed his jaw line, he just a bit bristly. He was district attorney now, and he and Mamma were members of *the* country club: the Forked Oak Country Club. Oh, God, Sarah thought, feeling all overflowing with love and hopes for her family, is that all they want? All they can reach for? And am I a snob, a foolish prig to think what I want is so much better than what they desire? The artist thinks himself so much above people, so much better, and why? (Mishinoff had asked when his ulcers bit.) Sarah's doubts, the mood didn't last for long. Mamma and Aunt Kate came out "all gussied up" and they went out to dinner at Mattie's Fish Shack, where they had a shore dinner: a pot of clam broth, steamers, lobster in butter and sweet corn on the cob, and even watermelon. An Eastern Shore sea food dinner was always part of Sarah's strong memory of her youth.

The student concert at Franklin Hall was a great success. It made a great deal of money for the charity to put Negroes into perfectly reconditioned Philadelphia colonial houses. It showed Sarah at eighteen, at her best. There were cries for more; she, "looking so ethereal" (Mamma) in flowing blue, did Chopin encores.

Matthew Davis turned out to be a balding young man with a thin voice and great knowledge of music, and a fear of colds. He hardly ever took off his topcoat. He stayed on two days in Philadelphia after the family left, and listened to Sarah play for hours in the small school hall.

He had a habit of breaking off his conversation to cough politely behind a fist, but he did not waste time in praise of her playing. "I shall advise Mr. Solly we could work up a Chopin and Debussy concert tour for you. Bring you slowly east in a series of recitals—San Diego, Denver, Kansas City (cough), St. Louis, then spring you on New York after our publicity department has done its job. Yes, in some big traditional hall in New York City, a week (cough) after Thanksgiving."

"It's the way it's done?"

"It's Mr. Solly's way. We could send you to Moscow to win a Lenin Art Prize, or have you discovered by Lennie or Stoky or some other solid baton waver with media power. But I think we can do you straight."

She watched the young man, fist to mouth, nod as if reassuring himself.

"And if it doesn't work out, Mr. Davis?"

"No negative thinking." He seemed worried and patted the back of his head with an open palm. "No, it's all in thinking in the right direction. You have the talent, perhaps more than talent. The thing is to see that what you have *and* the musical world meet properly."

He left, and Sarah sensed he was not too sure of her. But a week later in New York with Aunt Kate, Leon Solly had her seated in a comfortable chair in his office. A neat walnut-paneled place, Sarah saw, with too many pictures of very famous dead and living people in the concert and theater world—all marking off their sentiments in ink approving Leon Solly as friend and defender and a peddler and lover of the arts.

"Your Aunt Katcha will travel with you? Good. Davis will be setting up dates, halls, interviews. We have a nice little group of concerts planned to take you across the country, little lady. Right until fall. Then we'll bring you in, with luck. It's *tocus offen tish* then. You have to show them you're what we've been saying. Only more."

He shook her hand and said he was off to meet a plane of Israeli actors who were coming over to tour *The Golem.*

Sarah relished the trip west. With a small steamer trunk bought secondhand, and Aunt Kate with a handbag of instructions. They planed to San Diego to begin the tour. Sarah felt that she wasn't nervous and not upset or fearful of failure. It seemed wrong to feel *so* sure of oneself.

CHAPTER

6

At first, the Southwest seemed all Esso and Richfield signs, Bar-B-Ques, Holiday House and Free Wine Tasting.

Aunt Kate turned out to be a formidable manager of Sarah's first concert tour. Armed with a heavy handbag of some thick-hided animal, she had a weapon, a defense, a bag that contained, it seemed, everything needed for air, train and bus travel. For motel and hotel living and emergency cosmetic and female problems. She boldly (and loudly) faced auditorium owners, hotel personnel, theater box-office staffs, college concert bookers. To demand respect, running water and a good piano. Aunt Kate watched over their four suitcases, saw to dry cleaning, demanded clean beds and flush plumbing in dressing rooms. She fought the deficiency in air conditioning, short and damp bed sheets, and the slack plane connections on faltering small airlines. A world of huge supermarkets in empty deserts at dawn: Alpha Beta, Safeway, Ralphs, Market Basket, Ranch Market. They also saw a great deal of the country.

Sarah became used to sleeping on the cinder-smelling

plush armrests of worn-out railroad stock, to primitive groaning plumbing in cow colleges. Even the strange and peculiar pianos that often turned up in new million-dollar halls and modern buildings of fancy design. No one seemed to consider the performer. The piano got the least attention in many otherwise splendid places.

It was for Sarah an exciting time, an awakening to the size, scale of the world, to wonder at all the empty space, mostly in the Southwest. Such vast horizons, and dialects of the natives—sun-baked folk wary of outsiders—balanced by the earnestness of the young in the colleges. Who, raised on record players and radio, sat entranced at a live performer while she played the well-worn classics; only now and then sneaking in some modern item during an encore.

Matt Davis, who had set up the routes, and whom they saw at least once every two weeks when he flew in to check reviews, box office bookkeeping, insisted Sarah play what had been decided upon and not experiment with the program.

"Mr. Solly doesn't want any experimenting. Just a break-in tour, get used to the feel of an audience."

She was becoming not as innocent as she had been—aware of the commercial side of concerts and public support of music. There was still wonder in her at the real world, and the glow of being a performer. No matter how small the audience or remote the college, as a solo performer, Aunt Kate agreed, "She got her kicks out of it."

As for Matt Davis, Sarah said, "I feel a change of pace is good, at least in encores."

"Not so many encores either," Davis begged.

"Up your kazoo," said Aunt Kate. "Your job is to see the lock works in these peckerwood hotel rooms, there is a privy, and not two flights down or out in the yard. And another thing . . ."

Usually Sarah withdrew from these details of the tour. Aunt Kate wanted it to be, as she put it, "first class all the way. And it's my job to see it's all hunky-dory." Her card read: *Katherine Walker Ormsbee, Personal Management of SARAH PEDLOCK.* She took her work seriously.

The personal-management claim Leon Solly overlooked as a bit of window dressing. It salved the bad plane and train connections, and the dismal public food of American towns. Luckily, both of them had the digestive power of goats.

Aunt Kate began the press interviews—dressed in loud colors, talking more than Sarah to the local reporters before concerts in Denver, El Paso, San Diego, Bakersfield, Reno, at the University of New Mexico, University of California, the various colleges of animal husbandry here and there, on which Aunt Kate frowned when she saw them listed. Yes, Wagon Wheel, Utah, which, amazingly, produced a large modern hall and a Steinway grand.

After a concert there was resting in a plywood-walled hotel room, or some motel compound with country music all around on the radios, and love-making or drinking vocal in various units behind the Coke, Dr. Pepper, 7 Up and Royal Crown Cola signs. Aunt Kate and Sarah would relax, and Aunt Kate would produce a couple of bottles of Blue Nun, and usually in two toothbrush glasses they would drink the wine and compare impressions. Sarah, limited to two half-glasses, let Aunt Kate do most of the commenting. Both with their shoes and dresses off, on the beds sitting up, Aunt Kate sipping, sipping and retelling with gestures and critical sounds the events of the day. The rotten flight in, on some "rubber-band-powered" connecting line, the dusty ride to the motel and the prissy small college music professor, or gushy art guild hostess of the town concerts. The dreadful lunch. "There isn't good food in any place with a population of under a hundred thousand. A grease culture; cheeseburgers, franks, ribs, chicken sections, ugh!" There was also sweet talking or cursing the lighting man at the theater, complaining the piano didn't stand level, had two keys that seemed to have gone dead. And the local media. Assuring the reporter of the local weekly, or college campus paper, they were not really freaks. "No, Miss Pedlock is not an American Indian . . . no truth that she's an heiress of the Pedlock copper fortune. Some distant branch of the family. Let's talk music, shall we? She's going to play tonight something really exciting."

"This Da Bussee . . ."

"Debussy. Claude Achille . . . a tone poem . . . and some of the Preludes and Etudes."

Two months on tour: native factory-made pies, southern-fried everything, septic-tank johns, motels where everyone —male, female and waitresses—wore cowboy hats. They sat in nylon slips in unreliable air conditioning, sipping wine, in a cottage of the Crazy Horse Motel in Dankin, Wyoming, after a concert at the local college. Sarah unhappy over the way the Chopin Fantaisie Impromptu had gone.

Aunt Kate, however, was keyed up, not just from the kicks she got on the tour, not the second bottle of Blue Nun she was finishing all by herself. Sarah was recognizing in Aunt Kate the "Ormsbee streak," a kind of eccentric attitude Mamma's family was supposed to inherit and pass on. Of course Mamma always denied the streak existed. But it was there—in Aunt Kate—an easy turning to anger over something small, like a lost package of nylons at an airport, or smelling a very wrong egg at breakfast, and making, as one waitress said in Omaha, "a federal case of it." And all the interviewers riled her, those who wanted to do a fake color story on Sarah. Even the college hosts who brought the talk around to Genêt, Cage, Warhol to show they weren't hicks.

Sarah wondered if she'd ever develop the Ormsbee streak. Like the double sharps in music, a whole step above normal on the scale. This evening she was very tired and Aunt Kate had her turn over on the bed, and began to massage her neck and shoulders. Sarah never had any ache in her fingers, wrists, arms, but after a two-hour concert it was hard to move her neck without feeling it was put on wrong. Her back and shoulder muscles seemed hung with lead weights hooked into her flesh with fish barbs.

Aunt Kate rubbed, slapped. "Honey, you think you can keep this up for a lifetime?"

Sarah laughed and sighed at the pleasure of her body being kneaded.

"How long is a lifetime?"

"Matt Davis, he figures piano players go on forever. Matt

talks of this Artur Rubinstein, hitting eighty he is, been at it nearly seventy years. How's the neck?"

"Ah, nice, *nice*."

"Monday we'll take off from this whistlestop, get some good un-American food in Las Vegas. Go on the town. How about it?"

"Sounds good."

"Fix you up with some dude. I mean, what the hell, we're not nuns, are we?"

"Right now, I don't want to fall in love."

"Who mentioned love? I didn't say we'd do anything serious. But face it, you can't just go on banging the keys and think that's all there is to life."

"Dear Abby, I know it isn't. But it's all so—confusing."

"You mean that Hunky teacher in Baltimore? Don't tell me how far you went with him. But I know it shook you up."

"It was—besides, Sandor, he . . . oh . . . nothing."

"Okay, now you tuck in and get some sleep, we plane out tomorrow for Vegas. You do a school concert there in the afternoon, Kit Carson High School. Then we'll do the town a few days, before we fly east."

"Why not, Aunt Kate?"

"I'll not wake you when I come in. There's a poker game in Cottage E, and Eddie, this rodeo rider, could be a spitting image of Gary Cooper. I'll leave the bathroom light on, huh?"

Sarah didn't reply. She was already moving deeper and deeper into a kind of half sleep and she only grunted, made a little moaning sound of satisfaction. More and more Aunt Kate would leaver her alone nights.

Aunt Kate went out after dabbing a bit of Chanel Number 5 here and there. Sarah began to sink deeper into sleep . . . wondering about Sandor; she hadn't thought of him in weeks and weeks. And of God on the ceiling of his studio—and of her fever. Was it really God who had been there, watching them? If not, it was just the fever. However, if it had been God? She'd think about it more, some other time. Love. A man. Going to bed . . . It was all something pushed aside just now. The tour, the concerts were all. Ahead loomed—like an advancing tidal wave—the big breakthrough in New York . . . throwing up a new star. She could not fail, the ache in her neck and shoulders was gone and she slept. Slept soundly. She didn't wake when Aunt Kate came in around four in the morning, a bit loose in her joints, and smiling a slack grimace she wasn't aware of. Aunt Kate undressed in part, saw the wine bottles were empty—a few minutes in the bathroom and she was in bed and turned away from Sarah's bed and began to snore.

The next morning she told Sarah the cowboy, Eddie Kincane, was going their way—and he'd show them the sights in Vegas. Eddie wasn't a cowboy, just dressed like one. He was a crop duster. Flew a couple of old crates— Cessnas one-seven-fives—with a partner here and there, taking on contracts for cotton, lettuce, Imperial Valley melons. Had had a good season and was celebrating. Aunt Kate needed some headache pills, but seemed happy. Eddie would meet them in Vegas.

Matt Davis of Leon Solly's office turned up in Vegas. They were in a motel—Eddie Kincane too, a place called the Comanchee Pioneer. Aunt Kate liked hotels and motels with Indian names. Eddie was nice-looking; long neck, red, weathered ears, a bit paunchy for Gary Cooper. And seemed pleasant enough—with pale blue eyes, salt-and-pepper hair, a lock worn over one eyebrow. He had a belt buckle all shiny brass lettered *Wells Fargo and Company. Alert and Faithful Since 1852.* He told Sarah he had paid a hundred dollars for it in Fresno.

"Only really good thing I own, this and my crate, and that isn't much, needs a new motor."

He and Aunt Kate went off to the Fremont, where Eddie liked the higher percentage the slots paid off there. "It's all rigged, of course, for the house—but there they lay a mite more on you." Sarah decided Eddie was pretty bright after all—the cowboy boots could fool you.

Matt Davis had a new dispatch case, and larger silver-rimmed glasses. He sat with Sarah in the coffee shop of the Comanchee Pioneer and explained to her Mr. Solly had decided she'd better come to New York in two weeks. "It's your first big concert. Mr. Solly, he's springing you on the town. Mr. Solly feels the PR planting, two months of it, has been good. Lots of media items. Can't overdo it, or the critics, unlike the theater scribes, film writers, resent too much hoopla in advance; it looks solid, however."

"I feel it isn't real, Mr. Davis, but that's natural, isn't it?"

"Natural and expected. On these papers, now, I need your aunt's signature as to expenses for Mr. Solly's accounts of the concerts so far. You want to see them?"

"No, at dinner I'll give them to her."

"Can't stay or I'd join you—have to fly to the coast. The Kiev Bolski Ballet are defecting so fast we're suggesting to plug the holes recruiting local dancers, if we can get permission. I'll see you in New York. You'll be at the Waldorf; Mr. Solly wants an atmosphere round you. TV interview coverage, all that, in your suite. Big party after the concert. The whole *megillah*, as Mr. Solly puts it."

When Davis had gone, with dispatch case, furled umbrella, Sarah felt alone, and she didn't want to go out this early to the high school and test the piano for the concert. She tried not to think of New York. Of her launching, as Matt Davis put it, as if she were a space ship going into orbit.

That afternoon she played well to three hundred and fifty students. She felt a lassitude, so she had to be careful not to just play, but to project. She had been performing such concerts for a couple of months now, and there was this tendency to just make it one more concert before New York.

The lobby of the Comanchee Pioneer seemed filled with elderly losers who had died in deep club chairs and not been removed.

Sarah slept for two hours after a large Negro woman with Indian features had given her a rubdown and talked about how only damn fools would think living in Nevada was worth living at all. Sarah only half listened as the large woman poured some scented oil on to her big pink-palmed hands and rubbed Sarah's body into a purring contentment. "Tin-horns and call girls, call that living? And skimming to cheat the tax folk by the mob boys. And sand every place. You sing and dance?"

"I'm a concert pianist."

"Now ain't that nice. I'm from a piano family myself. My pop was a honky-tonk boogie-woogie player on the old uprights in East Texas. I wanted to play, but my hands was too big. You look too delicate for it. Bones like in a river trout. I'll just leave you here in the sheet. You kin put my service on the bill. Whatever you want to add for me . . ."

Sarah came awake suddenly to find it was nearly dark over the neon façades—with a deep blue sky when she opened the drapes. A color from a child's book, a Maxfield Parrish sky, now turning darker to become sugared with stars. And for miles and miles around she imagined desert, a landscape like the moon.

Eddie and Kate came back and were, as she said, "feeling no pain."

They went out to dinner at Caesar's Palace. Eddie had a nice earnest quality, not all that educated, maybe, but honest and good to laugh with.

CHAPTER

7

At Caesar's Palace at dinner Eddie told them he had been a logger ("never call 'em lumberjacks"), had captured and corralled wild horses and burros destined to be cooked up by the dog-food canners. After three years in the air reserve of the National Guard, Eddie and a partner, Chuck Moon, had bought two old Cessna crates from a disbanded air circus that used to stunt at country fairs. Crop dusting was a living, even if the planes were crocks. Next year he'd get some cash maybe to buy a Grumman Az-Cat or a converted Canadian CL waterbomber.

It was a world Sarah had never suspected existed before her concert tour. A way of life in the dry high places of the Southwest where the women seemed larger, and people often lived—in their telling of it—on whiskey, chili (called a "bowl of red") and hardly singed steaks. A world of pink Caddies and fifty-dollar jalopies, western-costumed city lawyers on palominos and wetback stoop labor with short weeding hoes.

After the Caesar's stage show of stale dirty jests by an aging comic who refused to quit, a man moved around from behind them. He had that tailored look of what Sarah now knew was an easterner, and by the smell of his after-shave lotion, the pattern of his Countess Mara tie, New York, rather than Philadelphia or Boston. And the voice was Manhattan. "Hello, Eddie, you seem overloaded, *all* the beautiful women."

Eddie looked up from his roast beef, waved an overlong arm holding the fork. "Oh, this is Mr. Salt, Julie Salt. He wants me to write a book. Mr. Salt, Miss Ormsbee, Miss Pedlock."

"Julian Salt," said the man, "*not* Julie. Eddie could turn out a humdinger of a best seller. But he's writing shy."

"Hell, man, I can print some. But that's about it."

Julian Salt motioned a waiter for a chair and sat down, and Aunt Kate invited him to have some coffee and dessert with them. Sarah, of course, knew who Julian Salt was. Once a German refugee, his publishing house, Park Square, was often in the news, and Julian, too. He was a talk-show celebrity, collected works of American folk art and published them in volumes; some said edited by his staff. Julian was always welcome on public platforms, was seen at theater openings and, as a keen businessman, managed to collect a group of authors; some were best sellers with no literary talent, and some masters of the modern novel but with small sales; he called these window dressing.

Julian was trying to impress Sarah and he was a good talker. It was a contest between him and Aunt Kate, and he kept insisting Eddie could write a great personal story of growing up in the Southwest, all his natural ways of life, his various adventures. Eddie didn't even have to write it. Julian would furnish a writer. Eddie would just have to answer some few basic questions on tape. Julian fascinated Sarah. He and Leon Solly were the real New Yorkers, she decided. Not that she knew New York.

Sarah enjoyed the evening, and the next day and that evening, Julian, very attentive, was amusing and entertaining. He told her he hadn't thought girls like Sarah still existed. There was a visit to Hoover Dam, and Sarah knew he was feeding her a line as he kissed her going down in one of the high-speed elevators, and they walked from one state to another, hundreds of feet down through solid rock under the dam. He hugged her and when they were a little ways behind the rest of the party, Julian, very seriously, and as if reluctant to give out the information, said she was the most beautiful, most delicate and even fragile, graceful person he had ever known. Sarah wondered what had happened to his line—and why was she so drawn to him? She knew he had a wife and several daughters, also he had a reputation of having once been the lover of minor film actresses; "if not stars, at least featured," he once explained. Sarah, attracted, wondered, does he see me as prey? On her part was it some hunger, desire? Admittedly he had polish, he had a New York gloss which entertained after all the weeks of south-westerners. He was a comfort, too, after the months on tour in that part of the nation all raw desert and empty plains, or sunburnt towns of J. C. Penney, Sears, chili parlors and Birchers' Halls. Men in Stetsons and bifocals figuring profits on bits of paper, and raucous night goings-on in motels seeping through thin walls to keep her restless to the sound of empty cans of Miller's Highlife and Busch tossed out of windows. Aunt Kate usually out on some expedition of her own.

Julian Salt had known Gide, Betty Grable, been photo-graphed with Bernard Shaw, published a book about Stravinsky, and didn't eat his steaks an inch and a half thick, rare or well done. Julian introduced her to hot Bibb salad and told a funny story about Verdi.

Two crucial events happened to Sarah in Las Vegas, that strange town that seemed a mirage, a nonreality, no matter how much one gambled, ate, drank and did other things. Sarah went to bed with Julian Salt on the second night she met him—in a yellow two-room suite overlooking the pool at the Flamingo Hotel. She did it because she was suddenly frightened of the New York concert, and because so much male attention enlarged memories of the afternoons on Sandor's red velvet sofa, afternoons that had seemed to a very young girl the ultimate in physical ecstasy. Now she was—by her picture of herself—no longer a very young girl. She was nineteen and a professional artist. There was also excess vitality and a sureness in what she wanted from life that had to be satisfied. A minor shock, a surprise, was to find in herself a hint of bitterness. The thought that if Julian's wife had wanted to keep him, she could have; if she didn't want to, then someone would capture him. She was of course at the time of thinking this full of martinis and champagne, not clear-headed, only excited by the physical side of what she hoped was love. She said to Julian in the half-dark in the big bed, music seeping up from below, the low murmur of the people at play, "Julian, Julian." She looked over at him and grabbed his dark hair in both fists and she said, "Julian, I don't want to be wrong about us. Do you care?"

He insisted, of course, he did, and that she was the last love of his life. He was middle-aged, forty-seven, and he had found her. After a new bout of love-making, he phoned down for more champagne—and to be sure it was well iced. Sarah added she was hungry again.

They sat up in the bed, naked, and ate corned beef sandwiches on rye and drank the champagne. Body sated, fed, she had a clear moment to wonder about what was called sin and morality by creeds that preached against adultery. But as she kissed Julian on his city white neck and chest, she couldn't muster any reasons why people talked of sin. What was sin when a man and a woman were at each other as they were again in the sweet savor of their bodies. Near morning they slept. So Sarah, absent from her room, didn't see the note Aunt Kate had left for her, not until noon. *Going off, flying to L.A. with Eddie in his flying machine. Getting married in Reno. Davis will see you to NYC. Good luck on concert. K.*

Panic, fear was like an instant colic in her. Was this punishment for her pleasures? Julian, shown Kate's note, was splendid about it. He reread the note and folded it. "It's as if they planned for us to be alone, Sarah."

"I feel shipwrecked."

He was consoling, helpful, comforting and very amorous. Sarah spent two nights in his arms, abandoning herself to the idea love was all; aware she might be wrong. When Matt Davis appeared, Sarah was in that elated mood, a bit too elated in what Mamma called the "Ormsbee strain." Davis frowned, said little.

Julian Salt decided to accompany them to New York, insisting they all—even Davis—fly first class, and he gave Sarah the window seat as the plane began to warm up.

It was to Sarah, as they rushed off into space, a feeling she was leaving a familiar planet, taking off into a void. When she would again come down to some solid surface, it would be another universe—on something from a Ray Bradbury story that Aunt Kate read. Even Aunt Kate was lost to her, off someplace with her crop duster, in a creaky Cessna—nothing fine like this flying whale with overcharming hostesses. She looked down on the falling-away desert landscape, the wedding-cake structures that were the gambling palaces put down on the worn-down land that seemed the rind end of some world not fully habitable, but in use anyway as a crap table.

Julian was in sporting blue slacks, a patterned sport shirt, some hairy tobacco-colored jacket, a kerchief knotted around his throat instead of a necktie. He had not gone as far western as a cowboy hat or half-boots, but the kerchief was pushed through a miniature silver longhorn steer head.

During the steep climb—her stomach hanging back—Julian smiled and held her hand, spoke of New York with a sense of ownership. "Everyone west of the Hudson used to dream of New York as the only place to make it, came to paint, act, write, and just live. It's even dangerous now—which builds the excitement."

Matt Davis looked up from across the way where he was bent over papers taken from his dispatch case. "You have to move around in an armored car."

Sarah felt her ears pop as they continued to climb up to thirty thousand feet. The land fell away into washed-out colors and the backbones of mountains rose from the dusty expansion. That was Peter Barraclough's expression: *the backbones of mountains.* Poor Peter. Poor sonofabitch, Daddy had said of Peter. But poor Peter, his true obituary was that he was one of those whom Sandor called "the special few; special by something beyond the every day." In Peter's case, poetry. If it was poetry. As they leveled off, Peter was fading. Just as Sandor was fading. She looked over at Julian seated well back, a cigarette smoldering in the ashtray, a glass of Scotch in one hand. The airline tried, he insisted, "to get us as drunk as they can in first class."

Sarah encouraged her thoughts. Already three men in her life. Little Dedee of Hawleytown, Maryland, "the young Pedlock girl." Sarah hurrying to piano lessons up Blue Cape Street in her best dress, also playing in the auditorium at the high school, that dreadful Sousa march for students stamping in for a day's routine of education, giggling and whispering—hinting at secret romances. Now here I am as the earth below is still falling away, and we knife, bore, into fleecy clouds and all the world is just this people-stuffed shape carrying us, two hundred or so living, ticking humans, eastward. And for me, as the old song had it, "I Know Where I'm Going."

She sensed that she was flying toward the future, toward a career. She had as much optimism, intuition, as most young girls. Her intellect was satisfactory to her ideas and her sense of purpose was nearly that of a fanatic. She was certain that New York would be a victory, a triumph, and ahead lay the hope of a splendid life. She accepted all this as destiny, while the plane moved through the clouds with a sound that mingled in her mind with the Bach Concerto in C.

It was a dreadful thing, she knew, to be so sure one could peer in over the edge of the future. She turned to Julian and grasped his arm. He smiled at her, put down his glass, and held one of her wrists, rubbing it with a thumb. About Julian she had no inner signals as to their future as—she thought of the word with a grin—lovers. She had not known men who were so successful, so sure of their own worth, and, yes, even of their charm. Yes, Julian thought of himself as the smartest of publishers, and the most able to get what he wanted by his personal persuasion—what people who disliked him called funky.

Sarah was in love; like with Aunt Kate, she suspected heart led the mind, blotted out any messages, warning.

"Happy?" asked Julian.

"Happy," she answered, and decided words had no nuances for lovers; two alone said such banal things to each other. Even poor Peter. Lucky Julian didn't write poetry. As he had told her, "I publish the damn stuff, at a loss. It balances our list."

She dozed until they slowed, preparing for the descent. Julian's Rolls Royce was waiting at Kennedy Airport; they had only been stacked over Kennedy a half-hour, going round and round over the stone and glass city, the marshes on the fringe of Brooklyn.

On the ground past the baggage recovery, there were two little girls in the Rolls, a plumpish chauffeur and a woman a little plumper. Julian had kissed Sarah briskly with haste as they filed out of the plane. They would have lunch tomorrow at The Running Footman, he said, "One o'clock, I'll make a reservation. Matt will get your bags."

Matt Davis did, and led her to an exit. Leon Solly had a hired Caddie waiting, and he was wearing a fuzzy fashionable Italian hat a bit too small for his head, and shouldering a furled umbrella like a gun.

"Good, good." He grasped Sarah tightly, smiling, nodding to Matt Davis following them with her coat and a small vanity case, two books, and trailed by a porter with suitcases. "Good, good. Now, I have some camera men and *meshugana* reporters waiting. Project, little lady. Just the simple farm girl, born with a piano under her. Understand?"

"What do I say?"

"As little as you can, keep smiling. Don't have to act shy, you *are* shy, I see. You're shaking. Look, easy does it. Talk of what favorite music you'll play Wednesday."

"The Chopin Scherzo Number Three."

"Good, good—give it to them. Don't be smart ass, and remember, they're just hired hands trying to get a story from you. They don't write music critic prose."

"Bach's Traueode—Ode to Morning."

At the curb in a crush of traffic, she watched the Salt Rolls move away, aware she had for security only the piano and nothing else. Julian Salt would be there Wednesday with Mrs. Salt, and with Sarah from time to time, an hour or so, grabbed from wife and children, and the book business, his talks on folk art. Just as God had eluded her after his warning, so love, the true great love the novels were loaded with, had not come; perhaps it was all lies. Writers; liars selling fantasy.

There was a huge gathering of flowers into one big bundle in her arms, delivered by a Solly hireling, as she stepped into the car. And a telegram.

SARI
    WELCOME TO WHATEVER IT IS YOU WANT AND WHAT-EVER YOU CAN OFFER US. DINNER TONIGHT AT 7:30 NORTON-ON-HUDSON.

                         JUDITH PEDLOCK.

Strangely enough, Sarah's great success Wednesday night, her concert as reported, reviewed as the most amazing debut of a piano genius, was always very vague and misty in her memory. Family, lover, manager, the very posh audience in the great hall, all seemed etched on snowflakes.

BOOK TWO

The Ship

Everyone makes mistakes. The snake in the Garden of Eden was supposed to be just a tiny worm in the apple. But as it was the first time the design was created, the measurements got out of hand.

JACOB ELLENBOGEN
Waiting for the Messiah

CHAPTER

8

MUSIC NOTES

LAWRENCE STARKWEATHER

Piano World Magazine

The beautiful young musician performed with extraordinary audacity. Never was Sarah Pedlock in better form at the piano. Her fineness of perception held the audience at the Music Center of the Dorothy Chandler Pavilion in Los Angeles to an awareness that the solo work of other performers that season had been clumsy and unfelicitous. Miss Pedlock went at the Scarlatti sonata like a young avalanche, *fortissimo sempre crescendo e prestissimo sempre accelerando,* keeping her skill, moving through the syncopated passages, going down the flights of octaves and finishing unbeaten after a record-breaking, neck-or-nothing reading that would have made Rubinstein gasp and Van Cliburn faint.

Yet a week later in Carnegie Hall, after a masterful

and flawless rendering of Beethoven's G-major Piano Concerto, she announced through her manager she was canceling all the rest of her concerts that season. That was two years ago, when at the age of twenty-two, she disappeared from the public halls of music, with no explanations . . . Rumors of a breakdown have been denied by the dean of concert managers, Mr. Leon Solly. "Sheer nonsense—she's young and wants to enjoy life away from the crowds who engulfed her before and after every concert. I expect to make an announcement soon of a new extended Pedlock tour."

[From the scrapbook of Judith Pedlock]

Nearly all the northern Pedlocks were ardent travelers, maybe not all with a sense of languor or grace, but they racked up a good deal of mileage a year. Nathan Pedlock, chairman of the board of Pedlock & Sons, Fifth Avenue (Est: 1853), president of the Pedlock Stores, used to rush over to Europe twice a year to check on his buyers in residence in France, Italy, London. As for Marcel Pedlock, the 57th Street art dealer, he could usually be found in season at some auction of Christie's or Sotheby's, eying a suspected Turner seascape, a fine Degas drawing, an early 1912 Matisse oil. Judge Woodrow Pedlock of San Francisco and his wife, Nell—Sarah's uncle and aunt (the California Pedlocks, Judith Arneth Pedlock called them)—attended international legal conferences abroad when the judge sat on the Committee for Orphan Relief, or the one for Revision of International Water Rights.

The most traveled, and the oldest of all the Pedlocks, was Judith Arneth Pedlock, a solid mind, old maybe, but not gnarled. She was a major stockholder, "the wary Matriarch" (said her son-in-law, Lazar-Wolf) of the Big Store and the Pedlock Bank on Wall Street (Lazar-Wolf & Pedlock Brothers). In her eighties, Judith still felt life was "as exciting as a punch in the nose." Whatever her true age, Judith was lively and alert, the remains of her once startling beauty still there between the creases (like hints) on a well made-up face, the blue eyes a bit short-sighted, the Titian-tinted and teased hair, the work of craftsmen. The body creaked, bigger than ever, yet well formed even if too bulky, swelling somewhat in the ankles after one of her meetings (The Pedlock Fund—founded by her late husband).

When she cursed, or recited a childhood prayer, *"Dein bin ich, Gott; rette mich,"* she was aware that gone was the grace of the John Singer Sargent portrait of her that hung on the grand staircase of the house at Norton-on-Hudson. Lazar-Wolf said his mother-in-law was "a little wonky—*meshuga.*" But really, at times—only at times—she was *just* very tired.

Unlike most of the Pedlocks, Judith traveled only by train on land, on sea only by boat. She had made her early crossings in the great Cunards, the *Berengaria, Aquitania, Mary, Elizabeth.* In a top-deck suite with Nora O'Hara, her maid, in attendance, seated at the captain's table, always on his right when she was younger. Already smoking her little Schimmelpennick cigars, asking the ship's orchestra for Mahler, or Cole Porter.

The rest of the Pedlocks, indifferent to the past, flew in jets across seas and continents. "Comfort," she told Nora, "is merely to pick grace over speed."

This May morning, in her suite at the Plaza, preparing to sail, she said, "I'm no such a fool as to accept discomfort in metal and plastic birds." Nora O'Hara was packing the two big trunks, "It's safer than walking the streets of this New York, or riding in a car, choking on the air of them throughways."

"Just keep packing, Irish. My pills. And the leather-covered flasks. Gin in one, vodka in the other. A little booze keeps the pumps thumping."

Nora said, "We better get a move on, or we'll miss the boat. And a good thing it be, too."

Judith, standing at the pier glass, trying on a hat, smiled. "You, and my damn family—daughters and son—would like that." Judith tossed the hat aside. She liked staying at the

Plaza, feared all the talk of tearing it down. "Even the dusty smell of old lobby rugs has character."

"Better call the men for the trunks. If we want to make the boat."

"Lock the trunks." Judith stood at the window. "You should have seen the real gala days of sailing. I was a girl on the *Kronprinzess Charlotte*—1913. All the hand kissing and heel clicking. Mordecai, Mr. Pedlock—*Olva shalom*—liked the Cunarders in their prime. Not this Italian galley we're taking today. I suppose I'm *en pleine* decadence. And later the twenties, Irish, ah, the twenties—the *Normandy* sailing at midnight. Parties in all the staterooms, bootleg likker. We were all younger. You couldn't believe anyone would ever be fifty. And the men . . ." Judith turned from the window as if mulling over a different kind of memory. "I'm old, got the nostalgia rash, Irish, old and falling in on myself."

"If you say so . . . Hello, desk, send for the trunks in Suite 28-A."

Nora was giving no comfort as she locked the trunks. "You're no spring chicken, veetamean pills or no veetamean pills."

"Doctor Zimmerman insists."

It wasn't the vitamins that made Herself so bright, wise, holding the family together; she had more brains—forgive the expression—up her arse than all the Pedlocks in stores or the bank.

"Your niece is not sharing our suite?"

"No, no. She's got her own cabin. I mean, I don't want to smother her social life, crowding her in with us."

"There aren't any young men traveling the boats no more, if that's what you mean—hanky-panky."

"I didn't mean *that*."

"She's come out of herself?"

"Sari just decided she wanted true privacy, to practice and wallow in a bit of introspection."

"Is that it—introspection?"

The men were up for the trunks, and Judith marched down toward the elevators. At times, Nora was pure irascibility.

The world, Judith thought as she stood facing the gilt doors and a moving arrow in a half-circle, the world is lived by accepting it. No good trying not to accept it. Sari is too keyed up. Life at its best is a happy family, all its knees under the dining room table. Of course, what Sari needed was a romance. Oh, there was some gossip of a music teacher, also one of New York's sporting publishers, a real bastard, some said. Judith thought of her own past and sighed. Not in regret but, perhaps, in some remorse. There had been a few men—not as many as gossip claimed. Well, that was long ago, and only age brings a life *sans reproche*. She thought often in French or German phrases, but it no longer gave her the pleasure it had in her youth. If Sari only knew how to accept and not torment herself. But then most Jews have too many moral values; that goddamned Old Testament. She laughed at the unintended jest. Goddamned, or God-authored indeed! The elevator doors opened and she entered the golden cage.

"The Italian ship, lady?"

"The Italia-Iberia Line."

"That's what I said, din' I?"

"That's what he said, Dr. Knott," said Sarah Pedlock as the cab passed under the overhead parkway.

The taxi driver, looking into his rearview mirror, nodded, as if suspecting someone was putting him on.

Dr. Edward Conrad Knott shifted his weight in the back seat of the taxi. It was a bit crowded. Sarah had insisted Sean sit with them. Sean panted, open-mouthed, let about four inches of tongue hang out, and barked. The damn dog—too big for a pet, too stupid for good company. Sean, an Irish setter of a mahogany and gold color, never barked loudly, and that rarely. Sarah ran a gloved hand with a tender patting gesture over his shiny coat. Everything was so clear, detailed—the day was like a sharply focused photograph. New York City traffic was heavy, the sidewalks packed. She felt she was part of the city, a friend of all the people, at least just then.

How Negro the city was becoming, Dr. Knott thought.

It's never the same city generation to generation. Washington Irving, Henry James, O'Henry, O'Hara. It becomes a different Troy each time I return.

He glanced up at the reflections of Sarah and Sean in the glass of the side door of the cab. A slim, beautiful woman in well-cut blue traveling silk suit, corn-colored, honey-toned hair worn long. Blue-green eyes. A face finished off by a mouth of too much character. And mutton fat Sung jade clips on ears. Stylish, delicate bones, but as if made of wound-up springs. Did one still use that word, stylish? Stylish whatever they called it now.

Sean was quiet. Sarah's hand rested on the big dog's shoulder, he watched the people of the republic moving out on the lunch hour.

"As a little girl, I loved the sea, we used to picnic on the beaches."

" '. . . suffer a sea change. Into something rich and strange,' " quoted Dr. Knott.

"The Talmud," said Sarah, smiling, "put it better. 'When I was home, I was in a better place.' "

"What's home, Sarah?"

She shook her head as if at the absurdity of the question. "Once it was a place called Hawleytown on the Eastern Shore of Maryland, that was home. Was it Curtis? That was mostly hard work. Then after the concerts stopped—was it studying Chopin with La Chaise in Paris? Was it . . . was it . . . ?" She made a vague gesture, a girlish gesture—at twenty-four she often still suggested the school girl.

Dr. Knott brushed his smart gray beard, cut, he hoped, like an Elizabethan sea rover's. "For a mechanical nightingale, home is a cage; for us, it's this overcrowded planet. I rather like American crowds."

Sarah was amused at the thoughtful expression on the handsome but battered face, the too-often broken nose. Leaning toward him, her mouth a bit open, blue-green eyes very wide ("bugged on stems," her father used to say when she was a child and acting up, and she was still Dedee), she said, "Doctor, you have doubts about Aunt Judith taking me off, showing me Italy?"

"No, no, great idea to invite us." He patted her hand with two swift taps, almost playful blows.

"She isn't really my aunt. My family is from the Joseph Pedlock side, the copper refiners. Aunt Judith married the grandson of the founder of the Elijah Pedlock dynasty, the Big Store, the Bank. We're the poor relatives. Clear?"

He fumbled in the tweed jacket pocket, a jacket with leather patches sewed on at elbows and leather gun butt patch over the right shoulder. He was hunting for money as the cab came charging into a packed sailing scene under the Hudson River Roadway. Other taxis clanged bumpers. Private cars, trucks, pick-ups seemed locked in battle. Several police were writing tickets on cars left unattended. The ship's stewards were lifting up and carrying away baggage. Sarah snapped a thin steel leash on Sean, who panted politely. Unlike Dr. Knott, Sarah thought, he disliked crowds, American or otherwise.

It was not clear to me, she thought as the traffic grew thicker, that time between my last concert and this sea voyage; no, it's not clear enough. Why the breakdown? Was it the death of Aunt Kate, or that unfortunate affair with Julian Salt? Or an obsession with finding God? Was I terrified not by death but by a fear of impregnation, suddenly imagined while performing a concert? My being turned off from men for a while through the mixture of my experience with Julian and the wrath of God? But how would this relate to my playing the piano? It doesn't come clear for me. I want to forget about my visions and concentrate on my search for God, in the figurative sense, as well as my hunt for a Jewish or some religious identity, which was denied me while I was growing up. To face it. In me are medical *vs.* religious establishments fighting for my soul. Am I mad or actually "possessed," in this case by God? This possession is as frightening to me, awe inspiring, and I know as *dangerous* as that by the prince of darkness.

Dr. Knott is right—the God vision is an aberration; only, *only* what if he's wrong, the whole rational—so-called rational—world is wrong? And isn't my major goal full Jewishness? Or even why am I *not* really relatively coherent? It's so clear in *Faust, The Golem,* in the ecstasy of the saints, their confessions . . .

She became aware they were still in heavy traffic, but at the pier.

"Plenty people traveling," said the taxi driver.

"Would you mind," asked Sarah, "seeing my bags don't get scratched?"

Dr. Knott paid the taxi driver (who sneered at the tip) and took Sarah's arm.

She made a pantomime of overamusement, graceful arms, long torso, slender neck all playing a part. "I used to know a man who, to impress me, always gave ten-dollar taxi tips."

"Paranoiac."

"I was twenty, loved to go to Père-Lachaise cemetery in Paris with this man. He always visited the grave of Gertrude Stein."

Dr. Knott moved between two great mounds of luggage which stewards were attacking.

"Sounds like real fun, Sarah."

She held the dog leash very short and the dog looked up at her. *Fun* was a word he reacted to.

Dr. Knott motioned to a steward to attend to their bags. Two were Sarah's, his own was the old Gladstone of walrus hide. A vast bag, strongly strapped, brass locked, worn but sturdy. "They're ticketed, steward, by cabin numbers."

"Yes, signore."

"It's muggy weather—I need another bath." Sarah walked with a ballet-like step among the pushing, shouting, solid citizens going on holiday, they elbowing other boarding passengers, shouting at stewards, calling out cabin numbers. The snarl of arriving taxis, Sarah thought, was like a Schönberg scoring—thinking like that made crowds less personal, not so menacing. Doctor Knott, for all his lean height and a bit of a paunch, was strong and pushed her through the crowd, making room for Sean.

"I've some Jim Beam in my bag, Sarah."

"Aunt Judith will have champagne. And I'm not jumpy."

"Well, I am, thirsty anyway."

From the ship itself, high, white, all cubist forms, came the deep throat-clearing sound of the big siren. The people—passengers, visitors—packing onto the pier became more animated. The baggage carriers, Italian and Spanish youths, were shouting and gesturing in Latin excitement, sweating through their lime-yellow short ship's jackets, with the metal buttons and a pattern in red braid around the collars.

Sarah reacted better to the odors than to the crowd images. There was the smell of newspaper print, bodies on a hot day, peanut shells, dying hothouse flowers in Bon Voyage baskets, the tainted river water and sewage alongside the pier. Rather a vivid odor—not delicate—but living—life. A special sailing-day smell Sarah always remembered as being the smell of her thirteenth year, when she had gone aboard for a two-hour visit with a group of Baltimore school girls under a Miss Hatvon, a visit on a Dutch boat, the *Staatendam*. The pianist in the main salon played Weber's *Rondo Brilliant*. No one played that anymore, and Stacy Cohen said Miss Hatvon tried to kiss her neck. Stacy was always a creep. Hardly likely about Miss Hatvon. Stacy had married a builder of beach houses—and last time Sarah had visited Hawleytown, Stacy had shown off three fat babies. Sarah—some deep mother-urge—was tempted to steal one of the fatties. But no, children made problems. The ship's siren went off again, and she jumped: the present moment, this day, the ship—these were the only realities.

CHAPTER

9

[From the journal of Edward Knott]

MAY 24:

At the dock a Mack Sennett pace and a damp rushing about. Great confusion at the pier; no one could make sense in a mass of taxis, private cars and large Italian families weeping and hugging, to see relatives off to visit the Old Country. The ship very large and white, impressive, but rust-streaked, I observed, like a rash some of my patients get—rust in large blotches all over the noble white hull, and we two (and the damn dog) fight our way on board. Sailors, officers and staff, all charming Latins, all happy, gay and helplessly helpful; not well organized.

I had decided, I told Sarah, I would make this trip as a follower of Stendhal's le beylism, a system figured out by me from his works as a belief that all living of ourselves originates in sensations, impressions, sense perceptions. She'd buy that, she said.

Now I'm settled in. Sarah will go to greet her Aunt Judith. I begged off—till later.

My cabin on B Deck has gin-mill lighting, a hard mattress and an old man smoking a panatela—me. I recount my traveler's checks, and see I have two-dozen coat hangers in the closet. There are three orange life belts and pictures of an Edwardian gentleman, out of an illustration from an English pornographic novel, in various stages of putting on a bulky jacket. The ship is called the Lucrezia Borgia—*rumors are—so named by the wife of the president of the line after a party at a Fellini film opening and some drinking. The president went along with the name, he found his wife—his third—a very amusing woman.*

Sarah, today, is on a fine even keel and is cheerful—perhaps a bit too cheerful. But that's all to the good just now. I've been trying for the last nine months to get her to travel. Come out and feel the world moving beneath her feet. That damn fool Leon Solly, her manager, told her aunt she'd soon give concerts again. I certainly never promised that. *I have never mentioned her concerts to her after the first few weeks she was brought to me by Judith Pedlock. I sounded very hopeful, I know I am not in an honest profession.*

"*Scusi,* ist not."

"Not? *What* ist not?"

"Ist not open the service. Steward's pantry."

"I just want an ice bucket. We have ourselves brought caviar, crackers, tidbits, the whole damn schmear," said Judith. "*Capish?*"

"Ist not—."

"*E troppo.* Go get."

The cabin steward, a small man from Piedmont, waved his fingers as if drying them in the air. "Is closed, signora, the pantry service this side of A Deck. Broke, *si Lei piace,* ice machine."

Nora O'Hara, hanging clothes in the bedroom of the suite, turned around. "I'll manage the ice from the other stewards, and I'll open some tins of antipasto."

"*Scusi,*" said the cabin steward, pressing his way out into the corridor as Sarah came through the suite's door, dodging and maneuvering herself around the deck steward.

Judith, balanced, legs apart as if far out at sea, was

smoking a little cigarillo and shedding her traveling jacket. She smiled and held out a hand with only one bracelet on it, gold and some rare stones—and a finger with one ring, a four-carat diamond.

"Sari, Irish thought you'd missed the boat."

The two in affection made those pecking gestures of kissing cheeks, actually just a brushing touch, but it was clear to Nora they took to each other. That's the Hebrews for you, family feelings thick as a peat-cutter's brogue.

"What a mob scene, Aunt Judith. In the midst of it I had to get Sean settled in the kennel on the top deck."

"You brought the dog? *Gruss Gott!*"

"You have to have something to make you walk." Overhead sounded the metallic thunder of hoofs. "He's good company."

Judith nodded. "One summer at Norton-on-Hudson I was thinking of leaving Mordecai. Oh, yes—it was the season of my madness for some gentleman farmer in Kenya where he was growing coffee trees. I bought a dollar alarm clock and kept it wound up and lived with its ticking, letting my thoughts beat themselves to nothing. And so I never did pick coffee berries."

"An alarm clock?"

"Doesn't bark. So, settled in? Enough space?"

"B Deck, Aunt Judith. Big enough." Sarah began to remove her gloves.

"Forget the aunt. Judith is enough. Irish!"

Nora came in still wearing her tweed jacket, a lump of a hat set on back of her head. She carried a tray of opened glass and metal containers holding sardines, antipasto, crackers, smoked sturgeon and a basin of ice with a bottle of wine in it. "Located ice in the next steward's cubby. The boy was holding out for a bill." Nora smiled. "Miss Pedlock. I hope we all have a good trip. It's the eighteenth crossing we've made, Herself and I."

"Twenty." Judith twirled the bottle of Latour Fleurit in the basin of ice and looked over her shoulder at Sarah. "Doctor Knott is at the brandy, I suppose."

"It's bourbon, I think."

"The old coot. Used to reek with Freudian orthodoxies,

now mostly discredited by the young psychiatrists. All over Europe, Doc Knott, as a guest on the yachts of rich Greeks, or eating goat cheese on some goddamn Greek island with some shepherd boy to keep house; the old rip. Oh, the hell with waiting." Judith dipped up ice cubes and set them two in a glass. She loosened the cork of the champagne bottle, poured and handed Sarah a glass. "You been practicing?"

Sarah accepted the glass, shook her head. "Haven't been doing anything. Not much of anything but contemplating."

"Oh, that." Judith took a big sip of her drink.

"I no more want to be a wunderkind, Judith. Not again a wild romantic at the piano. I see me as a classic, cool performer when I play again, calm as a master. There was a time when Aunt Kate and—"

"No confessions, please, Sari. I promised your father I'd keep an eye on you. But don't you go believe it. Not me shaking a finger. I'm a lousy chaperon."

Sari sipped the wine slowly, feeling it the way wine always felt if it was a good one. Poor Aunt Kate—she dead, Eddie dead in that crop duster plane in that Kansas twister. Aunt Kate could belt wine like nobody else . . . She studied Judith, eating smoked sturgeon on crackers. What a knock-out big-boned beauty she must have been around World War I time. Wise-looking now, the mouth sensual in pride and poignancy. Were there actually sensual mouths, or had novelists improvised Eros on the image of full lips? There was a tilt of amusement at one corner of the old woman's mouth that suggested ironic introspection.

"Judith, have you religion?" The words burst from her suddenly, a thought turned verbal.

"You're goddamn right I have." She chewed, sipped, in thought. "My religion is life. That banal enough for you, Sari?"

"Too easy." Sarah tapped a neat show on a long foot on the green rug.

"It's enough for me. *Con amore.* You want more? All right, I agree with Spinoza: Man is God, God is Man. Beyond that it's all horse apples. Don't expect any fancy philosophy from me, Sari."

"You're a Jew. I'm nearly a Jew."

(75)

"Nearly doesn't count with the goyim." Judith laughed, handed Sarah a rye crisp with sardines on it. "A Jew is anyone whom someone *else* thinks of as a Jew."

"Daddy's father, my grandfather—who married a shiksa—was the son of the Joseph Pedlock, the copper miner. Mom's family called themselves Ormsbee in Hawleytown, but in Baltimore they were once Ornstein."

"Lucky girl. You can swing either way," said Judith. "My advice is, forget it. Fidelity to some things can be overdone."

Sarah chewed and swallowed the tidbit with relish. "Suppose, suppose there is a spiritual reason for being. That it's all true in some way we don't understand."

"In the beginning was hydrogen, somebody once said." Judith refilled Sarah's glass. "Why not? Take my advice. There may be some young man on board. Latch on to him. You can't solve everything that way, but it does take one's mind off things."

Sarah put down her glass. "I'm a real lousy hedonist, Judith." The ship's siren sounded louder than ever, the vast bulk of ship stirred, the cabin tilted a bit. The hoots of tugs were heard in contrapuntal dialogue.

"Oh, come on, Sari. You're no virgin at twenty-four, with that body, those legs."

"Physically, no."

Judith refilled her glass. "Physically is how they count it."

"I think the ship's moving."

On deck Dr. Knott was pressed against a tall man in a tobacco-colored sport jacket, a man who looked to be in his late twenties; standing there, not waving, not cheering, his hatless head of reddish curly hair a bit too thin at the temples.

"Sorry," said Dr. Knott in the crowd pack, elbows bent. The man, his face the deep peanut-butter color of one who had been under a sun lamp for several weeks, just nodded. Not a handsome face, Dr. Knott decided, but a good one—at least likable. He studied the man closely. A very careful shave, hair freshly cut, modestly cut, none of the popular fancy shaggy styling. Dr. Knott took out a leather cigar case and offered it up to the man. "Smoke cigars?"

The man looked at Dr. Knott as if suspecting to be asked for a loan. His hazel and deep-brown eyes seemed to have flecks of gold in them. His voice was good but somewhat hesitant, that of a man who wasn't too sure about the motives of strangers. "Wouldn't deprive you of one."

"No, no, have a couple of boxes below," Dr. Knott said. "You can also get Rafael Gonzales Havana cigars on board once we're past the three-, or is it the twelve-mile limit?"

"Twelve." The man took the cigar from the case, expertly rolled it in strong fingers, sniffed it. "You're very kind—"

"Knott. Dr. Edward Knott." He pulled out a cigar himself, and the tall man took out a small silver lighter shaped like a large raindrop. He lit both their cigars and they stood puffing pleasantly on the pungent smoke as the music grew louder, the tugs snorted in their assault on the ship and hauling cables grew taut from ship to tugs. Dr. Knott took hold of the lighter. "Handmade?"

The man nodded, seemed more trusting—almost pleased to talk to someone. "Indians made them, or did when silver dollars were around."

"Yes, an interesting folk art, Mr.—?"

"Beck, Gregory Beck." The man offered a hand which the doctor took.

"You may be the youngest male passenger aboard. It's a cargo of old crocks, mostly."

"What kind of a doctor are you?"

"No kind just now. Retired psychiatrist, if you must know. Traveling with two women friends . . . Oh, no, *just* shipmates."

"Relatives?"

"No, no. One of the friends and I—working on a book; the states, tensions and agitation of great musicians and composers. Wagner, Beethoven, Stravinsky, etcetera."

The other man laughed, mouth open fully for the first time. "Goddamn it, sounds like real fancy crap."

Dr. Knott cheerfully slapped Gregory Beck between the shoulder blades. "Oh, it will be. But my partner is serious

(77)

about it, and I'm an ancient maverick at liberty. The old lady is a grande dame. Look, I'll arrange for you to sit with us at table."

"I've already asked the purser for a small table in—"

"Forget it. I know Dino, the maître d'." He saw the young man seemed almost eager to have company—after his first wary doubts.

"You're sure the ladies—?"

"Not at all, and alone, Dino, he'll put you behind a door by the swill barrels. Unless you slipped him a fortune."

"It's been a long time since fancy food mattered to me."

"Good, settled." Dr. Knott looked around as if checking to see if there was any other choice he might have made.

With the ship moving down the bay, Gregory Beck didn't protest the doctor taking his arm on an offer to come below for a drink. The B Deck cabin contained one chair which Dr. Knott offered to his guest. From his Gladstone bag, tossing aside two shirts, a case of straight razors, he got out a bottle of whisky, and from a nest of silver drinking cups, half-filled two.

"Boon to mankind *if* not abused." He lifted his cup. "Well, death to our enemies, if any."

They sipped, while on decks the cheering and yelling seemed to grow weaker, the ship's siren hooted, the tugs answered. The cabin swayed in just a hint of what life moving over a liquid surface could be.

Gregory enjoyed the Scotch, his mood was now expansive—he had been rather doubtful on deck of sailing alone, deciding so quickly on the trip. "I'm a teacher. Rather, I was an instructor, professor of environmental studies. Actually, I'm an architect, not very active at the moment."

"I wish there were more like you, Gregory. I mean inactive. I'd like to dynamite *everything* modern built since Frank Lloyd Wright was fifty."

"Christ, lots of times I agree with you there. Modern architects often build mostly for photographers, Doctor Knott."

"Call me Doc, and let's have one more."

They had one more and another. Dr. Knott studied

Gregory Beck. He seemed melted from a kind of frost rime that had appeared so solid on deck. They talked of horses, the Berkshires in autumn, of Joseph Conrad, whom they both liked, and Henry James, whom they couldn't read. The more he studied the young man, the more his old professional searching out of character came to the fore. He had wanted a young man at their table—Lord knows there was little to choose from on this ship of middle-aged passengers. But this Gregory Beck was more complex than at first appearances. A sudden change of mood. A mistrust of my motives at first. Now an eagerness to talk—just to talk.

"Yes," said Dr. Knott. "The film made of *Lord Jim* was one of the most dismal ever made."

CHAPTER

10

The *Lucrezia Borgia*'s First Class dining room at night looked cheerful enough with Italian and Spanish versions of the mildest modern abstract art debased to respectability etched on what looked like steel panels. It suggested the lobby of an art-film theater. Gregory Beck came into the dining room past racks of fantastic food; displays of roast turkeys, suckling pigs in aspic, splendid pork pink smoked hams. Also chickens and ducks framed in truffles and minor organs. He heard the buzz of already feeding diners. (He was to learn later that the food displays on the rack were all made of colored wax and part of the room's décor.)

He had changed into a blue jacket and gray rep tie. Dr. Knott had told him one didn't dress for dinner first night out. Gregory was not sure how he had let the old crock con him into joining his table. He had looked forward to sitting alone at a small table and reading his copy of *Ego 5* of James Agate. He had *Ego 3* to *9* in his luggage and he enjoyed the texts, the trash bins of the late London theater critic. He, himself, hardly cared for going to plays, but the books with their inner circle quirks were delightful time-killers. But it was good to be with others. He had half-promised himself this trip to enjoy being with people.

The maître d' of Dr. Knott's section was tall, luxury-car-salesman-type, with larded dark hair and a rubber-band moustache. Smiling at Gregory, printed oversized menu and table list in hand, head to one side in some facetious charm, he asked, "Ah, welcome . . . name pliz?"

"Beck, Gregory Beck."

"But, of cuss, *capisco*. Dr. Knott's table. This way, pliz."

Gregory awkwardly slipped the folded ten-dollar bill into the maître d's palm; he had read some place that on a luxury ship one did this on the first day out. The palm was like an extension of a sleek elephant, a trunk that seemed to snuff up the folded bill automatically in one continuous gesture of grace and movement.

"This way . . . an honor, signori."

Dr. Knott was seated at a fairly large table, a martini in front of him, his steel-gray Viking beard and whitening hair seemed to have felt water and comb but were still in some rebellion. "Ah, Greg, the ladies are dining in their cabins tonight. Just as well. Dino, *non è vero*, a double martini for Signor Beck. And some caviar. Your menu is so damn long." He slid Churchillian half-glasses on his big blade of a nose.

"Doctor," said Dino, bending over the table, "may I suggest from the captain's buffet as special, the Oysters Mignonette, Consommé Rubis à la Modavia, Stuffed Cornish Hen with Sauce Périgordine. Pliz, *not* the pasta, notta the steak."

"We're in your paws, Dino, eh, Greg?"

The maître d' set a drink before Gregory, who took small sips of the martini. It was good tasty gin, and just enough vermouth, the proper twist of lemon.

Gregory said, "If the ladies object to me, I—"

"Of course not, and, damn it, you'd eat swill like many of the First Class passengers if I didn't alert Dino we know better, eh, Dino?"

"Pliz—a real gourmet warms my heart."

Gregory studied the long menu. "I really haven't been paying much attention to food, Doctor Kn . . . Doc."

The ship dipped a bit on the Atlantic, but it was a calm night. The meal was good, and the people all around them cheerful. The wine steward, a fat fellow from Naples, brought Dr. Knott a bottle of champagne. "Signore Doctor, this ordered for you before sailing. A gift from friends."

"I don't have any friends left alive. All died playing tennis or jogging." He took up the card. *Happy Sailing. Much Fun. The Staff. The Clinic.* "What do you know! Trained a hell of a lot of the best men there at Megandor. When I used to see some validity in psychoanalysis and believed in it."

"You don't anymore—I mean, believe?"

"Yes and no, mostly *maybe.*"

They drank two glasses each of the champagne. Dr. Knott suggested they go up to the top deck where he had a duty to perform. The animal kennels were up there under a huge funnel that belched diesel fumes and also, unfortunately, sucked in air for the conditioning system.

An attendant opened a kennel from behind the screen of which the Irish setter, Sean, was whining and thrashing about. Free, he leaped at Dr. Knott, placing his forepaws on the doctor's chest, hunting the doctor's face with an active tongue.

"Down, you emotional bastard. What slobs dogs are . . . Here, I have something for you." He opened a napkin and offered the dog half a Cornish hen breast. The dog did away with it with speed, and Dr. Knott snapped a leash the attendant handed him on to the animal's collar.

"Belongs to Sarah, girl in our party. Too jumpy to be in shows, but a nice enough dumb mutt. You like dogs, Greg?"

"Not very much."

"I've found people who like dogs too much don't give any big damn about people."

They walked the deck, the dog pulling hard on the leash. Two other couples were also promenading under the mechanical whirl of the funnel pouring out fuel oil fumes and sucking in air. Two long-haired men in crew-neck sweaters and open-toe sandals led two white poodles, and there was a fat couple with a mean little Mexican dog with a pendulous belly and a habit of offering to bite the world.

Gregory inhaled, exhaled, flexed, unflexed his hands and fingers. Overhead the sky was dusted with stars, and behind the ship the wake hissed like frying pans of bacon, at least a dozen frying pans. There was a sadness on a ship on this vast night sea, Gregory felt, in being alone. The yellow lights in rows on rigging were haloed in mist. On the bridge, sealed in glass, he saw flat figures as if painted on, shapes moving slightly, mysteriously; alert—he hoped—to the duties which controlled the ship.

"The officers, Greg, are all picked for their movie star looks, and their copulating abilities. It's a very civilized approach to travel in luxury. Be nice if they had sea experts, too."

"Sure they have, Doc."

The dog turned to look at them and whined. His mahogany golden coat looked black in the dark night, only his eyes shone, reflecting the violet and silvery lights overhead.

"It's all right, boy. Sarah will take you for a nice big deck stroll in the morning."

The dog whined again, coughed and vomited at the base of the funnel. "Son of a bitch," said Dr. Knott. "Never live with a neurotic dog."

Am I really at sea, and what hassle am I running from? Gregory thought as he lay in the bed the steward had turned down for him in his cabin. Trying to read, smoking the cigar Dr. Knott had insisted a man should smoke as a nightcap. A good cigar, better than the ones his grandfather used to smoke. Pittsburgh stogies Grandpa had called them. "Me and Mark Twain, we never paid more than five dollars a barrel for 'em."

(The old man was a stone-age Socialist, who made a fortune supplying drilling pipe in the Oklahoma oil fields. Secondhand pipe and drilling gear, Grandpa taking shares in the wells the wildcatters drilled, not selling the pipe or gear for anything but a share of the site. "Well, a lot of

dusters, Gregory, this old man backed. But when it hit, boy!
Yes, there was a God in those days."

(He had said to Gregory when he heard his grandson
didn't want to be a lawyer, but rather to study architecture,
"Why not?" They were seated in the town's Memorial Park
near the depot, Gregory's bag set down by the cast-iron
bench. A young girl passed, swinging with no discretion all
she had. "A delight," said the old man. "The ass not bad."
He still had an eye for life and women. And while he had
lost his last fortune—he used to say—not the pleasures of
admiring women.

(When Gregory's bus was announced on the public-
address system, Grandpa had handed him a fifty-dollar bill
and an address written out boldly on a bit of paper torn
from the flyleaf of a volume of Tolstoy the old man read in
Russian. "No, no, no goddamn protests, Gregory. Drink
good bourbon and learn to spit in the eye of the world—if
you don't, it will spit first."

(Oh, boy, the old man was so right.

(Grandpa had no use for organized religion. But he
attended schul, even owned a prayer shawl and skull cap.
Could rattle off Hebrew better than any reform rabbi . . . A
tough old man, Gregory thought, my grandfather, who had
been a tough young stud in the early frontier wildcat oil
fields from Tulsa to Beaumont. And a middle-aged hedonist;
pictures of him were on the parlor piano. In a bowler and a
tubular overcoat, handle-bar Buffalo Bill moustache, along
with Big Bill Hayworth, labor leader, and an older grayer
one pictured with Emma Goldman. Grandpa always was
torn, Papa said, between proving he could make money as
easy as a Rockefeller, and pissing it away for some socialist
dream.

(Grandpa agreed at the bus depot that day Gregory left
for college: "A folly in my thinking was I felt I could ease
the schmerz of the world." He had been married four times.
And had slept, he swore, with Pavlova. *"Goldenen Jahre* I
had. Don't kock yours away, Gregory. Go catch your bus.")

The ship's bed was too soft. Gregory took the mattress
and put it on the floor. Soon he slept, rolling a bit to the

movement of the ship. The dreams were confused, but he had had them for so many years that the images, the people, even the events were worn down like pebbles in a brook.

Sarah prepared to go tumbling off to sleep soon after getting into the cabin's bed. Just a few moments of vagrant thoughts first—thoughts that she relished, a sort of half-dream summing up the day, her feelings, the cozy sense of being in bed, covered, warm. The rocking of the ship was like the old wooden porch swing at home; she used to recline on it full length when very young. To let herself fantasize on summer nights while at the other end of the porch behind her, the bright orange lights of the living room windows made squares and there were voices of some gathering of family friends, a party, or a grown-up birthday. It was so safe, being small and petted, knowing you were backed up by the love of all those people who loved you. Aunt Kate's voice a bit louder, somewhat more boisterous . . . Sarah twitched and turned in the roll of the ship, moved to a more comfortable position. It was hard to accept the fact Aunt Kate was dead. How unfair of whatever decides our destinies that some storm had knocked Aunt Kate and Eddie out of the sky, thrown them across power lines, mashed, singed and crushed them—so indifferently—in the Kansas night.

She had never believed in death as a child . . . somehow she would escape it. But the telegram announcing the death of Kate and Eddie had grabbed at her heart. She had given a concert in Boston that night. What came was a real pain, and a stomach filled with ground glass. *Dead was dead. Dead are gone.* But it took so long to accept the final end of people so close.

She slept, curled up, burrowing the left side of her face into the pillow. A good sleep until a wilder roll of the ship, some unexpected heave of the sea, and she was awake, unable to orient herself. Where? Who? Then her mind cleared. Trip. Ship. A new face. Yes. Why did waking remind her of the time when she was four when she asked Daddy, "Is it true, like Stacy Cohen says, you made me by putting an egg in Mamma's navel?" Daddy said, "Stacy needs to get a clout in the ear." Sarah had thought about it some more and then said, "Please, Daddy, I don't want an egg put in my navel." And for several nights she had dreamed of huge serving plates filled with hot scrambled eggs, the way Tessie, the big black cook, made them; eggs soft, salted and peppered, being spooned into her navel. To awake screaming in incoherent terror, yelling for Mamma to come and hug her and say, "Dedee, whatever it was, it was only a dream."

Much later, the egg theory of impregnation sneaking into her dreams had caused her six months of terror before dislocation of the image, that fear from her subconscious. This was after *it* had suddenly appeared in the middle of Beethoven's *Lustig-Traurig* Bagatelle in C. She was on stage in Toronto, at the Steinway concert grand, thinking *there* is Tessie standing over me holding a hot platter of scrambled eggs and the big kitchen mixing spoon, and hearing Tessie say, "Lift yo' dress, Honey Chile, and I'll git these nice an' hot all up yo' navel . . ." Somehow Sarah's fingers had not faltered on the keyboard. She had closed her eyes to the image and played on. Superbly, the critic wrote.

"Audacity and self-confidence," the critics had added of Sarah Pedlock after that concert. She remembered the words: "A bedazzlement without guile." She no longer liked to recall herself as a prodigy, a wunderkind. She was now set on a deeper, wider goal. The purpose of this sea trip, Dr. Knott suggested, was to clarify just *what* she would do. To piano again, or not to piano? Turning onto her other cheek, she slept again, solidly, and if she had dreams she would not remember them.

Judith Pedlock, after deciding not to call Sarah on the ship's phone, slept on her back, breathing through her mouth, giving now and then a coughing sound, then a snort, and turning on her side, muttering "*Vielen Dank . . . wir leben . . .*" Sleeping deeply, a large body on the bed, the hair held in a net, the one feeble light under frosted glass over the dressing table making shadows and ominous fissures on the old flesh as if mocking what had once been of so much beauty, so desired. Nora stood by the door from the living room of the suite on A Deck. Nora in her long braids, standing in her blue, short-waisted bathrobe, the large peasant feet in sensible slippers. Herself, there, was breathing so she's still among us. Nora went back to the second and smaller bedroom, recited a prayer for her old Aunt Sibonne, for her two nephews she was supporting in their study for the priesthood.

She put her dentures in a glass of blue water, made some comic gestures with her now flabby lips, and got into bed, thinking of death and salvation and Father O'Connor intoning the absolution over her mother's casket: *"Deinde, ego te absolvo a peccatis tuis . . ."* Remember the morning coffee, Herself likes it hot and waiting . . . *"in nomine Patris et Filii et Spiritus Sancti."* And then Nora slept, melding from a dream of sinful pleasures and languorous cruelties, vague and confused, to a tired sleep of one who had been busy all day since before dawn.

Dr. Knott had finished the cigar and the little left of the Scotch—a two fingers' drink as he thought of it. Something very secret, very interesting in Gregory Beck . . . And was soon asleep, snoring loudly from a deviated septum, and clutching at the blanket that came up under his chin. His pointed goat's beard aimed at the ceiling of the cabin on B Deck. He slept with an old man's pleasure in sleep, and from time to time dreamed incompatible, wonderful bits of the past, of his boyhood and youth. Nothing he could fully remember when he came awake, but of boyhood chums, friends, wisteria vines, skating, water bugs, an Ivar Johnson bike . . . some hint of the naked immediacy of a sensual drive that had not left him to taper down until he was fifty. He remembered some fragment of Gestalt psychology he had discussed with Sarah that now intruded into his sleep—oh, the windy crap, the humbug of philosophers. He caught glimpses of the girls and boys he had made love to, of the men and women who had been his lovers, most all gone to the inevitable final urn of ashes . . . It all seemed now part of Wu-nien, the Zen no-mind, the training he had taken at one time in hatha yoga, in metabolism and respiratory controls.

Dim hot spots of color, far apart little bulbs burned on the windward side of B Deck over the shrouded lifeboats. Gregory Beck had awakened after a short sleep and come on deck in a topcoat of tan fuzzy wool, a garment long out of style, and a large cap on his head. He paced off the scrubbed deck planks, walking at a good rate—4 mph— head bent down, walking as if walking had a purpose, even if it had no final door to admit one. At the turn of the deck he reversed automatically and went on without losing the rhythm of his pace. The wristwatch showed 2:35, a plain watch of no great value but old and so kept in rather odd affection. From his past. It was about all he had left of those early years; to recall too much of them gave him a racking nausea. He walked carefully, trying to make no clatter, for there were sleepers stretched out in complete commitment behind the portholes. The stewards were most likely snoozing with open shirts, shoes off, in case, just in case, some sleeper awoke to call for attention. The engine gangs on duty, officers yawning on the bridge. And Doc, that old fart, why has he latched on to me?

Gregory Beck decided twice more around the deck and he'd be tired enough to go back to his cabin, that inner cabin with no porthole, and lie down again on the mattress on the floor, get some troubled sleep before morning. The cabin was like a monk's cell, and small rooms for some time had given him night sweats. So far the sea trip had not produced all its expected results. Not that he wanted wild gaiety and orgies. So it was only the first night out, and there was Doc and his so far two invisible ladies.

A little sailor came out of the double plate-glass doors, carrying a bucket. He was in his shirtsleeves, or rather a kind of short sea garment. He seemed shy, and lowered his head as he said something in soft Italian. *"Permesso? Scusi."*

Gregory answered, "Good morning."

"Buon giorno," said the little sailor and went on with his bucket.

That *"Buon giorno"* proves I'm really at sea—not in the middle of one of those dreams. Or is this a dream too?

To the east over the slate-gray sea he saw there was a suggestion of a warm line of color. He thought of Ionic pillars of red porphyry and looked at his watch again, put it to his ear. It had stopped; he had forgotten to wind it. It had been a gift from his now dead wife's family, given to him at the engagement party. Then the wedding in Carmel, at the Sand Piper Inn. He remembered the wonderful glow of the lava rock fireplace at the Inn, and the charm of the host and hostess making them welcome. A Jew among gentiles, set to carry off the Christian daughter.

Pop, the old bigot, had come down from Seattle. Grandpa was too old to travel. Pop was in good form: "You, the great-grandson of the chief rabbi of Budapest," his father had said. "Of *all* of Hungary—marrying a *shiksa*." He had also quoted the Torah and, irascible as ever, at their last meeting in the bedroom before the ceremony, had disintegrated into fearful Hasidic cursings. Pop always had a ferocious agility with oaths . . .

Gregory slipped the watch from his wrist and walking to his cabin wound the watch slowly and carefully so as not to overwind the spring. He fell asleep as soon as he put his head to the mattress.

Only Dr. Knott appeared for breakfast in the main dining room. When Dino remarked that it was a fine day, the doctor recited:

> "I'd like to be the Weather Man
> And wigwag with the sky."

"The kippers, signore, and perhaps some eggs and de very good Canadian bacon?"

Dr. Knott went on deck smoking his first cigar after a big breakfast—feeling well fed. Gregory came out on deck dressed in the same jacket and slacks he had come aboard in.

"Late hours, Greg?"

"Didn't go to sleep until very late, Doc. Walked the deck till all hours. My watch stopped."

"You'll be at lunch? Meet the ladies."

"You still think I'm not—?"

"Intruding? Hell, no."

Several women came past them, large women making screechy laughter, their colors a bit loud, their hair somewhat overdressed.

"Schoolteachers. Downy lips, sure sign of passion," said Dr. Knott. "Frozen ovaries. Nature's unused products."

"You're a mean bastard, Doc.

> "O Faithless Love
> You pass my door
> You pass my gate
> But you can't pass
> My .38
> Bang! Bang!"

Gregory said, "Had a grandfather once who knew twenty verses of it. Taught me all of them when I was a kid."

"Greg, you're a gold mine. Sometime soon, teach me all of them. Now let's just let the day at sea seep into us. You bet on the pool for the day's run?"

Gregory said no, he never won anything in contests. He didn't add he didn't make friends either, easily. Doc was stalking him, no doubt of it. Even if Doc was freakish—could bet he was by now, most likely, too old for it. No, it was something else. Maybe just he was bored and needed somebody to bounce conversation off of. Needed an audience. The old gal in his party—Gregory had had a glimpse of her and the girl—the old dame was formidable, would like to monopolize the conversation. And the girl, almost too frail; a delicate beauty—like a surprised deer—yet held in a pose like a doe he once saw in an Oregon forest clearing—ready to flee, but not moving, just great eyes staring. He had lowered his gun—let her escape. The doe.

CHAPTER

11

So, è una bella giornata, Marchesa" (to a maître d' every rich old American woman was a marchesa).

"How is the Sogliola alla Marinara?"

"*Al solito.* Better the Piccione Arrostito."

"I can't stand their little bird claws pointed up at me from the plate."

"Chicken alla Cacciatore? *Con permesso* to advise it, Marchesa."

"*Si, se vi piace,* Dino," said Judith Pedlock. "But be sure everything is *very* hot." She turned to Gregory. "This is your first trip across, Mr. Beck?"

"No, spent two years as a student in Rome and Paris. Baroque to de Stijl, to Mies van der Rohe."

Sarah looking very gay and slender in pale yellow, rearranging her cutlery carefully. "You like modern buildings?"

Gregory looked up from his food. "A few."

Judith said, "I hold them all in low esteem. Mule barns."

The main dining room of the ship was well filled. Little groups of discontented waiters and busboys seemed, Dr. Knott remarked, to be having union meetings in corners. There was a noisy clatter at service enclaves and around chafing dishes. But the table Dr. Knott had arranged for with maître d' Dino was off by itself, far from the serving noises and yet close enough to the kitchen doors to get the food to their plates at the proper temperature. Their waiter, Chico, under Dino's snapping fingers, was thin, serious and of great skill. Dino bowed and moved on after handing Chico the table's listing of the main course and the desserts.

Sarah ate with relish but with dainty unwasteful gestures. "How long ago was that, Mr. Beck? Last time on the Continent?"

"Too long ago. I was nineteen. Damn callow."

"You'll find Europe chasing its tail wildly," Judith said. She looked across at Nora O'Hara. "What's the ship news today?"

"Market down. War here and there."

The maître d' had a tray at Judith's elbow. "The Gorgonzola?"

"No . . . made of church candle ends and goat droppings. Pedlock Stores lost a few points this week. Something's stirring."

Dr. Knott said, "Have you noticed, Greg, there is a drifting back to Europe of Americans, as if a countercurrent of all the louts, peasants, rebels who came in the nineteenth century are going on a pilgrimage, a return to the old sites of their beginnings?"

Sarah peeled a peach. "You are a snob, Doc. Perhaps they just want to recover the image of themselves."

"Doc's halfway right, Mr. Beck." Judith took up a handful of cherries from a bowl. "Not many green spots left on earth. No landscape that is not suffocating with too many people. No real jubilation. Cars, bus tours, planes. A rush by the European natives to make money out of their own debasing. Notice it. And why do we Americans feel so damn superior?"

Gregory watched the waiter serve, the busboy follow

with a coffee pot. "I haven't been traveling much, so I'm not up on conditions."

Sarah cut the peach into four perfect parts. "If you haven't seen it for some time, you'll sense Europe is out of focus. You come from a small town?"

"Redwood City till I was sixteen—population sixteen thousand."

"Hawleytown, twenty thousand," said Sarah.

Gregory grinned. "Only kind of places to come from."

Dr. Knott rubbed his lower lip with the corner of his napkin. "The species we call man began small. Just a little clan gathering, so defenseless, really. Yet he soon got busy building, remaking the face of the planet."

Sarah looked up, just a hint of peach juice on a smiling mouth. "Doc, you're a poet."

"Man reminds me of an army of ants," said Dr. Knott, now on his second after-meal brandy. "I saw them in South America once marching like men at war, in formation covering the fields. Yes, soldiers, in formation, attacking with flanking military procedures. Ants, damn it, with a perfectly trained army."

"What, no navy?" Sarah said.

Dr. Knott reached for his cigar case. "The ant and man are perhaps Nature's great mistakes. Grasshoppers I like."

Sarah winked at Gregory. "Prove it, Doc."

Nora O'Hara as she sipped black coffee quietly crossed herself in the region of her navel. She hoped God had not heard all this unholy table talk and would not strike the ship and sink them all. She broke wind daintily and silently. After all, she and the dago passengers in the tourist section were good solid stock, the Pope's Catholics; shopkeepers, fruit growers, even gangsters, middle-aged now, returning to visit their old parents and to see St. Peter's. It was not her fault nor the 'talians that they were sailing with these faith mockers and a Black Protestant like that bloody blaze of a doctor. Also that daft girl setting her bonnet for the surly-looking Jew feller.

"You'll excuse me, I'm sure," said Nora rising from her chair.

"Of course, Nora."

Gregory watched Sarah. Her large blue-green eyes, as his grandfather used to say, were the blue of a Dutchman's pants. They were looking at nothing, amused but as if far away. She leaned forward, touched his arm with long pale fingers that yet were in proportion to the rest of the hand, the wrist. "Will you, Mr. Beck, put that leftover chop of Nora's into a napkin? Sean likes meat with a bone."

"Dogs," muttered Dr. Knott to no one in particular.

On the upper deck, the kennel deck, the wind whipped the halyard flags taut with a snapping sound. The plumes of smoke from the giant funnel went off quickly to be torn by the wind into fragments. The sea was running briskly with quaking white tops, but not high, and small spills of waves ran into each other behind the ship mingling with the bubbling and hissing of the wake.

Sarah stepped out briskly with Sean on the leash. A graceful figure, Gregory thought, out of Greek art? Those little clay figures of the graces? Limber torso, fine legs as if freshly sculpted, not grown. The head held back proudly, yet without hauteur, so that two old men standing at the rail were waiting for her to come around again, the Irish setter leading her.

Gregory held out a large bone and the chop wrapped in gray paper. "Miss Pedlock, Dino also sent this bone up for the dog."

"Wow—he'll really drool. Walk me to the kennel; we'll give it to him there. No, Sean. Not on the clean deck. *Walk!*"

"Not so well trained."

"Sulks at times. A real Irish mystic and brooder. He isn't really mine. He's on loan. I'm delivering him to his owners in Italy."

After the dog and bone and chop had been deposited in the kennel assigned to Sean, they both stood watching the dog through the metal mesh door as he gnawed the white bone after gulping the chop with guzzling sounds.

Sarah held the paper in which the chop had been

wrapped. She looked down on it. "Hey! it's the first pages of the score of Telemann's *Comic Cantata*."

"Never heard of it."

"*Der Schulmeister–The Schoolmaster.*"

"My mother spoke German."

"What a frugal ship, using old music scores for wrapping paper." She took out a pack of English Ovals from a shoulder bag. "Lord, no matches."

He pulled out the tear-shaped silver lighter. "This works on pipes and cigars. Turn your back to the breeze."

Heads close together, hunched over, four hands cupped —as if in some child's game—they at last got the cigarette alight. Sarah inhaled deeply and like a ritual lifted her head and slowly exhaled plumes of white smoke from her nostrils. It was so personal a gesture that Gregory felt as if he were peering by accident through an open door.

"Live dangerously, Mr. Beck. No filters."

"I've been smoking up Doc's cigars."

They stood at the rail watching far out funnel smoke make calligraphic shapes over the low silhouette of a freighter creeping along the ruler-drawn horizon. Behind them they could hear the sounds of Sean crunching the bone.

Gregory said, "You realize we're nearly the only passengers on board under fifty?"

"You trying to spook me?" Sarah asked.

"A Hawleytown girl? Me?"

"Let's go have a drink. Redwood City. Really?"

[From the journal of Edward Knott]

MAY 26:

At sea there is a chemistry that drifts people together in a kind of solution, a coagulated mass. On a sea trip it is often a tribal sort of herd instinct—sometimes a good one—a proper tribal blend. Having rejected the captain's table, we—Sarah, Judith, Gregory—are now permanent table mates. Judith and Greg are still not adjusted to each other. Sarah is chummy with the ship's young priest. New York slum background—jerked to Jesus by hopes of getting the poor made good and the city's garbage collected (cynical and unfair of me—yes).

At the bar the marvelous sound of dice rattling in a leather cup. (I rolled three kings and a pair of tens.) The cheerfulness of the Latin crew pleasing. But there's no paper as yet in the writing room. Judith reported no extra towels in the steam bath, and the posted bulletins of ship's events mean nothing; most of them old forgotten items. Greg ignores them. Judith insists on news bulletins. She is heavily involved in the stock market, I have discovered.

Second night out Bingo Night. Didn't play. Judith did. For $2 a card the elderly turn up hearing aids and grow excited. The sea remains fairly calm. A schoolteacher said to Sarah as she walked on deck, "It's always morning someplace in the world." Sarah asked her if it was her own line. Sarah seems in a good mood and retains it.

There's a five o'clock morning Mass which Nora O'Hara attends. There are Italian movies but I've missed them, too. Sarah, Judith and Greg go. The sea is roughing; the boat dips and rolls more. I hope to keep on my feet and stay all together—the food and me. I'm trying a spiritual system against seasickness; with a little brandy to help I win so far. Father Umbargo, a real Dead End Kid out of Mulberry Street, the ship's priest, admits to seasickness. So many young priests are so unhumorous, earnest. Father U at least has a big city sense of life.

I do not plan to join any of the ship's activities; dancing, bridge lessons, lectures on the art market, bingo, deck games, skeet shooting, but am a fast starter at the five o'clock public cocktail hour.

Sea rougher now. Sarah and the priest—a face of honest ire and love of us all—at tea talked of St. Augustine's Confessions. ("Make me chaste, O Lord, but not just yet.")

Greg is still not fully relaxed with us. He seems at times wound up tighter than ever. Noticed dog hair on his jacket. I am acting out the wise old duffer; I play it rather well I think. Judith is playing bridge—wonderfully well. After lunch we sit in deck chairs. Sarah has talked Greg into going to another Italian movie. Judith is reading Chekhov. "Of all *writers, Doc, I love him best. Camus once said to me—sorry, I'm name dropping—at a dreadful Cocteau film, 'All writers are merde, stomping on everything in some damn quest for an apathetic self-esteem.' But Chekhov is different, an all-comprehending compassion. Sari says she finds him too close to the bone. Listen to this:*

" 'Behind the door of every contented happy man there ought to be someone standing with a little hammer and continually reminding him with a knock that there are unhappy people, that however happy he may be, life will sooner or later show him its claws, and trouble will come to him . . . and then no one will see or hear him, just as now he neither sees nor hears others . . . What is terrible in life goes on somewhere behind the scenes.' "

"Not after lunch, Judith. Spare me. The sea is rolling about a bit."

The ship is like a moving sanitarium after lunch. We doze, we lie like cocoons in blankets on deck. The sky changes from apple green to old rose. At dusk the public address system announces dinner. No one ever invented something better than eating too much on a boat trip. First it is announced in basic English, then in Italian. In English it is "Is now serving da dinner. Pliz be sure to use hand-rails of using da stairs."

At the next table an old lady with walleyes does her daily recital of the Rosary: "Nunc et in hora mortis nostrae. Amen." We smile our thanks for her prayers as she finishes, and we dig into our canned fruit cup set in crushed ice. Sarah and Greg tell us of the fun of not fully understanding the Italian movie.

On deck afterwards the black Episcopal behinds of two Church of England clergymen walk slowly with practical rhythms in front of Greg and myself. God is well represented on the ship. The four of us are smoking cigars. Greg has several times almost begun to tell me something very personal, then changed his mind. I can wait. He will talk soon. I think he suspects I have picked him for some role playing. Well, let him struggle—I think I can position him properly. He already finds Sarah attractive. I have set the brakes at friendship. And he himself, I sense, wants no deep emotional attachment. My purpose is to thaw them out a bit, but not fully unfreeze them. Very delicate work, doctor. Oh, yes, I know. Always was a risky bastard in my med school experiments.

BOOK THREE

The Sea

Moshiach (the Messiah) will only come when for a single
instant everyone is completely good or everyone is completely
bad. It is not enough just to offer a glass of water to a
drowning man.

JACOB ELLENBOGEN
Waiting for the Messiah

CHAPTER

12

The young priest had spent two hours talking to Sarah. He could use a steam bath. There were two fine saunas aboard the *Lucrezia Borgia*, set in the stern of C Deck. The women's was in pink marble, the men's in Swedish pine and frosted glass etched with impossible muscled athletic figures. The grapevine was that after midnight the younger ship's officers and some of the morally liberated schoolteachers steamed and reveled and took delight in each other in mixed saunasing. The captain, a cheerful, moral man according to his own lights, told Father Bruno Umbargo, "*Avanti Cristo*, padre, these Protestant heretics have their little capriccios, if you say so, but all that *non vale un accidente.*"

"Captain," Father Umbargo had said, "you must really think I'm a fool trying to sell me that."

Father Umbargo, a lean young man, tough and earnest, was acne-scarred like Sinatra. He wished he had more time to read Chardin, Kafka, I. B. Singer. He had been a star basketball player at Notre Dame, and wore a medal with Pope John's image under his dog collar.

The captain had muttered, *"Basta, parole d'un pazzo per caso?"* as Father Umbargo went down to the male sauna to steam out. Here in the thick steam echoed the sounds of hard resilient slaps delivered by hefty masseurs on neon-pink flesh. After undressing and covering his troublesome genitalia with a towel, he found Dr. Knott and Gregory Beck seated on the top steam bench, naked, slippery with sweat and water. They were lashing on each other with wet whisks made of birch twigs, and laughing like children at play.

"How are you coping, Father?" asked Dr. Knott. His body was hard muscled for his age, spotted here and there with the pigmentation of the elderly, the body hair white but sparse.

"I'm not ahead, Doctor. I'm in a hassle with the captain about the swingers carrying on so boldly. I'm not their moral guardian, but it's getting too noisy."

"You mean we're the last to hear it's orgy time on board?"

Greg, his body sun-lamped to a good tan, wiped his forehead, neck and shoulders with a towel. "A good turnout for the scene?"

Father Umbargo averted his eyes from a body that reminded him of a beautiful St. Sebastian bound to a stake and stuck full of arrows, a painting by an academic mannerist that Bishop Kelly had in his private quarters in Yonkers.

Dr. Knott said, "Truth is, Father, it's part of the tour."

"And human nature? Tell me that again, Doctor."

Dr. Knott leaned back against the wall, closed his eyes. He enjoyed heat. "Father, fleeting pleasures are all we get here on earth. It's the animal in man, and that's why there is confession and absolution for your crowd. All this being put into a state of grace *after* sin. You're always reading of the hornyness of saints, before they were saints, of course."

Gregory began to dry his chest. "I think we all need an afternoon booze. Father, you'll join us?"

"Thanks. I need a shot of Scotch. You a practicing Jew, Beck? I mean the tallis, the *twelum?*"

Gregory dried his genitalia, grimaced. "As long as I'm alive, I'm a Jew, but without the dogma. It's enough being a Jew, isn't it? Unlike Alyosha Karamazov, I can't return my ticket to God."

"I meant—"

"Me Orthodox? Practice the rituals, the Yiddishkeit? No. Will agnostic do? Even if folk are descended from Rabbi Moses Isseries, the Ashkenaz seer."

Father Umbargo shook his close-cropped head. "I've been talking to Sarah Pedlock, or rather she's come to me. She's like you, Beck, a Jew in limbo. She wonders if she's moving in the right direction, in any direction."

Dr. Knott got off the bench and examined his arms. "You mean towards Rome?"

Father Umbargo smiled, but not with any ego drive behind it. Yet there was a special timbre to his voice. "They come to us, not we to them. Protestants have cockeyed ideas about us."

Dr. Knott said, "I'm just a retired hedonist. I remember Cardinal Tepilo—oh, I was a teen-ager then; he invited me to the Villa Sapri, the old goat. He used to say after a few belts of grappa, 'We are all Jews *con amore.* Always remember *that.* Without Jews there can be no Christ.' "

The priest shrugged. "No theology, Doctor, please."

"I don't think Sarah will decide—not soon anyway—up which creed God resides."

Father Umbargo stepped into a shower booth as the two men dried themselves vigorously with big towels. Dr. Knott wiped his knees and thighs briskly. Gregory wondered about the life of contemplation of priests.

The priest came out of the shower, a towel around his loins. "I'm not going to press Miss Pedlock to come to an understanding, Doctor, but I'm not going to turn her away from help."

With the palms of both hands Gregory pushed back his mop of reddish hair. "Well, it's not a ship's daily run, so we can't bet on it."

Dr. Knott slapped Gregory on the bare ass with a loud, comradely bang. "Booze time! What say to double daiquiris?"

Those who did not steam in the sauna or take dance lessons in the main salon, watch travel films or have instruction in camera art in the ship's movie theater, usually lay on their spines in deck chairs beaming radiant tranquility, and either slept, read or gossiped. A few walked the deck in the measured paces of their Hush Puppies, and a very small group toured the engine room, the radio shack, the bridge. The Episcopal ministers gave a tea at four every afternoon in the card room. Six passengers of both sexes hardly ever left the bar except to eat and sleep.

The ship's beauty parlor had only a dozen stalls and six operators, and so reservations were hard to get unless one knew how to reach Signora Chimi del Monte, who had protuberant crystal eyes and who ran the cosmetic salon— reached her with a crisp five-dollar bill and nothing under. All the operators were very expert.

Judith and Sarah sat under dryers, huge metal hoods over their freshly set hair. Sarah was relaxed, eyelids lowered, nearly asleep. Judith was examining her newly made up eyebrows in a hand mirror. "Chaos dueling with chaos. Don't ever get old, Sari."

"That sounds like good advice." Sarah didn't open her eyes. "What's the trick?"

"Lord, I feel like one of a stuffed habitat group in a museum . . . You getting on with Gregory?"

Sarah opened her eyes. "Why, Aunt Judith, should I be getting on?"

"You're both under eighty years of age. And it's a damn dull sea trip, my dear, without a little intrigue. *Nicht wahr?*"

"Judith, just what did my family tell you when they turned me over to you—I believe the expression is to keep an eye on me."

"I don't lie to you, girl. Your father said, 'She's had this mild little upset—not a nervous breakdown, understand that,' he said. 'She's just given up her concerts and she's off by herself too much. I guess I don't understand her—me being just a country lawyer' (ha, he's smarter than a fox). 'I don't understand creative artists or genius,' he said, 'or what the hell she is up to.' That's what your papa said to me."

"Sounds like Daddy."

"Sari, he also said, 'So if you'll just stay at my little girl's elbow, a shoulder to lean on.' Actually said that, and added, 'I'd be grateful, and so would Fran.' "

"That all?"

"The whole *megillah*."

"And Dr. Knott?"

"A goddamn clam with me. He maybe came along to drink."

"That's nicer than saying he's my attending psychiatrist, isn't it?"

"Ed Knott—he used to be something marvelous, vital, in the twenties. But then we all were. Boys, girls, he didn't care. Weekends on Arnold Bennett's yacht. For kicks a Black Mass with Aleister Crowley. And he helped people—creative people. He wasn't just an expensive head-feeler then. *Cospetto!* no."

"He was a great man in his field, Aunt Judith. His book, *Warnings and Apprehensions,* is an accepted classic."

"Did you ever finish it? Did anyone not a highbrow specialist?" Judith laughed, wide-mouthed, showing splendid teeth and costly inlays. "Look, Sari, all I asked you was how you're making out with Gregory Beck. I think a good time with a charming, well-endowed man is the best reason for a sea trip. All right, I was a high-kicking Edwardian–King George the Fifth bitch. But no regrets."

"Cleo," said Sarah to the attendant, "I'm ready to be combed out I think. Truth is, for me, Aunt Judith, right now, not again."

"Don't call me aunt. That was decided—that attitude—when you gave up your concerts?"

"No. And it's not an attitude. It all came years later when I was trying to get the knots out of my tensions, agitation."

Judith patted Sarah's knee, a knee covered by the linen robe. "Love, when you fall into it, it's like taking an asser off a horse. You must get up, brush yourself off, and get right on again, or—"

"I know all that advice, Au—Judith, shut up! I don't want anything but a calm sea trip."

"Temper, temper. That and feeding a stupid, crapping dog. Nor is asking *shailas* of God."

"Cleo!" shouted Sari, her skin flushing rose pink.

Judith said softly, "Keep a sense of gravity, girl, even if I talk out of turn. Now me, I might be thinking of marrying again. Oh, no young rip, or hard-breathing American allrightnic cutting velvets on Seventh Avenue. No. Some elderly scholar of the Hasidic cult, Aramaic texts. What I want is a human being I can touch, talk to . . . *Where* are you going, Sari?"

Sari was out from under the hood. "To walk the deck with my damn crapping hound."

Judith sighed as Sarah walked toward the dressing room like a little girl leaving a party, head up proudly. Judith took out a cigarillo from a flat gold case, and Cleo, a northern Italian blonde, held a flame to it.

"*Con permesso,* Marchesa" (more shipboard flattery).

"How do you feel about love, Cleo?" Judith made the Italian fist gesture of copulation.

"*È sempre l'ora . . .*"

Judith nodded. "Good girl." She inhaled, coughed, exhaled. The tobacco tasted sweet, pungent, satisfying. She closed her eyes and fell back against the chair to dream of the human capacity for self-deception and how satisfying it sometimes was.

After a light birdpecking lunch, as she called it, and a refreshing nap, Judith decided to write a letter to her daughter, Gertrude (Gittel), married to Saul Lazar-Wolf. Saul had practically taken over the Pedlock family bank on Wall Street, in fact had increased its business. A letter to mail in Lisbon:

Dear Gertrude:

The ship goes on and I have to go along with it. The age of the great Cunarders—wolfhounds of the sea, we called them—is over, I know. Last night after dinner I went to the dance salon where there was

Italian jazz, and pop tunes sung by a thick Naples accent. Sari said, "Just as if an American Indian were to try out for the opera *Aïda*." She is rather frisky these days when she isn't snippy to me. My fault—I give advice.

You want to know how is the doctor coming with Sari? As your late father—*olov asholom*—used to put it, psychiatrists need their heads examined. Dr. Knott's got some idea to involve her in a love affair—might be good for her. Thinks I don't know.

Love, Judith

She addressed an envelope for the letter:

Mrs. Saul Lazar-Wolf
282 Seabreeze Road
King's Point
Great Neck, Long Island, New York
USA

Enough address to choke a horse, she figured.

Gertrude was the only one of her children she had any maternal optimism about. "Me, I just wasn't in the tradition of a good Jewish mother." She had been happy enough to give Mordecai children, but after they popped out they were messy, wet, smelly things. Happy to have the frauleins and nannies take over . . . Certainly I'm a flop to the true Jewish mother legend. Gertrude and Saul they have six, my grandchildren. I'm happy to visit them and happy to have them swarm around for the gifts. ("Just bring us something small, grandma . . . only it doesn't have to be too small." Sharon, age four.) Bold, large children, not delicate, beautiful, full of sensibilities like Sari. It's as if Sari came from another world, not a Pedlock world.

Truth was, Judith had to admit as she blotted the envelope, she herself didn't much care for the family's social habits, the social status urge of the old ones trying so hard to appear important, ultrarespectable and respected. One needed stamina to declare oneself out. *Not* to get on the board of the Museum of Modern Art (like daughter Naomi Penrose), join the Sag Harbor Yacht Club (son Marcel), Temple Emmanuel (the Lazar-Wolfs), the Harmonia Club (son Tom).

She had never fitted in with the store and bank Pedlocks. That was so damn true. The Arneths, her people, were Bohemians, corporation lawyers who drank too much, uncles who committed suicide after fabulous embezzling (well, only Uncle Philip). And the cousin killed in a Hispano-Suiza car . . . or one who lived too long and became old and lecherous (poor father, to die in the arms of the red-headed Polish upstairs maid). No, she'd never be a Pedlock, just Mordecai's wife, widow now. But, dammit, she held the family together now; the Store, the Bank. Oh, Saul Lazar-Wolf would end up with the Bank, chairman of the board—Saul, a Jewish Snopes out of I. B. Singer instead of Faulkner. *Niente affatto.* What the hell, you can only live one life at a time. I picked my life, lumps and all. I liked it.

No wonder she was so attached to Sari, more so than to her own brood. Sari had a quality of reacting to things as she herself once had. Now? While she lived she'd keep the family functioning, keep the Pedlock & Sons stores showing better and better quarterly reports, the famous Fifth Avenue department store stretched up on its toes for higher sales. She wondered about the other, the distant branch of the Pedlock family, the Joseph Pedlock side that Sari came from. That old rip, Joseph Pedlock, he must have been one fine sonofabitch before and after he made it in Montana copper smelting. Judith suddenly felt alone, deserted. She cried out:

"Irish! Irish! Be sure this letter is mailed in Lisbon. And get me the radio report on the Wall Street closings. By six they have the closing prices on Pedlock Stores. And I'll have a big generous brandy. I think I'm getting too old for these trips."

"That'll be the day, when you take up hooking rugs."

"Stop mumbling. It's a sign of being addlepated."

Lord, if I had Sari's youth, looks—that almost doll-like

freshness, never mind the piano playing—I'd not mope over a godhead or wonder what a Jew is.

A Jew is not *what,* a Jew *is.* The trouble with Sari was being a cockeyed genius. Everybody called her genius. I don't know one end of a genius from another. I'm lucky being what I am—was—and not Van Gogh, Dostoevsky, Poe; those poor bastards, driven, starved, brains a mess of fancy worms. Oh, Sari girl, give yourself a chance—don't handicap yourself like a race horse carrying extra weight. Saddest thing in life is not disease, poverty, death. It's never having lived—just existed. Well, I better keep my fat mouth shut. Sari is a little bundle of temper if you let a spark fall on her to set her off.

CHAPTER

13

Sarah and Gregory were on their way to a showing of an Italian film, he to translate those parts of the dialogue which were beyond her tourist and music school Italian. Gregory was trying hard to recall the Italian he had managed to acquire and handle in his student days as a Prix de Rome scholar in Rome. One problem of the films shown on the ship was that there were no English subtitles, the pictures being in the main works that were not suitable for the American market and so were not dubbed for export. The all-comprehending gestures of the actors helped sometimes.

A half-dozen men and one woman were shooting at clay pigeons released from a machine in the hands of one of the deck boys into the blue backdrop of a clear sky. As Sarah and Gregory passed by two of the men were blazing away not at the clay discs but at some sea birds, slim creatures with pink beaks, birds that Gregory couldn't identify. The shotgun pellets had little carrying range and the birds with swooping perverseness stayed out of range.

Sarah shaded her eyes with a hand to observe the scene. "You hunt, Gregory?"

"My father used to hunt deer, and once I went with him after mountain goat in Utah. I was twelve."

"Foolish of Jews to hunt. They've been hunted so often themselves that as sportsmen they are on the wrong side in the chase."

"Doc seems to think we have great talent, capacity for self-deception."

A voice sounded behind them, raised in outrage. A red-faced German woman with thin knotted flesh was warding off Father Umbargo's restraining arms as she lunged at a deck boy. She was dressed in an awkward-fitting sunsuit, her gray hair with brown ends all in disorder. She continued screaming at the sailor who serviced the deck chairs around the stern of the ship on B Deck. "*Ya Ya!* That was mine blanket. I olvas haf it. Mine blanket. Go get it from whoever hast it. *Gehend!* Go, go."

The deck boy smiled, didn't move. "All blankets are the same."

"I want the one I haf this morning. Why don't you go. *Gerade aus.* Go, go. *Schnell.*"

Father Umbargo said, "Easy now, easy, Mrs. Landeau."

"You sailor, you *smutz*, you yelling at me?"

The deck boy was a very solidly built young man and moved about carrying an armful of blankets with the grace of a dancer, not at all feminine in his movements. He smiled. "Say *please.*"

"I am yelling at a *dumbkopf.* I demand you do what I say. Father, you tell him passengers are in the right. Mine blanket."

"Say please to me, signora."

Father Umbargo shouted, "Both of you, listen!"

She faced the deck boy. "To you I haf not to say please!" She turned sputtering, appealing to all the people tucked in on their deck chairs, but she saw no sympathetic faces. "What kind of a ship is this ship."

Sarah and Gregory moved on as Father Umbargo gave up, saying, "Why do I interfere?"

Gregory said, "Can you understand the killing of Germans?"

Father Umbargo shook his head. "I don't understand killing."

"Unless," Sarah said, "it's by the Inquisition."

Father Umbargo smiled. "I wasn't there, Miss Pedlock."

In the elevator going down to E Deck where the film theater was, Father Umbargo said, "There's something out of gear in that woman. She's been whacked up like that since we sailed."

"You wonder if Germans are God's work, Father?" Gregory asked.

"I'm not playing your game, Beck," said the priest.

Sarah waited for the doors to hiss open. "The men and women in Italian films seem so natural, and amusing, too." She hunted in her handbag, jacket pocket. "Oh, hell—pardon me, padre—no cigarettes. Never mind, good for me to cut down. Sex interests so many people; I mean the way it seems to fill the foreground of their lives."

"Does it, Miss Pedlock?"

"Can I see you, padre, this afternoon?"

"At five, in the small salon. I think I'll skip the movie."

As they approached people milling about, Gregory said, "The folk from Tourist climb all over you and stomp on your shoes. Where, Father, are the smiling, happy Italians of song and story?"

"Maybe waiting for us in Naples." He left them, his hands clasped behind his back.

The film was a very beautiful one as to color and costume. The period was the 1920s and the plot was a confusing one about how to avoid paying taxes, ruined nobles selling their antiques—mostly fakes—and the granddaughter of an old princess, who was a cat burglar at night so they might keep their position in society.

It was tea time when Sarah and Gregory left the theater, shoved and pushed around by some of the Tourist Class Italians. Sarah limped from trodden toes. "Damn, they've twisted my foot a bit, ruined a pair of stockings. And I'm meeting Father Umbargo in an hour."

(*112*)

"Let's find a spot and I'll get the tea. You like the priest?"

"Oh, come right out with it! Am I converting? I don't know." She winced in pain, rubbed an ankle. "We'll have tea in my cabin, and I'll change my stockings."

Sarah's cabin smelled to Gregory of fruit still in a Bon Voyage basket, also of the intimate life of a woman, and of new leather luggage that reminded him of the horse harness of his grandfather's buckboard.

"Order tea from the steward, lots of little sandwiches. Fresh, be sure to say *fresh*."

After using the phone and explaining carefully, Gregory saw a bit of newsprint on the rug, fallen from an address book by the phone. It was an old concert review clipping.

"The program had opened with Beethoven's Fourth Piano Concerto, which introduced the virtuoso, Sarah Pedlock. She is clearly an artist of rare bravura skill. Even rarer, she also commands a sense of poetry. Everything about the performance of the G-major Concerto was wholly convincing; an intimate approach to the work in the first two movements and the rondo finale a climactic impact. She sustained crystalline clarity with frequent little shifts in focus. These illuminated subtle, unsuspected details. Others made the proceedings tense and magnificent. The slow movement was subdued, delicately shaded, a lovely, other-worldly dream. One could only marvel at the flexibility and originality of Miss Pedlock's interpretation . . ."

She turned from the wardrobe, fresh stockings in hand.

He said, "You're really good."

"Oh, that's a long time ago. My mother always said a girl with a run in her stockings was a slovenly girl . . . I used to think at age ten slovenly meant sluttish, lascivious. Kind of sinful, too."

They had the tepid tea and the small sandwiches, avoiding the ludicrous, overcolored Italian cakes which he assured her "are always better-looking than they taste. Like chewing old candles."

Sarah, sitting on the bed, rolled down her stockings and skinned them off, revealing a splendid thigh in the process, a slim leg, hairless as an egg, and marvelous ankles, rather large feet with overlong toes. She threw the discards into a corner. "See, slovenly . . . More tea? Judith carries her own tea, loose Chinese tea and a silver tea ball, scalds the tea pot, the whole *Geschäft*."

"Fits her." Gregory refilled his tea cup. "Doesn't seem affected, or at least it's not an act. Wonderful old gal— really what used to be called class. I gather from Doc she is a genius as a businesswoman, old as she is, and holds a whiphand over all the family."

"Don't let Judith hear you call her old. I think she's maybe hunting a husband. Some prop for her old age of disillusionment. Acting as if she isn't already old *old*. I hate getting old, Gregory. The whole idea of death . . . You ever think of death, Gregory?" She was very close, very earnest, almost apprehensive.

"Some years, yes, all the time."

"And now?"

He lifted the teapot. "I thumb my nose at it. I say, up up yours, death! I just want to be a sort of bystander, amused, not cynical or aloof in some facile religiosity. Not involved. Yes, that's it, not involved." He set down the teapot.

"Oh? And what would you design to replace it, the copout?"

"A long long life with simpler human plumbing, and then pooped out, when you feel it's all too much . . ." He snapped his fingers in the air. "You just dissolve in the bathtub like a lump of sugar. Down the drain. No stink, no worms feasting, no undertaker's revolting rackets. You just become a pleasant liquid flowing to the sea."

"That kind of talk calls for something stronger than tea. Strega?" She took a bottle from a dressing case. "I got it from Juan at the bar."

They drank small cups of Strega and talked over the film.

Sarah was laughing. "Hey, we're getting *non compos mentis*. Hey, this is strong . . . Ever think, Gregory, existence is just the impossibility to exist? Hey?"

Gregory wondered if they were getting drunk.

She looked around her, head loose on shoulders, and found herself in Gregory's arms. He was kissing her throat in

(114)

sudden darting attacks of his mouth. She began to wriggle, then to toss her head around. He kept muttering, *"Sarah, Sarah,"* which conveyed nothing to her. She continued to struggle politely, almost provocatively. After a while she stopped wriggling and her struggling became a kind of quivering. He was nuzzling her cheeks and she felt his mouth on hers. It was a pressure of some quickening hopes—moist, male. She could smell him now in his excitement. All she could think of was Sean, Sean up there in the kennels, and she thought of Sean the times he made love to a rolled-up section of rug. Poor, deprived doggie.

She cried out with a fearful, birdlike sound as his hands cupped over her naked breasts. Something tore at her stability. She screamed again so loudly he lifted his head, his face flushed, color coming through the sunlamp tan.

"What the hell . . ."

"Crazy, crazy," she said. "Crazy ever to think . . . you . . . just . . . oh, God, I feel—I—I—"

Her fingers twitched spasmodically as she clutched his hair. He inhaled deeply and released her and her fingers grew slack. He stood up and beat his fists together, a puzzled man, as if sorting out the falsity of his thinking. She lay on the cabin lounge, legs at an odd angle, nylon naked legs, head wedged down among pillows, making sounds that suggested hysterics.

She supposed he had a hardon; they usually did. She controlled herself as if beginning a concert, said softly, very far away, "I'm sorry, Gregory, truly sorry. I haven't been well. I mean, I need tranquility. I didn't want us to—"

"That's all right, Sar—Miss Pedlock. We've been boozing on that Italian varnish, and I should have controlled my inclinations—which I figured were mutual."

"You don't understand . . ." She looked up, eyes very wide. "I'm not—not a cockteaser—it's, it's—just . . ."

"Oh?" His tone was crisp and sharp. He felt—why this outburst over a self-induced shipboard intrigue?

"You're hurt." She hunted some words. "Male pride, virility . . . hurt."

He put his hands in his pockets and looked over the

cabin, its open trunk, cosmetics set out, luxury leather, ceramic and silver, womanly tools. He said, "Christ, no inventory, please."

"It's not that I'm a damn schoolgirl, or a virgin . . . It's . . ."

"I know—it's you don't want a casual affair. I haven't heard that old favorite since college."

She said in a far-off voice, "Go ahead, say it."

"Say what?" he asked.

" 'Fuck you, Sarah Pedlock,' " she said, falling prone on the bed.

He stared at her, then began to laugh. She did not join in the mirth, and something seemed to change the direction of the drama in the overheated cabin. The fruit was positively rotting before their eyes.

"You see, you see," she said as if talking to herself, moving around on the bed to curl up in the fetal position (he almost expected her to put her thumb in her mouth), her words running together at a dead level. "You can't ever know, no one knows the way it is to be, I mean there's a sly madness."

(Why, she thought, am I acting like this? There is no real motive for my rejecting of this man, his body. He doesn't smell like Julian Salt. He doesn't even make me feel guilty of a too sudden sexual confrontation. That's why I'm mad, I have no reason for so many things. Or, or is there a fear of God appearing on the ceiling of the cabin shouting I am a sinner, I am a polluter of the Holy Books, the godhead. I don't know, just don't, why I don't open like a flower to him and accept, accept. Deep, dark down I know there is no doubt a fear that has no name for me at the moment. Oh, give me time. I'll come round. So keep talking, say something pleasant, be charming like the little girl Daddy liked.)

"You know, my father used to say, Dedee, you shoot a great stick of pool . . . summer we'd all pile into the jalopy, go to a beach house and live like . . ."

He turned away frowning. *Were they both drunk?*

"Gypsies . . . out by the strong smell of night-blooming

jasmine . . . Daddy had to carry a twelve-gauge Marlin under and over shotgun. It was grand when the hunting season opened . . . the ducks came and we'd sit in the blind of cat-tail reed by the Indian Bay salt marsh and I'd blow the duck call and it was warm, cosy—me and Daddy . . . my feet on a hot brick, drinking hot chocolate from the thermos . . . Daddy reciting Aeschylus: 'Take heart, suffering when it climbs highest lasts but a little time . . .'"

She turned and said, "Please get me a damp towel, Gregory, I'm all right."

"Sure you are." *Oh brother!* She washed her face, blew her nose, sat up and covered the exposed white flesh above the stockings.

"It's all fine now. You still want to come to bed with me?"

"Not today."

"You're a decent guy, Gregory."

"Read minds?"

"Sure. The Ornsteins, my mother's people, intermarried maybe with real storefront Turkish gypsies a long time ago. We have this seventh daughter of a seventh daughter tradition stuff . . . Why don't we wipe out my little scene of rejecting you?"

He poured himself a glass. "One for the road."

"I'll be frank," she said. "I don't know how to handle sexual experiences just now."

Gregory tossed off the drink, pursed his lips at the aftertaste, made a small bow, said nothing. Sarah sat up, wriggled her toes, observed them, studied them, didn't look up.

"You see, just now I'm not very good at sex—not inelegant maybe, but, well, lousy is a good word. Oh, I've had it. Some schoolgirl rolling around, seduced by my music teacher. And then, then just one big—oh, big experience when before I was twenty with—"

"Sarah, I hate explainings, so don't."

"Was I explaining? Can I have a drink?"

"Just one."

She kissed his hand in a sudden gesture as if of submission as she took the glass.

The public address system in the corridor came on with a

frying sound of static: "Signora, Signorina, Signore, Signori
—first call for dinner . . ."

Later, alone on deck (Judith, Doc and Greg had gone to
play bridge in the small Capri salon), Sarah stood at the
Lido Deck, smoking a cigarette, inhaling deeply, sparks
flying from the burning tobacco as it glowed in the stiffish
breeze. She stood erect at the rail, a pale-blue scarf with
overlong ends moving about her, that one solitary late
stroller walking by.

"Evening," the stroller said.

"Evening."

Why, she wondered, had she acted up with Gregory as
she had? It wasn't as if she was Miss Purity . . . Was it the
memory of old hurts done by Julian Salt? The dreadful
months of being a hidden object, of hasty fornications in
second-rate hotels. Once at a party in Stanford, Connecti-
cut, the two of them rolling together on a bathroom floor
behind a locked door, a very nosy hostess (who patrolled
hallways at night) banging on the door. Not a very good
housekeeper, for Sara got lint and dustballs in her hair from
the dusty floor. It had been a sad decline from the delight of
love and loving to shameful urgings on her part to be told
"we are still lovers." He had excuses for not keeping
appointments. He was a busy man who could, if urged,
spare the time, find the time (a better term) to see you, be
with you.

Also, frankly, Julian protected himself. Flamboyant
though he was in his love of public attention, of being seen
and admired, he did try to keep her in the shadow of his life.

Sarah had found in time this gay and well-tailored man,
the lover who had once declared his admiration of her
freshness, her grace, her dewy schoolgirl charm (his words),
had become vulgar, coarse in his relationship with her. A
gloating sadist lurked in the man, at times an arm twister,
and once a face slapper (but only once). He had shown
himself as he was behind the façade of the adoring male she
had met in Las Vagas.

After months of meetings it had come to what Daddy
would call a "drag-ass end." On her part they had lost their

(118)

savor and on his they were mere continuations of his conquest of an artist who had been acclaimed as the piano prodigy of the generation. For Julian she was something to ornament himself with, to hang on his watch chain. Yes, he wore a watch chain to show a key that looked like a Phi Beta Kappa award, but wasn't. Sarah had walked away for good when he suggested she join him and a best-selling female novelist at a weekend party of way-out swingers in East Orange. Yes, he admitted, his wife always approved of such arrangements.

And then had come over Sarah a sense that there was sin after all in bodies, in combinations of bodies. And so now, in every man she was attracted to, she saw a bit of Julian Salt. And in herself, when aroused, the girl who had seen printed on a ceiling the features of a godhead who could punish, and shout.

Or, or . . . she was not clear just what had happened after she left the concert stage, went into a kind of long walk in a mist of sensibilities that hide reality. Now she found herself afloat and reality was a long, long menu three times a day, not forgetting the midnight spreads.

She shivered, not alone from the rising breeze, and decided to go below.

CHAPTER

14

The sea had become lumpy, frilled with big whitecaps. Gregory Beck took the newspaper clipping Dr. Knott had handed him. They were sitting at a table in the Da Vinci Bar, one side of which was open to the curve of the stern of B Deck. It was a day flecked with tiny clouds on a sky that looked like a slack stage backdrop. Deck sports sounded from above them. In the bar two tables away a man and his wife were engaged in a low-keyed snarling debate of some kind, both pausing only to swallow a reviving sip of their glasses of Barsac.

Gregory looked at the date on the clipping. "It's three years old."

"Read it. You asked me if there were more of Sarah's reviews on board. Happened to have this one." Dr. Knott brushed up his beard with the back of his hand applied under his chin. "Read, read."

MOZART, BRAHMS AND PEDLOCK

For the joys of pianist lovers happiness is hearing Sarah Pedlock play Mozart and Brahms. Last night at the Pavilion the fabulous girl honored the Philharmonic Orchestra with an elegant performance of Mozart's 17th Concerto (C major, K. 453) and a colossal Brahms' First. A joyous experience that made magic on the audience.

It also would be no exaggeration to claim that everything was ideal in the Mozart. Here the properly reduced orchestra did not succumb to stridency. It sustained delicacy and transparency. However, Miss Pedlock played with such warmth, taste and knowing simplicity, that little else mattered. She is not the sort of Mozartian who sighs over every lyric flight.

Dr. Knott decided his beard was in order and picked up the newspaper clipping. "Ah, you missed a hallucinatory immediacy—only about half of her on recordings. The way she sat, the way she mastered the piano, her grace."

"You feel that adds to the music?"

"To see her in a clinging gown, Greg, those magnificent arms at work, the fingers attacking, smoothing, commanding the keys. You feel you've looked upon a woman beyond rubies. Hell, I'm getting maudlin."

"She plan concerts in Europe?"

The quarreling couple had gone silent, and the woman—her face outraged—leaned over and slapped the man's face: *potch, potch*—one, two. The barman was reading *Corrida de Toros*, the bullfight newspaper, and continued indifferent to what was taking place. The woman rose and went out, the muscles of her naked calves hard and gleaming below her shorts. The man sat very still, twirling the glass in his fingers, his face expressionless, merely the flush of the slap discoloring one cheek. He moved his lips but no sound came out, gripped in some shocked inadequacy.

Dr. Knott replaced the clipping in a frayed pigskin wallet. "The family hopes Sarah will give some concerts. Offers from Paris, London, Berlin. But she'd never play in Germany—too many relatives went into the furnaces, furnaces melted down, she says, to make Mercedes and Volkswagens. You're a music nut?"

"Not really—just, well, average interest for a man with a stone ear."

"What I meant about her, the woman, the sex quality, it's gotten to you. You are interested in her even without the piano."

"Am I?"

"Greg, I'm such a savvy bastard I sometimes scare myself I'm so good. Well, no longer full time, but when I was running the clinic it was a damn fine one, better than a lot of the fancy pathological ghettos that get overwritten about. I've known you a few days, cased you, studied your reactions. Got you pat, how you talk, walk. So? I don't want Sarah to walk into some unfortuitous chaos that is your past. Each inside has an outside."

"You bastard," Greg began, then he looked intensely in puzzled earnestness at Dr. Knott. "You know who I am?"

"No, if you mean details, names, places. But I know sure as shooting you're a man who has just come out of prison. A pretty long stretch. The wary talk, the indoor sunlamp tan, the steward gossiping that you find the bed too soft. A pretty long stretch."

"Three years," said Greg, his voice low and controlled.

"You don't seem a criminal type to me."

"Doesn't a college professor fit your pattern?"

"You don't. What was it, raping a student, stealing an art treasure from a museum?"

"Embezzlement. That led to a great personal tragedy."

"Ah! Interesting, interesting. You weren't guilty, of course. No one even is telling of such things."

"Legally I was. I had charge of a huge grant. I had an assistant I didn't trust. But I felt I could keep an eye on him. Stupid story, really. I was having trouble at home, I was hitting the bottle. I signed checks. My assistant swore I took my share out of the books he cooked. Stupid."

"Intellectuals are fools in the handling of money. But that isn't the tragedy you got the wound from."

"I was teaching at Berkeley. Anyway, I was supposed to have come home on Peppertree Lane, found my wife, Agnes, in the bathtub, and beat her to death with some blunt instrument, then gone to an art show of Daumier prints for an alibi."

"Supposed to have?"

Greg smiled sadly. "You know about hallucinations, doubts that can be instilled into people under stress. In court I kept thinking maybe I did it, blacked out remembering. Everyone seemed so sure I had killed Agnes. Even my lawyer, a high-priced shyster with the nose of a greedy ant-eater. He swallowed my houses, my car, my savings, turned in my insurance, sold my library. Even he from his angle of vision seemed to think I maybe, maybe, did it, murdered my wife. He liked to use fancy talk, like 'the duality of human consciousness.' "

"Motive? What'd they claim was your *why?*"

"You saw that man slapped in here a minute ago? Motive? Maybe she wants a bigger house, wants him to take on a bigger-risk job. Maybe he's a flabby lay, or has the sex habits of a porno film. Will he strangle her before we land? Will she shove him overboard?"

"What were your motives? The ones the state claimed?"

Greg began to play with the ornate book of matches beside the ashtray. "For some time Agnes had been demanding I give up college teaching and take an architect's job offered by some Los Angeles firm that was putting up dreadful vulgar boxes on an old film-studio lot. We had come to a lack of expectations in each other. She drove off one rainy night after a party, calling me a Jew prick, a washout. Drove off in our car leaving me stranded in alcoholic lethargy, and muttering in front of the uptight WASP members of the Bayside Club, I said, 'I'll murder her some day for these tricks.' " Greg smiled and tore out matches and laid them into a new pattern on the table. "Oh, once the DA gets the case in front of a jury everything looks black. Why, asked the DA's bright boy, did I stay in Denver on our fifth wedding anniversary? Who saw me with a redhead having cocktails at the Top of the Mark? 'The mystery woman,' the press called her. Hell, she was a daffy woman who just wanted a gallery designed for her collection of social status avant-garde junk. But the jury thought —who knows what dirty little thoughts?"

"If not you, who? A lover?"

"No, no. Agnes wasn't interested much in anything but getting there socially, making it. 'Lots of loot' was her expression. Being with what she called 'the right people.' Living in a posh neighborhood, Beverly Hills, Palo Alto, Pasadena. Being a society aide at the art museum, Junior League work. That sort of thing. Me being Jewish kept us out of the best old clubs. That drove Agnes to fits. No, no lover. Just the disintegration of a marriage. Whose fault? Who knows. Anyway, the jury said not guilty on *that* charge."

"Who killed her? You must have had a defense?"

"He spoke of a tramp, a drugged hippie. Oh, he put on a great show. A passing-through degenerate was his pet idea."

"Good, very good."

"I got three to five; embezzlement. Paroled. Permission by the parole board to go to Europe on a half-promised job for some low-cost housing the United States is giving funds for."

"They pay for this trip?"

"No, Doc. I wrote a college textbook in prison. *Man, His Search for Architectural Form.* The book caught on, something about civilizations functioning at their worst in buildings while at their height. And some civilizing of Gropius, Corbusier."

"I shan't read it, Greg." Dr. Knott turned to the barman. "Juan, *sacar el corcho*, two double martinis, *allez et retour*."

"I don't give a damn, Doc, if you believe me or not. I didn't kill Agnes. I wasn't unhappy with her—a bitch has a fascinating side—but I wasn't unhappy-happy enough to feel anything like a violent severance from her."

Overhead the deck sports had stopped and the shuffling of shoes sounded louder.

"Soup being served and blankets tucked in. Greg, I don't really judge people. I merely maybe label them, and often wrongly. Don't tell Sarah any of this. Not just yet. When you know her better, well . . . There comes a time in a relationship when lucidity goes, and two people, dazed by each other, accept anything."

"Doc, there isn't going to be any relationship. I mean beyond a shipboard sharing of a table and movies without English titles."

"How is Sarah's Italian progressing beyond *caro, carissimo, a vostro comodo?*"

Greg said without smiling, "Doc, go to hell."

Dr. Knott stood, stretched, yawned. "Get off the couch. It's over, the hour of truth, the half hour anyway. Didn't hurt, did it? You feel relieved and you don't really know why. As for me, I'm going to do my half-mile on deck before any serious drinking after lunch." Gregory felt the pressure of Dr. Knott's hand on his shoulder.

After the doctor had left, Gregory sat there, his drink half gone, thinking of the past, of the immediacy of the moment, of the genealogies of the Pentateuch . . . His grandfather had taught him and once given him a dollar for repeating them and all the awesome portents of the Prophets. And Grandpa a Socialist at that . . . He didn't think of Agnes. Sarah? He recalled her recording played on the prison radio at San Q. Most of all, Debussy's *La plus que lente.*

The barman was refolding his bullfight paper. He looked up. "Señor wants the refill?"

"No. You ever see, Juan, Belmonte, Maera, work the bulls?"

"I am too young, señor. My faddah, a true aficionado, he saw Chicuelo place the banderillas the day he was gored at Algeciras . . . The young lady, she will be joining you for the daiquiri? I will shave the ice."

He was about to say no, when Sarah walked in, all in gleaming white, and came toward him holding out one hand for him to take in his.

"You look twelve years old in that white outfit."

"I feel six and want to be naughty and drink and drink, and have you tell lies about how wonderful I look."

"What brought this on?"

"First thing you learn, Doc says, is *never* to ask questions when you feel real good."

CHAPTER

15

[From the journal of Edward Knott]

MAY 28:

Neither Gregory nor Sarah were at dinner or at the dance this evening. Judith and I sat watching the dancers. The dance floor is fairly popular but not crowded; the two honeymooners and some of the schoolteachers, department-store buyers in the arms of ship's officers. Two fashion models for the ship's fashion show sat at the bar, exhibiting marvelous Van Dongen legs, unreal film-star heads.

Judith is happy; to record her actual words: "We get no news reports of life on earth except a smudged sheet printed on board. A few stock market items."

"No note of levity anyplace, Judith?"

"Everyone on the dance floor looks as if recovering from mild orgies, and the ship's air conditioning roars all night. I shall go into a trance for the rest of the trip, or read a book on Halakah, the Jewish religious law, that Sari lent me. What do you think of her and Gregory not appearing at dinner?"

"There are buffets on deck, a snackbar."
"Doctor, I've come to think you set this up."
"Two brandies?"
(How to record the ironic tone of her words?)
"Yes, you damn fool, I believe you have tried to act the addled Cupid. Have you lost your mind, gone against your trade?"
"Ethics against senility? Believe what you want."
"Do they disbar shrinks, like lawyers?"
Brandy helps to face the fashion show put on by a third-rate designer of absurdly dull clothes. Only fun was the program note on the designer's life Judith found translated into English: "In her work Madame Salvatori . . . avoiding custom, tradition and intelligence . . ."
That finished the day's activities, unless one danced, romped or went to the midnight "Fiesta Party." "Hardly likely," said Judith. I knock on Sarah's cabin door. No answer.

MAY 29:
Sarah and Greg join us at lunch—an exchange of greetings. Judith winks at me, but it's a wink of wonder. Sarah looks perky and a bit overwound, even spleenish. Greg seems sleepy, his face a bit drawn.
They eat with relish. Sarah is not in a talkative mood and Greg tries to avoid any prolonged conversation. Judith and I decided to join Sarah and Greg at the film . . .
As soon as the film scene read FIN, *people charged out over our legs with no* attenzione *or* mi scusi, *hurrying off as if to a fire drill. In moments the theater was empty.*
Sarah and Greg had disappeared. Judith said they left soon after the movie started.

On the Kennel Deck the sky seemed vaster than in daytime. This deck, rarely visited at night, was barely lit but for some spots of gamboge yellow high on metal standards; so that the stars were brilliant as one looked up, seemingly in their millions, and now and then appearing to give a nervous vibration.

Sarah and Gregory stood at the rail looking up.

"Nothing," said Sarah, "nothing out there that has any connection with us. Just gases and planets, unthinking matter. Here, tiny as we are in comparison, we are the only thinking items in the universe. That rock you, Greg?"

"Be generous, Sarah. Maybe gases and rocks think . . . And your horoscope?"

She laughed and put a hand on one of his. "Don't you go spoil my morbid moment. I get my jollies that way."

"Not too morbid. But let's skip deep thinking. My mother when she got too serious always sang Schubert's *Lindenbaum*."

"Now that's class."

They were both aware the universe wasn't what they wanted to talk about. He put his arm around her and her first reaction was a shiver. Gregory felt the tremor the way he thought a young colt's hide will shiver when a blue-bottle fly lands on it. Hardly a romantic image. Then he sensed a relaxing of Sarah, almost a falling against him, no longer uncertain.

"I'm getting off at Lisbon."

"Suddenly?"

"Very."

"You told me your wife is dead."

"Four years."

"Fine to have had it."

"No, we were just two young people, rather callow, who could not enjoy any sense of properly living together."

"What she die of?"

Gregory tightened his grip on her without being aware of it. "An accident. In a bathtub."

"I'm not driving you off the ship at Lisbon, am I? I mean . . ."

She loosened her scarf, moved closer. "I'll tell you something, mister. I don't want anything to upset my self-sufficiency either. Don't go spoil your trip."

"Thanks." He came over to her and put his lips to her neck. "You have a salty taste."

From the row of kennels Sean heard their voices and gave a low, polite bark.

"Let's walk," said Sarah. "That quack Dr. Knott is on the deck below us, making believe he's just smoking a cigar."

Nora O'Hara was brushing out Judith's hair, fifty strokes, a brisk brushing every night, even if Herself's once-fine head of hair ("so long she could sit her arse on it") was thinning out and the dye job—they called it coloring these days but it was dye—was doing the hair no good at all. Nora brushed on. "It's at the Claridge in London where they do up your hair the best."

"I'm going to get a wig, Irish. When I was young, I had such a head of hair I'd get headaches just carrying it around."

Nora began to twist two braids with skill and speed. "There's that picture of you taken with the gentleman friend, with your hair—God forgive me—like something holy of Mary, by one of them Eyetalian painter fellers."

"Oh, that was André."

"Elegant, like a Dublin alderman." A little flattery will get her to sleep fast and skip the barbiturate.

"We had six months of it, then he found out I had come to him pregnant, legally set to spawning by my husband."

"Olov asholm," said Nora, handing Judith a cigarillo and holding a mother-of-pearl lighter to it until Herself had puffed it into life. It was to be a persistent memory night. "I was in a way, Irish, a good Jewish mother, when it came to adding to the Pedlock family line. I gave birth on a spring day. Our son, Marcel, born eight and a half pounds. A proper Pedlock for all his smooth ways as an art dealer. The Pedlocks used me as a brood mare . . ."

"How could you be sure, I mean that the tad he was a Pedlock?"

"Never you mind." She let Nora slip a silk gown over her large but not fat naked body, a body still pink and with a glow to it even if slack here and there. She looked into the wall mirror; the breast still had a proud lift and the belly that André had been pleasantly indecent on had the quality of a rather good Renoir. "You hear any gossip, Irish, about Sari and that Beck gentleman?"

"I don't listen to gossip. It's a sinful thing, Father McDermott always said."

Judith settled herself comfortably in the bed. "Don't give me that, nosy. You're chirping and chattering away with the stewards and with the other maids and nannies in the bar."

"It's good to hear the proper language spoken as it should be without all them expressions like *man*, and *yeah*, *sock-it-to-me*. It's nagger talk."

"So, nu, give." Judith pushed the ashtray on the night table closer, saw that her Agatha Christies, Simenons were ready in case sleep was short, and the vacuum pitcher, with which she always traveled, close, ready to serve her an iced white wine if thirst came in the night. A bronchitis sometimes assaulted her and pebbles seemed to rattle in her throat. The wine helped.

Nora adjusted the slippers neatly on the rug, stood back and turned off all but the blue light around the wall mirror. "You'll hear nothing bad from me. They've been cozying and nuzzling up among the dogs, walking with the darling Irish setter. And making with their hands, eating noses."

"Eating *what?*" Judith turned an astonished face toward her maid.

"What we call kissing in the Tralee parish. Leads direct to mortal sin."

"And?"

"The stewards on B Deck told the nannie with them Kreek people with the nasty child that spits that Mr. Beck, he's been to Miss Pedlock's cabin for some long hours at a time."

"What do you think, Irish?"

"Slap-and-tickle?"

"I mean do they—in confidence now—?"

"Go all the way? That's what you're asking me?" Nora's face went expressionless. "I wouldn't know, I'm sure. I didn't examine the bed sheets. Lor! Good night."

"You *are* cheeky tonight."

Nora turned and went to the suite's small corner bedroom. She knelt at the narrow cot, hands held in prayer. She said a few Hail Marys and a prayer for her two nephews studying to be priests: "Keep them chaste and free of lust." Then a prayer that Herself would come to believe in God, even a Jew God. "And don't let Miss Sari fall into fornicating sin . . . Take care of all the souls of the Hebrews, the good, the bad, for they were His people . . . Amen." So to piddle and to bed, tomorrow to iron the linen handkerchiefs.

Steadily through the night, the stabilizer fins of the ship working fairly well, the white vessel moved eastward, everyone on board asleep but the officers and men on duty on the bridge, and the engine room crews. How many sleep, Dr. Knott thought as he courted sleep; not the bakers preparing the morning rolls, men at work in the vast kitchens. The purser's staff at adding machines and punch-card systems that kept track of costs of drinks and the reservations for the tours to be taken in Lisbon. And in other holds from deep in the ship cases of wine and beer, supplies of pasta and canned sauces and bottles of American ketchup and English chutneys were being hoisted upward. In the laundry there was a steaming and wringing and drying and pressing—would they ruin his best shirt? Sew on a button? Dr. Knott imagined the radio room with two men listening, keys clicking; and someplace an inky man was printing the menus and the banal *Ship's News*; one-line items of a world busy with its murders, disasters, the Pope's advice to Ireland and the Pill users, and a murderous war against natives, fought, of course, with honor by the side with the bombers.

But otherwise, Dr. Knott thought as he turned in his bed, the ship's passengers slept, or tried like myself to achieve that state.

Judith slept on her back, making a whistling, puffing sound from time to time. She was not actually dreaming, but somehow with a note of levity she sensed she was young again and very happy, and the planet was a delight, as it should be for a young girl moving in the best of all worlds. Nora slept, too, in a prurient avidity for sleep, a slight sweat on her long, fuzzy upper lip. She was dreaming of her married life, over with so long ago she hardly ever gave it the trouble of thought . . . now her husband was taking his married rights on her body—she in a sulk, in a snit—in the dream he offering her something sinful to nibble on . . .

Dr. Knott slept at last, on his right side, it spared pressure on his old heart. He had gone to bed with a book on Gestalt by some schlemiel of psychic trauma, and the book had fallen onto the floor. He made small harsh cries in his sleep but was not dreaming.

Gregory Beck slept in a rolled up position—this night on the bed, not the floor. He had turned several times in his sleep without waking. The bed was still much too soft and wide. He wondered would he ever be able to enjoy a well-padded bed after those three years on the spring and pallet, the Lysol-smelling prison blankets, a fitful sleeping at Q—Block G—sucking in the night stench of a thousand men, their sweats, their moistures, vapors and gut gases.

Sarah slept in fits and starts, coming to surface in short awakenings almost like a goggle-eyed goldfish rising to gulp air. Aware she awakened from time to time, she never fully broke through the skin of the dream as she sank back into sleep. A sleep of images of rubber hammers and stethoscopes, a cataclysmic overflow of shapeless fears, she playing to huge audiences in the fields of heaven Prokofiev's *Overture on Hebrew Themes*. And as she looked down on her hands, the keys were dissolving under her fingers, the black ones turning to sticky licorice candy sticks.

She awoke early to stand at the window of her cabin, watching the crew wash down the deck in sloshing charges on the wooden planking. She had always liked the early morning, being alone, looking at the rising day. She felt vulnerable and yet happy in these solitary morning moments. Some great happy truth would be revealed to her—almost, but never was. Still it was a good feeling, like the feelings when she had first played the piano as a student, when she and Aunt Kate did that southwestern tour. As it had once been those first years of her concerts. She didn't "look like a great artist," one critic had written. She had retained the childlike appearance, even if she had filled out. Somehow the photographs in the press made her look frail, such a slim figure, wispy almost, attacking the big black body of the concert grand with its white teeth almost snapping at her fingers. She wondered if Gregory really liked music. It didn't matter. After all it wasn't a serious friendship; one doesn't see people again after a sea trip.

She turned and tossed off her nightgown, did a small series of dance steps, and said to her naked image in the dresser mirror, "Besides, I lie a lot to myself."

CHAPTER

16

[From the journal of Edward Knott]

MAY 30 (still, still at sea):

Too much fancy talk with Judith about Greg and Sarah. So I am hidden out on C Deck reading a copy of my College Alumni Magazine; *class notes reported in by graduates of that Ivy League bastion of fame, glory, New England horseshit I attended and later taught at. Here is the real stuff, a history of our time at a certain fatty social strata:*

CLASS OF '97. "My recent letter to Dr. Frank A. was answered by his son. Frank is 96 years old and was living at his Florida home (Orlando) until two years ago. He is now under excellent nursing care, but has been failing during the past few weeks. He has two sisters living in New York City, one 99 years old, the other 92. He gave up his surgical practice and his teaching in New York several years ago . . ."

CLASS OF '03. "I have been 100 percent out of commission and this is my first letter written in months. My wife and I went north in 1966 and early 1967 where I was hit by a partial stroke which has affected the right side and still has me restricted as far as accomplishing anything goes. We had been anticipating being in attendance at the 65th Reunion, but it is now out of the question, I fear, being so far from the base of operations . . ."

CLASS OF '11. Roy W. *"My daily routine is as follows: 1) Prepare and eat breakfast each morning. 2) Read A.M. paper. Repair to my shop-office hideout behind my house. Fuss with furniture repairs, etc., until mail arrives about 11 A.M. Sort mail and search for dividend checks. Enter them in my books of accounts . . ."*

These men, facing the Great Perhaps, yet merely lamenting the passing of Coolidge and Hoover, and clipping coupons as their prostates turn to stone. Why, Sarah once asked, can't we give away one's past like an old suit of clothes? . . .

(Called Greg's cabin. No answer. Expect the worst.)

Sarah and Gregory had spent a good part of the night in the E Deck salon of the Tourist Class passengers. At a wild festive dance, a dance with old Italian love songs, accordion music, flaring gypsy skirts, a pasta, salami and garlicky buffet and red wine. Lots of red wine. It was two o'clock when they left the party and Gregory saw Sarah to her cabin door. Panting, eyes popping, her face damp with the pleasure of the night, she grabbed Gregory's head to her with both hands and kissed him a hard smack on the mouth, muttering "um-um-um." Then she turned, was inside her cabin. He, still outside, heard the door latch click, and he stood, swaying, grinning foolishly. "A hell of a lot of the chianti on board! A hell of a lot." He spoke softly, walking away. "Sorry, ol' girl, real sorry. Too drunk for it to-to-night . . . night night."

She dreamed in tranquil solemnity that she lay in a man's arms, he sleeping that deep satisfied sleep of post-lovemaking. Sarah in a dream within a dream thought of the pervasiveness of the sense of the past. Her past. The last time she had lain like this with a man was Julian. That bastard, once her one and only love, was fading fast. The last time I saw Julian: the concert. To the standard version of Schumann's *Études symphoniques* I added the five variations deleted in the final edition. And logic was a strong point of my interpretation; no separate bits, rhythmic vagaries. I was to go to a party with Julian afterward. How I drove through the first, second and last movements of one of Chopin's Minor Sonatas. The Largo emerged as the most relaxed and eloquent moment of my evening. The Liszt *Valse*, the encores like orgasm after orgasm for Chopin's posthumous C-sharp-minor Nocturne, Brahms' G-minor Rhapsody, an arrangement of Bach's "Jesu, Joy of Man's Desiring." Julian was waiting in my dressing room. But I ran off stage, not bothering to change. Next day I flew to? to? Bermuda? Someplace.

The ship is rolling. I am at sea and not sleeping. The concert, Julian. Anyway, it was long ago in another country, and, besides, the wench is dead. (Am I going to vomit?)

Now, she thought, I must sleep . . . the ship's air-conditioning sounds in the wall like the whine of a piano accordion . . . Random thoughts bring sleep sleep *sleep* . . . the night world of unlogic . . . in the corner the shadow moved . . . close your eyes . . . sleep, court it by repeating authors. Conrad? "The best we can hope for is to go out nobly in the end . . ." Hemingway? the old crap, "Nothing ever happens to the brave . . ."

Julian . . . that you in the shadow there? You're not Julian . . . Dr. Knott? Old Merlin, libido's witch doctor, strong willed as an ox in clover . . . ? Oh, it is the Angel of Death . . . I believe, I believe in the Messiah in the dark, in the shadow . . . Play Thalberg's *La Sonnambula* for him and he'll go away . . . move with care . . . The Angel of Death has a flashing laser beam for a sword . . . a laser beam . . . Flee, Sarah, open the cabin door, go running on bare feet down the corridor . . . *Shema Yisroel adonoy eloyeynu adonoy echod* . . . still running as I fall, fall . . . my head . . . on a tray of broken toast . . . a coffee pot and . . . smears of strawberry jam . . . left outside a cabin door . . .

Dr. Knott, coming out of his cabin, hearing Sarah's voice, found her in only a fingertip pajama top, lying prone in the corridor, foam on her lips, eyes closed, babbling to herself, then singing softly: "The boat lies high, The boat lies low. She lies high and dry, On the O–hi–o!"

He lifted her up, her hair and face a mess from a tray of jelly and crumbled toast, and half carried her to his cabin. He gave her an injection, and as the needle went into the flesh of her left arm, she sighed the long drawn out sigh of no comprehension *and* full exhaustion.

CHAPTER

17

Judith awoke at five thirty in the morning and could not go back to sleep. She wrote another letter to her daughter, Gertrude Lazar-Wolf.

Dear Gertrude:

Last night I again missed both the midnight pasta feast and the native dancers among the Italian group on board. I think Sari is having an affair with G.B. I hope it does no harm. Yes, better this than that Father Umbargo, the priest-in-residence on the ship, should carry her off for a minyan with the Pope. The sailors, stewards and lady stewards are all polite, helpful. One senses the top-dog help from captain to purser, headwaiter are playing at being imperial Romans or El Greco's hildagos. The amount of bland food the elderly passengers put away in their stretched entrails is astonishing.

Got your gift—the two bottles of champagne. So we had the wine steward, who looks and acts like Stan Laurel—you liked him, Gertrude, when very young—

after mucho striving and polite windbreaking work at a cork to open a bottle for our table. Fine musty stuff, and I had two glasses. Delightful. Am saving the other bottle for the night before we get to Lisbon. Sari appears drunk at times, but I know she isn't drinking much.

Looking forward to Lisbon as our first landfall. Will be good to put toe on earth again. Not that I have any deep interest in Lisbon; it's just that I'm a land creature and the sea in the last half of the 20th century is stupid, not too dangerous, and very uninteresting. So far no whales, sea serpents, mermaids, thirsty sailors on rafts—not even another ship. Almost suspect Melville, Jack London and Conrad were telling great lies.

More when we touch land. Hug Lazar, kiss the children. Remember the prayer I taught you? *Dein bin ich, Gott. Rette mich.*

Love. J.

Father Umbargo held a daily shipboard Mass at six in the morning in the small writing salon, as was noted in the copies of *Ship's News* pushed under every cabin door sometime during the night. This morning as usual at the Mass there were half a dozen Italian women, one Moustache Pete–type, an old man who dozed throughout the service, three Boston Irish passengers from First Class. A young second-generation Italian-American beatnik–type of fourteen had been enlisted by force as altar boy, in a soiled lace soutane. Father Umbargo went through the Mass with practiced ease, trying not to show how irked he was at the small turnout of the faithful as he chanted:

"*Asperges me, Domine hyssopo . . .*"

Sarah sat in back of the room, half hidden by the magazine rack, not part of the service. She sat on one of the bridge chairs and felt sleep still misty on part of her brain. She watched the service, the nose-picking acolyte and the earnest young priest with his East Side accent. The Italian women from Tourist, in black with kerchiefs on their heads, were very attentive, Moustache Pete came awake with a snort and then settled himself back to doze again, puckering up his toothless mouth.

"*Confiteor Deo omnipotenti . . .*"

Sarah felt the mystery, the color and the faith behind the incense, the whisk flicking holy water. Yes, there was a mystery and Father Umbargo was part of it, and projected his faith and his involvement in it. He had found the Good Great Place.

"*Vestri omnipotens Deus.*" The priest turned, gave the boy a hard knuckle blow for yawning, and went on with the service. Sarah felt it must be true ecstasy to believe as this young priest did and still not be sunk down in sentimental awe, be able to face with deep faith the hard edges of life. In two talks with her Father Umbargo had not presented theology or dogma, had just listened and let her talk without restraint.

"*Te Igitus, Clementissime Pater . . .*"

How comforting, Sarah felt, to believe blindly, hopefully like that. And as Pascal had said, If the faith *is* the truth, you have a chance for salvation, eternal life. And *if* it's all a myth, *what* have you lost? She felt that for Pascal it was too much like a gambler's odds.

After partaking of the Host by the women and the Boston First Classers and the last drone of Latin, Sarah went up to Father Umbargo. He looked serious, particularly undocile. Then he smiled, wrinkling his face and showing the faint traces of adolescent acne scars.

"You have come to see the Christians, huh? With no lions to toss them to?"

"It's always an impressive ceremony."

"Oh, come off it—that's contemptuous talk. All that holy jazz, as some people say. Only glitter and color to attract people. But behind it, the few people here this morning, they see the Rock. Yes, the solid stuff of eternity. Isn't doubt the Protestant sin, not ours?"

"You don't get discouraged—the small turnout?"

"I take what's offered," he said, cheered up, amused by her questioning. "We get them all back—those who didn't show up—when they're dying. The last thing we remember in life is dying; and that being just mortal can't be the answer . . . Do you mind if we don't have a serious talk this morning? I'm bushed. Been sitting up with a sick man from the engine room down in the sailors' section. Not going to make it and he's scared of Hell, the idea of his wife's relatives seizing his olive trees."

"No talk—but, Father, come have breakfast with me and Doctor Knott on deck."

"Let me put things to right here." He shouted at the boy, then cuffed him. Yelled in Italian, made a cluster of all the fingers of one hand and shook it under the sneering features of the boy. "I catch you drinking the sacramental wine again, *capisci*, I'll kick your ass from here to the captain's bridge and back!"

"Is that Christian?" asked Sarah as the boy went off with a Jimmy Cagney strut.

"When I was a kid the nuns in school used to beat my hands bloody with their rulers. I was a bad kid. And now how can I feel the wine will turn to the blood of Christ when that little crapshooter has been sipping it in secret from the bottle like it were Pepsi? There's a housekeeping side to every godhead, you see."

On deck on the shady side a steward had set down a basket of fruit, all golden oranges, silver pears, assorted grape tones, on a table with a crisp white cloth. Dr. Knott, wearing a yellowing Panama hat, sat eating scrambled eggs and little sausages, a bottle of iced mousseux at his elbow. He didn't rise but waved Sarah and Father Umbargo to chairs.

"I don't usually enjoy feeding in the open air like an ox, but there are no insects flying the sea, and there may be ants and termites on board but I haven't seen them. Good morning, padre."

Sarah pulled off white gloves. "I've been observing Father Umbargo's Mass."

Dr. Knott sipped the mousseux. "Impressive when done by the right man, and the setting is satisfying, palpable."

Sarah drank the tart fruit juice, and broke off a bit of roll.

That and black coffee would be her breakfast. "Doctor Knott, don't you find an empty space in our life, refusing to accept the spiritual? Am I stating it properly?"

"Sarah, Sarah, you live in the prospect life will drop its seventh veil for you."

The priest picked up a roll. "Why not?"

Dr. Knott poured himself a cup of tea after sniffing the pot's snout. "Because the answer is reason, logic and science. Which never seem to please the pious and the myth lovers. Actually life arose on earth by chance, man is alone in a dead universe, there is no rational foundation for any belief that man's existence serves a purpose, is part of anybody's plan, or is progressing towards a higher end, has any discernible goal but the biological goals common to living organisms. Survival of the individual and of the species. It's all there, in the nature of proteins and cells and of the human central nervous system."

"No, no," said Sarah. "Horrible, *horrible!*"

Father Umbargo took two kippers from a tray offered him.

"The Church, Doctor, doesn't see life as a Macy's Christmas parade."

Dr. Knott sipped his tea slowly. "There are scientific faiths as strong as Rome's. Vitalism, Bergson's *élan vital* or Shaw's life force. The universe has or is something like a mind or soul; all phenomena are best understood as part of a larger structure. Take your pick and pay the cashier. No refunds after package is opened."

"You're in a rotten mood, Doctor Knott," Sarah said.

Father Umbargo remained silent, deboned his kippers.

"Not really," said Dr. Knott. "It's a beautiful day, and I live by what I believe. Father Umbargo lives by his codes. You, Sarah, live best by art, by music. The religious folk suffer by the inability to sin decently, naturally."

"You chop away too much of morality," said the priest.

Sarah frowned, looked at Father Umbargo, who was buttering a roll, bit her lower lip and walked away.

Dr. Knott said, "I think you've got her, Father, if you shake out your net."

"I didn't try to move her away from the Jews. She came to me."

"She was waiting for you to stand up against me. Give her a holy, comprehensive image of the world to grasp. She may walk out on you."

The priest set down the roll untasted. "She isn't walking away. Like most people, she'll circle. I used to keep pigeons on the roof when I was a kid. I'd let them fly loose and waved them off, and they always came circling back. They knew what was best for them."

"You don't fool me, padre. You were stealing other people's pigeons from other cotes, sending yours out to whirl and turn. Right?"

The priest laughed, picked up his roll, took a big bite of it with his perfect white teeth. "Bull's eye, Doctor. That's why I gave up pigeon breeding. Seriously, aren't you pressing Miss Pedlock a little too hard? She's high-strung, what you head feelers call—"

"Neurotic? Don't be ashamed, Father, to say it out loud. Hell, you show me a person who isn't neurotic, more or less, and you've got a human vegetable."

The two men sat and enjoyed the sea breeze, the cloud effects, so spectacular, rimming the horizon. They greeted people walking their daily deck duty as if on a military drill. From a deck above came the barking of a dog eagerly choking himself on a taut leash. Sean no doubt.

[From the journal of Edward Knott]

Bad scene with Sarah and Father. Talked too much. Hope lunch will be better. Got caught by a fat fellow who knew I knew a doctor in Miami. A monologist. "So you're going through to Rome, doctor? The fountains, don't miss 'em, must be a thousand—say a couple hundred anyway . . ."

The sea is glass smooth, the day focused by a lambent sun. And tomorrow Lisbon. I was eighteen when I first saw Lisbon. There are to be three-hour and six-hour bus tours. Must make it clear to our group; no tour sights, no smelly old churches, no old art, good or bad, no bones of saints or proving the lack of progress made in public toilets. Judith insists our group will most likely hire a car and drive with some English-speaking driver around a bit, eat native. ("Please, no octopus, Sarah. Just look over the trash for sale, and hope to buy nothing.") The city I remember from when I was here with the Prince is beautiful, the country and seaside well worth looking at. Aboreal and rocky, sea swept. We found—the Prince and I—there was just so much of a landscape that can be taken in at a time, and that sight after sight was not a piling up of goodies but rather a numbing of the senses in time. The Prince said, "As I grow older I no longer try to pull life towards me with breathless joy or anguish. You are young, my friend Eduardo, you'll learn." Well, I'm not young anymore—haven't learned yet.

So not really depressed with some schizoid images of my youthful visit to Lisbon, worry over Sarah, I turn back to the Alumni News:

CLASS OF '19. The news of the month is Jim D., who finally realized his life ambition by finishing in the Grand National at Aintree in England on March 30. The news coverage made us proud of our rootin' tootin' classmate. The biggest cheers Antree has known for years went up. Jim D. has done it, finishing 15th among 17 out of 45 starters. He had completed the course; that's all he wanted to do. D. was the oldest man ever to ride in the Grand National.

Wondered how my own story would read if I were foolish enough to write it. Would it mean more than the items I had been reading? Like the rest, I was chained to a dying animal. Still? I began to compose an item for the Alumni News I shall not mail.

CLASS OF '18. Dr. Edward K. reports he is a mean and scatterbrained old man. Drinking too much, thinking a great deal more. And his mind has atrophied a bit. Has become very unethical to his training and trade. Been playing God to a young couple, well, not a major god. And things are out of joint, going wrong. Keeps bolstering himself up with juicy quotes from the masters, and like all medical men acting as if their errors were brilliant strokes of pure genius. Having been discarded—a husk—by the pleasures of the flesh, lost *or peed on the honor of his profession, Dr. K. reports he isn't actually feeling much regret. He finds to his surprise he is fairly happy. (Boy, would that set the swine on the magazine back on their heels!)*

CHAPTER

18

The warning of the morning gong was ringing its hard brutal metallic insistence of "off the fartsacks"—the hacks in their prison blue were banging their clubs on the railings. The air was heavy with the smell of stale bedding, the musk of males. He could taste it before he opened his eyes; spilled sperm all along the block tier, and the reek of the toilets and the scratchy disinfected blankets. The cell was small, painted battleship gray; the big black man over him in the upper bunk was muttering obscenely in which the word mother was maligned. He heard from two cells beyond his the voice of Princess Grace bitching, yelling out, "Don't beat my ass, kiss it."

He knew the parole board would sit in two weeks, and again most likely turn him down. He would then calmly, with wary secrecy, climb up four tiers of cells and launch himself into the open space at the concrete floor . . . William Blake slid down from the upper bunk. *What is Eternal & what Changeable & what Annihilable.*

"Where did Superspade go to?" he asked the Englishman facing him.

"The Imagination is not a State; it is the Human Existence itself . . ."

No use arguing with spooks—they were to the prisoner now frequent visitors. He got up and the prisoner found the cell shaking. William Blake blew him a good-bye kiss. *"The long-promised earthquake all California had been waiting for."* The prisoner in panic turned and found himself at sea, the ship rolling, he hearing the hiss of the air conditioning . . . its slight smell of fuel oil recalling the prison yard at San Q, and the smoking stacks from the workshops . . . From the position of the hands on his watch he figured it was near noon . . . He had overslept . . .

Gregory sat for some time on the edge of the bed, moving his body with the actually pleasant roll of the ship. He could just as easily go over the side some dark night as jump from four tiers up at San Q; just leg up on the railing, drop into the salty air, sink down into the dark purple of the night sea, making bubbles all the way. Go down down, and some place where the will to rise is beaten, open his lungs to the briny. Much pleasanter than the thought of a jump off the four tiers that had kept him sane—the freedom to mash oneself onto the concrete floor—anything he wanted. Just now, while he still felt transitory, he wasn't alone. There was Sarah Pedlock.

This day he had no desire to do away with Gregory Hirsh (Grandpa had insisted on the Hirsh) Beck. There was a luncheon date with Sarah and Dr. Knott. Judith skipped a lunch when fear of weight was on her mind. A long walk around the Kennel Deck with Sean on a leash. First a drink at the open-air bar in the stern of the ship with Dr. Knott making ironic comment on life. The old boy sounded senile at times—maybe because he belonged to another age: Hemingway, Fitzgerald, Redtop's jazz pad in Paris, the 52nd Street speakeasies, the overripe nostalgia of the Twenties, Thirties. Time the world got bored with all *that* crap about fun, tail and drinking calvados, marc, apéritifs. Doc misunderstood how he, Gregory and Sarah were progressing into a good friendship. The damn boat of senior citizens, retired vice-presidents, was a walking graveyard, a portable Forest Lawn, only four other passengers under thirty on board. Two were faggots, the owners of the white poodles, and the other two were the ship's honeymooners. "Trouble, trouble," he told his mirror as he shaved.

Gregory was puzzled by a coolness between Sarah and Dr. Knott as they sipped their drinks before lunch at the open-air bar.

"*Es usted el pianista Pedlock?*" someone said, stopping at their table.

"*Si.*"

"*Cuyas manos beso el pianista Pedlock,*" said the dark little man with the pale-blue beret, lifting Sarah's right hand and kissing it. He bowed to Gregory and Dr. Knott, and then smiling he walked off with dignity.

"Your fan club," said Gregory, lifting his sunglasses and looking after the departing figure.

The deck attendant of the bar section came up to them. Dr. Knott pointed to the man in the pale-blue beret talking to a bearded man in loose tweeds. "Who is the gentleman?"

"No gentleman."

"Really?" said Sarah.

"He play in ship band. Make musik." The attendant acted out the involved gestures of playing a violin. "Band musik, dance musik. You order more drinks?"

"Bloody Mary for the lady," said Gregory. "A bull shot for me. Doc?"

"Scotch, soda on side."

Sarah said, "Change mine to broth and vodka. *Chicken* broth and vodka."

The attendant said, "Dank you," and went off.

Gregory said, "In the army they always asked you to name your godhead. I never held much with the probings of the military psychiatrists. 'Shrinks,' the enlisted men called them."

Dr. Knott sipped his drink. "So now can you accept life as it is?"

"That old chestnut? What is life?" Sarah held the bowl of broth with two hands and drank slowly.

Dr. Knott smiled. "What you mean to say, Sarah, is, 'I can't *perhaps* know *who* I am.'"

Sarah said, "You think Father Umbargo is avoiding us? You gave out some nasty answers this morning, Doc. He should have said, 'Balls to you.' "

Dr. Knott said, "A member of the crew died. The priest is holding the service secretly not to upset the passengers." He looked off to the horizon, a bland, insipid line, he thought, merging sea and sky. "Why can't we just say, 'I am.' "

"Just, 'I am'?" Sarah asked.

"Not just say it, mean it. 'I am . . .' "

"I am," said Gregory.

"I am," said Sarah.

A polite gong sounded. Gregory said, "Lunch *is*."

CHAPTER

19

"The white?"

"It will soil."

"Always go ashore in white. It's civilized."

"My whites are crumpled. I packed badly."

"Never mind," said Judith, inspecting items of her wardrobe. "We don't get into Lisbon until tomorrow morning. Irish will take your things down to be dry cleaned and pressed."

Nora was pulling pins from a folded sunsuit. "They're having a wake or something in the sailor and servant section. They have a dead one on their hands."

"It's one of the crew," said Sarah. "Father Umbargo gave him the last rites."

Nora crossed herself, muttering from a mouth one corner of which held six pins, "Gawd rest his soul."

"I feel odd. Death—and we're thinking of fun ashore . . . What is there to see, do in Lisbon?"

"Sari, let's leave it in the hands of Doctor Knott. He seems to know the country."

"Greg wants to see some church architecture, where

early explorers are buried on top of stone elephants set up high on a church wall."

Judith threw up her hands and laughed, then coughed as she got tobacco smoke in her windpipe.

"It's all the angle of perception, Sari. Let's just say [cough] even-steven, I gave [cough] as good as I got with the jeunesse dorée . . . Slap me on the back [cough]. Christ! I'm choking."

Sarah pounded the wide back with glee, got Judith a glass of water. Judith sipped, grunted, tears running down her face.

"You . . . see, an old windpipe gets emotional . . . But I don't think my view of things is out of date. Now, even if sex is like dropping a letter into a mail slot—among nonprofessionals, that is. The sexual act no longer brings with it an obligation. It used to mean a dedication to a passion, to a victory at last after some long and pleasant dalliance."

"Honest Injun?"

"A kind of glorification of a culture. Ah, Sari, the best horses and a landau out of Henry James, private dining rooms, a wide Paris red velvet hat and shaded lamps. Great clusters of hothouse grapes and roses they no longer grow. Believe me, it was better than ten-thousand-franc roulette. Love in the scent of his hair oil, and Ylang Ylang and your rice powder, while all the time there was unlacing and unbuttoning and unhooking, and removal of layers of silk and satin and Alençon lace, whale-boning and garter gear. It was a blessing, Sari, I can tell you, when the Twenties came in with the flapper's rolled stockings, just a slip and a loose high waisted dress. And those helmet hats and shingled bobbed hair, with spit curls . . ."

"Well, I must decide on what to wear ashore."

Sarah smiled, patted Judith's shoulder (poor old girl), turned and left the cabin. Judith looked down at her glowing cigarillo end and some tears rolled down her cheeks. She felt weepy, sweetly sad for the past she had lived. Many small victories, some two or three great defeats. Sad that she was so old, that she felt her body turning against her, and for the fact she was still emotionally prone to desire as she had been at seventeen, at twenty-five, at forty. Or nearly so. She smoked, and all the images, memories blended into time passing, things done. Men's faces, playboys and sportsmen—murmur of parties, theater nights . . . Names, colors, out-of-style hats, women with white camellia skins, men in Stone Age motorcars. And always the satisfied feeling that she, the head of a dynasty, yet even now was still seeking, still prepared to be the fool, fear God. Yes, she had never been able to shake out the upbringing of upper-class German-American uptown youth. A Balzacian Jewish Comedie Humaine. The very glossy temple of Rabbi Wise, so Uptown. Dinners at the Harmonie Club, where no Russian or Polish Jew was a member then. Jewry was a monied, banking class, a social status world, and the rabbis shaved, and hatless, as her Aunt Selma once said, presented Jehovah with "a Protestant nose." Even the Hebrew had an English actor's accent. Yes, it was true: God will find you behind a thousand walls.

Father Bruno Umbargo watched the two sailors below him among the great chains and the battered hatch on the foredeck carry in the light of night lamps a long bundle to the motor launch set on blocks at the bow of C Deck. Gregory Beck stood at his side, the wind disordering his hair and tugging at the priest's long black jacket.

"They used to carry out a dead convict in some prisons like this at night, Father, just in case the guards had beaten him to death, and if it were known it could cause a riot among the inmates."

The priest motioned the burdened men to move with care as they placed the long, canvas-covered bundle in the motor launch. "Nothing must upset the passengers. Death mustn't intrude. Get it? After all, a lot of the old characters we're carrying could be dead by morning. So Arturo will be slipped ashore before we dock at Lisbon in the morning. So as not to upset you folk going ashore. Company policy. Just like the honeymooners."

"The honeymooners?" Gregory watched the sailors rope the bundle in the launch. For sailors, they didn't know rope very well.

(152)

"Yes, the honeymooners; they're hired. Most cruise ships carry a pair. Gives the trip a sort of added glow. Maybe flares up old banked fires among the passengers."

"They seem a very affectionate couple."

"I insist that at least they be a married couple, married to each other. Actually the Weltons are a fairly okay couple. It's their third honeymoon trip. They're saving up to buy a friend's Kentucky chicken franchise."

"Not very romantic, Father, is it?"

Father Umbargo went over and tucked the tarpaulin over the long bundle. He made the sign of the cross and whispered a short prayer: *"Deus est qui regit omnes . . ."* Turning to Gregory, he shook his head. "This is my last cruise. I dreamed as a kid of going out among heathens. But the age of missionaries is over. So no fuzzy-wuzzy spear in my gut. And I don't want to run an adding machine in the Vatican's business office."

"My father used to recite a prayer for the dead: *'Bimheyroh yovo eyloyenu im mosheeach ben Dooveed.'*"

"Thanks—sounds good."

"How do you see your future?"

"I'm trying to get a position as secretary to a bishop in Chicago. A wise old mick, has lots of ideas like Pope John—one great humanitarian pope in a thousand years isn't bad . . . Beyond that I'll just pray and wait."

"Good luck, Father. I'm staying on in Lisbon." Gregory offered his hand. "If I don't see you in the morning, it's been interesting talks all around."

"I hope I counteracted Doctor Knott's irony about life . . . When that poor sailor—he was in the engine room crew—was dying and I was giving him the last rites of his faith, I kept thinking of my own doubts: Why this good man, a little sinful maybe with women and other people's money, but a skilled man, a man mad about his children, enjoying the vine, the pasta . . . why at his prime end his life—the bursting of his heart? Dying, the physical part, is a hell of a mess, believe me. Yes, well, good luck, Mr. Beck."

"You, too, Father," Gregory said, and he went away to the bright lights coming through the portholes of the main salon.

The priest stood leaning against the motor launch, its metal side gathering night dew. He looked after Gregory's figure. Poor bastard of a Jew, he thought. Tragedy someplace in his life. Now he has found the Jewish girl and he's running away. Maybe tonight I'm thinking like the street gang kid I was down below 14th Street, with the old Brooklyn Bridge always overhead, while my old man peddled paper bags of fresh roasted coffee beans from a pushcart and had pictures of Mussolini and Karl Marx on the bedroom wall. On each side of the brass crucifix and the faded red ribbon of the Unione Sicilia, a ribbon he had gotten when he was a young punk and a bootlegger for the Malinettis. Beck at least could do something with what he carries between his legs. I'm one of God's capons. *Dei gratia.* Too bad he's getting off at Lisbon. Miss Pedlock is a puzzle. "A classy broad," as my brother Dommie used to say. Dommie not a very important clog in Washington with the Justice Department. A classy broad. A soul, too. Hunting a faith—a home for her faith in God. Always wondered as a boy what a soul was like—a mist, shapeless as a wad of chewing gum? The burning heart for faith in God Jubilla on a holy picture in all those bad colors? The sighs my old lady gave after a day working her vegetable stand on Rivington Street and then preparing food for the six of us, her feet swollen big as grapefruit, and me bringing her the pan of hot water to soak them in. The sighs my old lady made as she put her deformed feet into the hot water, was that sound, was that her soul? Doubt can take you too deep—the dive so far down you can't rise again.

The night dew was thick, the priest felt his long jacket clammy, the damp cloth feeling heavy. He went below, down down to his windowless cabin where the air conditioning seemed to expire without losing its fuel oil odor. He stripped to his shirt, removed the dog collar, as he still called it. His thoughts remained in the main on Sarah Pedlock. Not sexually. He had learned how to sidetrack that stuff—*no wet-dream music, please, O Lord, tonight.* Usually he escaped by thinking in haste of other things . . . Should he press for conversion, no matter if she was as yet not fully convinced? the way the fancy bishops did it, capturing all the rich old dames. But if she came forward *one* step, he would take two steps toward her—*dextro tempore*. Red Rover, Red Rover, let Miss Pedlock come over. He had played that kid's game under the arc light of Canal Street, and walked Maggie Gross home and put his hands into the hem of her drawers, pulled, probed, felt her, so warm and moist, and then—*Disco pati*—he shut off all that image and picked up a small book. Father Kelly, of the wise perceptive eye and despair for the Church, had given it to him when assigning him to the *Lucrezia Borgia* a year ago. He opened the volume, or rather the book seemed to open itself, to a page he read, reread often.

I am gall. I am heartburn. God's most deep decree.
Bitter would have been my taste; my taste was
      me . . .

Down in his cabin, Gregory, having just been thinking about death, was now brooding over the subject of love. As far back as he could remember, he had always been in love with the idea that women are marvelous creatures. As a very young child, he was in love with his Aunt Mona's naked arms in an evening dress, later with various little girls. Florence, in grammar school, he remembered best—maybe because she had a habit of wetting herself (a weak bladder) when the teacher asked her a question in too loud a voice. Puberty he found a delight; his body fairly hummed with healthy glands. He remembered all the high school girls he had secretly cherished, and some he had fondled at parties. Others he had dreamed about, to awaken tacky and filled with wonder over an emotional experience one could work up over just the thought of a particular girl. He had surges of pleasure in being in love with various girls before he went away to be educated. The first adolescent sexual experience had been amazingly puzzling, and while satisfying, yet he had wondered what could make one girl mean more than another girl. Given the same qualifications of height, color, wit, appeal and permissiveness.

He found out the difference important to him when he met Agnes, and went into what Dr. Knott would most likely

have called "a temporary madness akin to true insanity."
Well, stuff you, Dr. Knott. It had seemed the true,
sixteen-jewel ideal of love. Too bad that soon certain
disturbing human elements, social relationships entered into
their lives. To end so tragically.

Gregory, seated in the cabin's one chair, stretched, lifted
his arms, yawned, flexed his shoulder muscles. The ship's
band was still playing someplace for the late dancers;
others, gluttons, would be drifting toward the midnight
buffet, for the cold cuts and the white chicken breasts in
aspic, and gluey Italian cakes that looked like a disaster
before one even tasted them. He hoped no one would think
he disliked Italians because he objected to their confections
and because they ran a confused happy ship.

Now to return to a personal problem—love was back.
"Like a swift kick in the ass, this love business" as Grandpa
had once called it. "Only it's a kick in *tocus* we don't mind
and after a while we like it, and even rub the sore spot with
pleasure."

Gregory, as with most men who have a loving attitude
toward women, now in the present or in the past (it had
been a hard three years in prison—better not to think of
that), didn't fully understand women. He was capable of
loving them, enjoying their company. Liking to hear them
talk, savor their laughter, see them walk on long legs. And
when they had moods, giving comfort, seeing it all as part of
their alluring mystery. How good and warm to the touch,
symmetric, like a perfect building.

He was not a lecherous man, not given to great driving
lusts. Fully sensual as he could be, he had had several good
friendships with women that had not ended in bed, even if
in the end it had frayed his nerves a bit.

Now he faced the fact there was Sarah, Sarah so slim,
elegant, a creature that in less lucid moments he thought of
as a creature from some ancient Greek grove, and in his
more adult periods as someone with whom this whole, so far
casual, adventure was wrong for him. It was falling into the
very serious condition of being deeply, fully, in love. And he
wanted nothing fully, deeply just now. Wasn't sure he could
handle anything so intruding on his solitary journey.

Gregory moaned, sighed, and lightly beat his fists together, smiling all the time. Lurking in the back of his mind had been for a few days the thought, just a hint, that Dr. Knott had trapped him, played him like a trout on a nylon line from the moment of their first meeting. Brought him so skillfully into the table grouping on the ship. All for the purpose of Gregory servicing Sarah Pedlock. It was clearly so. "That's it," he cried out as he rose from his chair and paced the small area of his cabin. Yes, it seemed plain, as plain as could be, that was the truth of it. And he had fallen into the trap and it had clicked shut. Patsy, sap, stooge, he called himself silently. Kick yourself in the behind, boy. It had begun with Agnes, that same feeling under your breast bone, of something like happy gas pumping under the ribs. It's now gone to the point when Sarah comes in sight you have no more control over your adrenals than a high school kid on his first back seat romance. She was now special, standing out from anyone else on board. He created at night fully imagined scenes that came and went quickly, like a blush.

It wasn't, he told himself, as if he wasn't mature, he had been through some dreadful times close to suicide. He knew the world was Kafka's world. "In your battle with the world, always bet on the world." Love, love, love. You've got an attack, you poor bastard. Examine it. Give it the saliva test. You're deeply in love.

And as with all men in love he was sure that if she had faults, problems, all that was needed was his love, his presence, to cure everything. But not him—he was jumping ship, getting off at Lisbon. Destroying Dr. Knott's little game. Not an easy decision to make. So much in common. Sarah liked his company; they could talk confidentially about almost anything, share certain private emotions. Still, that didn't mean she felt as deeply as he did. She was of another world, a cock-eyed genius; not that he felt he was qualified to pass on musical genius. And there had been men in her life—many men, most likely—so she did not take this matter of men and women in love as seriously and deeply as he did. He wondered: what malarky to think I can now fully analyze myself and Sarah.

He began to pack his bags. Lisbon in the morning.

BOOK FOUR

On Shore

I am aware there was a world before Genesis. When daylight was all the time and night slept beneath the waters . . .

Some of us remember how we were before the Deluge and know angels are the thoughts of God—but suppose they are terrible angels . . . ?

JACOB ELLENBOGEN
Waiting for the Messiah

CHAPTER

20

[From the journal of Edward Knott]

MAY 31. LISBON:

We slid with unjustifiable and lucky complacency up the Tagus River and into Lisbon during the night. At dawn we were tied to what looked like a Santa Monica pier—in fact the waterfront looks like Santa Monica, California. Most of the passengers had signed up for a six-hour bus tour, but I had advised our group—Sarah, Judith, Greg—we'd hire a car and just do as we pleased. Turned out to be the wise thing. Found a Mercedes taxi and a native named Vasco, who had been a sailor all over the world for ten years and spoke better English than many of the passengers. Sarah excited, Greg pensive, Judith in festive dress and jewels.

From the waterfront we saw a California city, a busy waterfront, the usual vulgar public monuments to war, kings, heroes and pestilence, fine old buildings but also the usual modern shapes, belligerent, foolish, sterile—boxlike and all windows. The Belem Tower saved our sense of the past. The nation is well off, Vasco said, people well fed again, well dressed. Street traffic along the Avenida de Liberda mostly all small European cars and Mercedes, Greg observed, no Caddies or Rolls in sight. Armed police and military every place, but no one paid them any attention. All very polite to us—natives and cops. "The nation is a police state, of course," said Judith. "The only native color touch is at the markets, with the women carrying burdens on their heads."

We drove on past the city into the countryside, past several fine new structures. Very rich Long Island or Palm Beach sort of section where the rich in power live. Passed a house—empty—where Lord Byron, incest prone, once lived.

But I wasn't seeing the modern countryside. I was remembering when just eighteen (two days short actually of that age) I arrived in Lisbon with the Prince. I had been studying in Vienna and in Zurich with men who were associates of Freud, Yung and Adler. I was a pre-med student, undecided yet whether to train to be a surgeon or an expert on cardiovascular disease, or the rising science—if it was a science—of the probing into the unconscious. I was very young, and blatantly aware of my good looks and charm.

The Prince, he called himself old but he was just fifty-two, was a tall, slim man with the dignity of heightened perception and the grave Old Master's face, the great nose of the S. family, as painted by Titian and a follower of Bellini. The S. family had owned great estates in the Veneto. Still owned at the time of our visit to Lisbon a sinking palace, the Palazzo S., just off the Grand Canal, within a pasta plate's throw of St. Mark's in Venice. The grape orchards that produced the tart purple wine they owned in Bari and Taranto before Garibaldi marched north were long lost. But the Prince told me they still held ancient olive groves in Sicily at Siracusa, Paterno and Nicosia. He represented grandeur, grace, grievances and debts.

"My dear boy, we may die out as a family before the century is half over. You know Bianca, the princess, is barren. My first wife? Only daughters."

I knew damn well the Princess could not conceive. I had

been her lover in Venice in the damp decaying Palazzo S. and now, tit-for-tat, the Prince was my lover. It had been a discreet trip to Portugal on a ship carrying timbers to Lisbon. The Prince was very wise, very much a gentleman (he left our shared cabin to break wind). He had never learned to shave himself, and I did that for him with his case of seven long razors, one for each day.

(I suppose memory of this past event keeps me from observing what Greg and Sarah are up to.)

The day before the Prince and myself had come to Lisbon, we sat in deck chairs, the smoke of the coal burning in the engine room escaping from two rusting funnels like funeral plumes on the horses drawing hearses that carry the dead of Naples to their rented graves.

"You are young, Eduardo," said the Prince—he was smoking a short Dunhill pipe. "And I want to set a good example as to our conduct. To do anything simply with grace is as hard as being good. I have tried to be good, oh, yes—but find myself often forced to an acceptance and adjustment to society. Let us not delude ourselves with the hope that the best is within the reach of all, or, dear boy, that emotion uninformed by thought can ever attain the highest level."

The Prince was fierce and ardent in what he felt was his last vitality, and he would speak in French, which he used for more intimate talk.

"This is my last adventure, Eduardo. I go back to the Princess, and shall take the waters at Baden for gravel in my kidney, and my lawyers will fight to regain the vineyards."

"The family will survive, Prince."

"I have only three ugly daughters by the first princess, and the lawyers will perhaps press out dowrys for them somehow to marry among the Di C., and they will retain as part of their name that of S. I've scattered my seed in my careless youth. I have this genius, Eduardo, of being in love many times with women, with men. As Dante puts it: color d'amore e di pieta sembianti . . ."

Of course, being still young and callow, this was mostly lost to me, only memory recalls it. We had good weather most of the time in Lisbon and drove in a big Pierce Arrow for hire. The Prince was at that time always pressed for cash, so we visited churches. "Real monks buried under floor." Kings and queens and great explorers entombed in wall niches, caskets held up by huge stone animal figures. Coffins of explorers, stone portrait figures asleep on the lids, all very dirty and dusty. The Prince said the missing wall statues had been stolen by Napoleon.

I was catching the night boat to England. I was going to spend a year in Scotland under a great surgeon, Frazier McDermont, studying the blood vessels of the brain. (Standing by an opened-up head he'd say to us students, "Aye, laddies, that's the thinking box.")

In the hotel suite the Prince kissed me good-bye as we waited for the man to come for my luggage.

"I shall not see you ever again, Eduardo. You have your life to plan, and I must become serious about producing for my three ugly daughters. They will need big dowries, not because they are ugly but, you see, the S. family is of Jewish decent. Which makes silver for us cost like gold. Some uncle once said we are descended from Josephus, who wrote that history of the Jews, he who came over to the Romans when the Temple was destroyed the second time. Whatever or how, there is that Hebrew strain and more in our line—but we may survive . . ."

The Prince died ten years later, wise to the end to the pathos of mortality, according to gossip. I wrote several times to him, witty, cynical letters, but he never answered, except for one year when I graduated from the medical school in Vienna and there came a silver and gold pin in the shape of a salamander, set with rubies, and the seal of the House of S. on its head. DUM. FORTUNA. FUIT. The Prince's hopes for family survival were dashed by World War II. The three daughters—two were already widows— and their children were taken from their wonderful estates, packed in freight trains with other Italians also classified as Jews. The Prince's grandchildren died first in trains crossing the Alps to some camps near Merano, frozen to death, those who didn't starve. One of the daughters killed herself by running up to a high voltage wire fence and grasping a

*strand. One was blown up in an air raid. The third daughter
lasted out the war, but trying to reach Palestine in a leaking
Danube River tub, she and her shipmates were all turned
back by the British to Cypress, a cargo of three hundred sick
and barely alive Jews. She died of typhus, the last of the
princely house of S. Their fate, somehow, makes me relate
their destinies to Sarah's.*

Gregory Beck did not go with a bemused Dr. Knott and a
queasy Judith into the Church of Mosteino Dos Jeronimos.
He stood outside the church, gazing at the waterfront in the
late afternoon, when someone touched him on the shoulder
and he turned to face Sarah, near ecstasy bursting from her
eyes. "You missed something wonderful. Big, big. The old
monk took us into this special chapel and he sang for us, and
six *different* musical echoes came back. Six!"

"I'm not musical enough to have caught it."

"I gave him a dollar for each echo, Greg. A dollar." She
took his arm. "You're set to leave the ship. I know. So I ask a
favor . . . Listen. There's a marvelous little place back of
town in the hills, Dr. Knott told me, where they serve a fish
like no other, and a sunset like no other. You're going to
have dinner with me there."

"Am I?"

"Just the two of us." She turned her head to look at him.
"Dr. Knott said it's a tradition—the Vinho Verde Inn. It's
two hundred years old. He ate there long ago when he was
here, just traveling with some duke or prince, or somebody
impressive. What a snob he is."

"How do you know it's still there?" He was not so sure he
had moved far enough away from the danger of full
intimacy with Sarah.

"I called. I phoned, or rather our driver did for me, made
reservations. A reservation at sunset."

"It's cutting it pretty close. My train leaves for Alcacerdo
Sol at ten thirty."

"Plenty of time. Lots of time. Come on. We'll walk down
to the square, walk around, get a taxi. There are marvelous
gardens up there Dr. Knott says."

"I want to say good-bye to Judith, to—"

"You did that in style at lunch in that waterfront restaurant. I told Judith I just had to see those gardens at the inn, have dinner there overlooking them. She can't join us, got some tummy rumbling, and Dr. Knott seems sad to be seeing this country again. He'd spoil it for us. No romance in him."

Greg smiled and pressed his hand into hers. She was like a little girl saying pretty please, *please*. "Sarah, I don't have another damn objection left. But I must make that train."

They walked down the square, away from the church; both very much at ease, he certainly, Gregory thought, now that they were so near to terminating what could have been an awkward, entangling situation.

In her cabin, reclining on a sofa, Judith swallowed the two pills Dr. Knott held out to her and took a sip of water. "You've failed, Doc, failed."

"What the hell are you talking about?"

"Your old-fashioned romantic plot with Greg and Sarah."

He took out a cigar. "Oh, you are sure I planned anything?"

"Don't smoke. I'm ill. Something I ate ashore. You're really an old-fashioned romantic, something out of Henry James, for all your Freudian patter. It was as plain as a clown's lit-up nose, what you were up to."

"You think Greg caught on?"

"He panicked, didn't he? Is running away, isn't he?"

"I thought it was so basically simple—was sure it would work."

Nora came in with a bowl of hot milk on a tray. "No good Irish milk on board with the butter fat floating on top. But—"

"I'm too ill to swallow anything. That sardine salad! You amaze me, Doc. Such a trashy plot."

Dr. Knott put the unlit cigar in his mouth and left. Henry James! That old tea fighter never wrote a character with a hardon you could notice.

CHAPTER

21

The exterior of Vinho Verde Inn was solid, rather preposterous in its use of stone, low-lying on a leopard-colored ridge over the city of Lisbon. An inn not particularly impressive from the outside. The terrace to the rear was paved with a scattering of old millstones set between a hairy grass border, and the gardens were splendid. Sarah and Gregory sat there in the dusk, fireflies animating the fast-darkening twilight beyond the flower gardens. He had admired Sarah's exquisite bone structure under the ivory skin more than the tortoiseshell sunset; a sunset that suggested some marvelous state of idiocy. They had tasted the Croquetas de Camaroes (which turned out to be deep-fried shrimp balls), which went with what they assumed was the wine of the country, *vinho virgem.*

"Doctor Knott talked so much about this place I felt we had to have one meal here, a last meal. I don't mean a *Last Supper* by Da Vinci."

Gregory sipped the wine. "The old boy seemed rather

affected by today's trip around the country. Not his usual ironic, crusty self."

"He's hard crust all the way down. No soft spot in him. A flinty bastard. Laughed when he told me this inn was the accepted hideout for a prime minister or some general with an opera singer or an actress. This was the place for it. *The* place. I'm hungry for the dinner."

"I hope they go easy on the olive oil. Your aunt must have gone back to the boat rather queasy in the stomach from the native cooking."

A thin old waiter came out on the terrace. He was actually carrying a folded napkin in the crook of his left elbow. Gregory had thought only waiters in movies or on the stage did that. His eyes were large and black, and his soft leathery skin was all wrinkles. He bowed. "Ist, please, ready for de dinner, sirs."

Sarah stood up, just saving her wine glass from falling to the terrace as her elbow struck the little table beside her chair. "Ist ready."

"Be so gracious ast to follow, sirs."

The interior of the Vinho Verde was dimly lit by candles covered by smoked-glass chimneys. Gleaming copper instruments hung on the old wood walls; Sarah could not decide if they were for kitchen use or were torture tools. She shivered at the idea of skillfully applied pain and remembered Julian Salt—but only for a moment. The waiter led them two steps up and then through a red door into a small private dining room. Just room for a table, a large pale-green divan. He opened a narrow door. "Barf room, sirs. Shall I please start serve of de dinner?"

"Please," Sarah said, sniffing the air of the windowless room. There was an odor, faint but there, of overseasoned soup, old hangings, wormy wood, and spices dried in attics. Where, where, from where did she remember such details? Drying spices?

The waiter pointed to a small silver button set within reach of the table. "Only come when you press de bell, sirs."

"Oh, Christ!" Gregory looked at the array of silverware. "He thinks we're either officials or generals."

"How grand. And I'm, oh, a prima donna opera singer, or Lisbon's most popular courtesan—no, whore. Whore is a more honest word. You ever go to whores, Greg?"

"I'd only lie. Yes, if I didn't; no, if I did."

It was a splendid meal, and not too much of it. A chicken-rice soup, baked cod which the waiter told them was "de dish invented at this inn. Ist called Bacalhao Fresco a Portuguesa . . ." The brandy in balloon glasses after dinner caused them to laugh after a few sips and make private jests that seemed very amusing at the time in the small, intimate room. Laughing, sipping, they were sure of their abilities for lucid exposition.

"Seriously now, Greg, very seriously." Sarah was smiling, sipping her brandy, her head in a slight delightful roll from side to side. "Seriously, I felt we had to get off the death ship. Good ole *Lucrezia Borgia*. We can't part, not without getting to know ourselves, you know? You follow me? The ship was restraint, a barrier between us."

"You're too serious, Sarah."

Sarah sipped, smiled, grabbed his arm. "When you talk like that, you're like my father. I mean, so damn determined to set me right. 'Make plans,' he said. Once we went camping on a soft crab inlet on a sea island off the Eastern Shore. The whole family, even Beanbag, our dog. It rained, it really rained, poured, you see—poured. Daddy said the storm would pass, and we set up the tent and sat for two damn pouring days in the tent, the wet wood smoldering and we eating cold beans from cans. And why? Because Daddy had set aside a weekend from court cases . . . made a pattern, couldn't change it."

The food, the brandy seemed to transport Greg into a kind of new reality. Sarah across from him in the low-cut gown, an apple-green sheer molding her body, earrings of small green stones, in "real pierced ears" she had assured him. Hair piled up and falling away behind the beautiful neck. An animated girl, yes, very animated, he thought as he put down the brandy snifter with rather too much bang, misjudging distance. "It's getting late—my train—"

The waiter came with a tray, coffee pot and cups.

"*Caffè nero?*"

"Black," Sarah said. Gregory agreed; he peeped at his wristwatch—early yet.

"No crim, no zugar?"

"Black."

The waiter set down the tray, bowed, went to the door, adjusted the spring lock. "You will nut be disturbed. Ring if de sirs desire anyting." He bowed again, closed the door. Gregory heard the spring bolt click into place from the inside.

"Hey!" Gregory felt this was too much sophistication, turned toward Sarah. "The old crock thinks we—" But Sarah wasn't there, adding to the grotesqueness of the situation. From the bathroom doorway she stood laughing. "I know what he thinks. Be right with you, Greg."

"Phew. I mean, what—?" He took a good solid slug of the brandy. Damn strong, stronger than you think. He stood up, felt his brow, warm, damp. The room was too closed off, still there was some sort of system of ventilation; maybe those slits in the ceiling between the old wooden beams. Looked like ship's rafters as in some of the old houses. Grandpa had built one for himself on the edge of town . . . "Ship's beams. Came from the clippers that got stranded in Frisco harbor when all the sailors ran away to the goldfields back in 1849 . . ." Gregory took one more sip and put the glass down. Yes, my grandfather used to talk of the private rooms at the old Palace, and at Seal Rock . . .

The memory of Grandpa recalling the hedonism of his youth was cut off for Gregory like a strip of film tearing in his mind. For he was staring at the doorway of the bathroom and Sarah, naked, there, posing in the opening, one hand on hip, one near her pubic area, she laughing. "Oh, God, Greg, you should *see* your face."

He could only croak a shocked homily, "What the hell do you think—?"

She came toward him, little Greek statue breasts so well formed and lifting. Narrow waist but flaring hips; exquisite, enchanting, his lower nature had to agree. Tapered thighs, very slim legs. And yes, a crisp thick pubic bush. All this, he assured himself, taking it all in at one glance, was real;

before lifting his head in unresolved tension so he saw only the rafters.

He felt the brandy vaporize in his system and he was in shock, very sober.

Sarah put arms around his neck and pressed closer. "Oh, darling, darling, don't look so shocked. So *unglaublich,* as Judith would say."

"Not shocked. Surprised."

She seemed very warm to the touch and there was a spark, a high glaze to her eyes focused directly on him. She was breathing both through nose and mouth. Then she pressed her open mouth to his and he felt no self-confidence, only a kind of unreality. Yet still able, oh, *so* able, to feel sensation, feel that Sarah was solidly there and he was certainly real. The moment? the time? the place? All were a kind of envelope that sheltered them, hid them, gave an instantaneous impulse of vitality.

"Greg." More of a command than a moan—and the open mouths hunted each other.

But *this* was another time, another place. Sarah was unbuttoning his jacket, talking away, busy talking—he not understanding a word. His shirt gone, he found himself lifting Sarah, and the two of them there on the green divan. A quicksand pit of a divan, wide and soft. In the candlelight the shadows were that dried-blood color of bullfight posters . . . It was again as it had been in his adolescence, an intense ecstasy. He was de-trousered, never knew if he or Sarah had done it, and there he was, almost in a state of incoherence, but not quite.

Sarah's grip was strong, almost beyond his being able to bear. He said, "I love you. I love you, Sarah."

"I know, darling."

It was just magnificent, he thought as they embraced, skin to skin. He pulled back his head to enjoy her visually. She appeared quite frankly mad with pleasure. He'd never bothered to observe a girl this close at just this moment. No girl, woman, had ever looked so overwhelmingly involved with frenzy in the pleasure of contact. Large orbited eyes, chest inhaling, exhaling with quickened pace, mouth open.

Later Sarah was aware that she was pulling on his hair, had her fists buried in his red-brown curly hair, was yanking it as her orgasm seemed to revive and go into a series of aftershocks.

"Darling." Her voice was thick and deep as if coming from inside her. "Oh – Jes – us. Greg! Jes – us."

He wished for some perceptive poem, some remarkable burst of language to come to him to express the moment. But it didn't. It never does, he thought.

Sarah was very still.

"You all right, Sarah?"

She seemed unable to speak, just rolled her head, nodded a yes. He tried to break her fingerhold on his hair, but she refused to let go. He could smell the candles, the odors of food served here, but most of all Sarah, the good smell of girl, of woman, something like bruised fruit and damp salt. Her hair was broken loose from restraint and fanned out in a flow over the pillow. Her brow was beaded by sweat, and as she suddenly looked up he saw in her glance she wanted exclusive proprietary rights to his love. Slowly Sarah released her grip on his hair. Her hands fell to her sides. Her eyes remained enormous. She tried to speak. It seemed hard for her. Then words came; little girl pleading words.

"I love you, Gregory Beck."

"Gregory Hirsh Beck," he whispered in her ear.

She repeated it, tasting it like a new dish, "Gregory Hirsh Beck. Sounds like singing *Aim Kailohainu*. I shall become a Jew, too."

"You are a Jew." He felt her skin between her breasts where perspiration had collected; his finger traced a little river.

"No, I'm an Episcopalian. Mother, neé Ornstein, is. Daddy, he just goes along. I'm going to convert."

"Crazy, crazy," he said.

She bit his hand lightly but painfully. "It's the only way, darling. Oh, Greg, don't you see, I want to *be*."

They lay in each other's arms, glued in warmth and moisture. Then she slept in his arms, he feeling on his back a pleasant pain where her fingernails had broken skin, drawn blood. For the first time Gregory felt the prison gates had really opened. He was a keeper now with a prisoner of his own locked in the cage of his arms.

He was not thinking of railroad timetables. He was thinking what happens from here on in? No matter how high the ecstasy you'll come back with a bump to the fact you've got a woman depending on you. You're no longer going your own way. No matter how much the moments are high here at the old inn, is it for you—the sin-designed room from the past, even the damn goodness of having such a woman, being so lifted, drained of all the sour past, those few minutes when you die and live and sink and rise? Still, the real truth of what comes afterward has to be faced.

They had both said *the* word so many others had said before: love love love. For a moment he hated the word. Then found it warm and solid, a comfort; but the world out there intruded again. The ritual of departure was called for. They'd have to get washed, dressed. He'd pay the bill, the waiter would bow, the staff would nod knowingly, inwardly smirking. Or didn't they give a damn anymore?

That's the trouble with plays and novels, Gregory decided. They can lower the curtain, fade out, end a chapter. But in real life there are the shared little bathroom indecencies, the problem of what to do now after the first consummation. How to proceed? The best solution—the logical one—would be to rise, gently disentangle Sarah's arms. He looked at her and thought when defenseless in sleep how much she looks like a little girl who's had a treat; who smiles as she sleeps, sleeps so deeply, her skin glows as if blushing for the last hour.

Gregory turned his head away. Rise, dress, leave a note. Naturally he didn't have paper and pen, but the maître d' would provide. Pay the bill, split (as the expression was) in a taxi for the railroad station. His bags were already there. And ahead? A life of no ties, no duties to anyone. A free man.

Of course that was the only sensible thing to do. He could not imagine what his future would be if he didn't. Go he must. Go he would. Yet he didn't rise. He didn't do anything but stare at the naked little girl's body. Out loud he said, "Doctor Knott, you bastard, you've won."

Somehow with this confession he felt elated, even if his stomach protested at the same time. There was still a little brandy left but he didn't reach toward it. Sarah moved an arm about, muttered something in her sleep. He grasped her hand.

CHAPTER

22

The cruise ship *Lucrezia Borgia* went down river from Lisbon. Headed its plunging knife-edge bow for the open sea. Time 10:04 in the morning. Damaging in the process the side of a government dredge, a mere scrape in passing. Two of its crew left behind in a Lisbon jail for drunken assault. The ship's chef had traded a half ton of beef for six packets of heroin in hopes of a fortune in the Harlem market. Several of the officers had hangovers; there had developed some nonspectacular liaisons with four of the schoolteachers.

Judith Pedlock was under the care of the ship's doctor, Professor Ercole Baldovini, she having developed what the doctor called "da Portogees stomach flu, *è meglio una volta che mai.*" However she blamed her condition on some poisoned native dish. Her temperature was 102, and feeling very ill she informed Nora O'Hara that a copy of her last will and testament, the latest one, was in the false bottom of her cosmetic case. Dr. Knott had passed out cold, sitting up in the chair in his cabin; passed out from brandy and nostalgia, and was to come to vowing never to come back to Lisbon, never ever. Sarah slept, having come on board at seven in the morning, floating up the gangplank in a state of ecstatic haziness. She never had found her stockings at the inn. She was in a deep, dreamless sleep; the motion of the ship, the toots of the tugs that had taken them down river did not break into her slumber.

Gregory Beck, back on board, unexpected, had gone through two hours of gesturing, and at last threatening to bust the nose of the ship's purser. His cabin had been allotted to a Swedish family of wife and husband and a small child; the purser insisting that Gregory had left the ship at Lisbon, had his baggage put on the dock, paid his bar bill. All signs that he was *not* sailing with them from Lisbon. *Avanti Cristo!* Americans were all mad.

In the end a ten-dollar bill and an offer by Gregory to agree he had spoken harshly and threatened the purser— very sorry—he was given a windowless cabin on C Deck. Once settled in, Gregory threw off his clothes, took a shower in a space as large as a coffin, nearly falling asleep under the caressing flow of the warm water. He decided not to brush his teeth and fell into the too narrow, uncomfortable bed. After a few moments of reviewing images of Sarah, he fell asleep, smiling, feeling as tired as he could ever remember. There had been a mumbled agreement with Sarah to meet for lunch. He had somehow shifted events so that he, not Sarah, had been the aggressor in challenge and fulfillment.

It was two o'clock in the afternoon when he came awake, the ship rolling now on a decided angle and his stomach felt it had to protest. Not so much the motion, but all the assorted wines and brandies, boozes he had tossed down. To say nothing of the rich oily food, all topped by a testing of his abilities and perhaps the innate folly of love. Yes.

He had come awake feeling his throat fill suddenly, and he sat up at once to keep from catting up the contents of his stomach. He sleepwalked to the bath closet, brushed his teeth, saw his drawn features in a square of sea-spoiled mirror. He noted his coated tongue, pulled scientifically on a lower lid and saw his eye was slightly bloodshot. He phoned Sarah's cabin and after a while decided the phone there was off its cradle. He wanted to send flowers, called and found the ship's flower shop was out of roses, so he ordered a dozen of "something big and yellow," not understanding the Italian name given him.

Gregory dressed slowly, feeling as if only tepid water was in his veins . . . The outer image he presented wasn't bad. Pale-blue shorts, his gray corduroy trousers, on his feet over gray nylon sox brushed Hush Puppies of dull pigskin. All topped by a conservative sport shirt of chrome yellow featuring a pattern of little brown fish. He decided not to shave. His cheeks would do after a rubbing in of some bath powder; Grandpa had called this procedure "a Jewish shave." He thought his grandfather would approve. The old man had died while Greg was in prison, but for three years he wrote long letters denouncing the inadequacy and incompetence of mankind. On his mother's side, Gregory Beck reminded himself, he came from a long line of famous rabbis, a great-grandfather having been chief rabbi of Turkey, an authority of the Zohar—the Cabala in Aramic. So what? But he had never felt a complete link, a commitment to anything. Not even his marriage. (If he had not murdered Agnes, he had certainly killed something vital in her just as she had murdered something basic in him.)

Now there was Sarah, so suddenly thrust into his life. He was back in flesh alley. He was in love again. Yet he had promised himself after the parole board verdict to hold to an avarice of emotions expended and a caution in his behavior in contact with any human being.

Gregory shook himself free of memories and went up to B Deck. There was a huge bouquet of yellow flowers and several message slips in front of Sarah's cabin door. The little printed sign on the doorknob read DO NOT DIS-TURB. He tried, by leaning against the door, his left ear alert, to hear her breathing, but he heard nothing. He had no hunger but needed a drink, and went out to the stern bar and ordered a double bullshot, something like a Geiger counter clicking between his ears.

"Hello," someone said behind him. He took a big swallow of his drink before turning around and saw Dr. Knott, seated, holding a glass of tomato juice with a raw egg and some dark addition to it.

The doctor gave a bronchial cough, sipped the pick-me-up, made a face. "You low-down dog."

Gregory went over and sat down at the little table, facing the old man. The beard, once neat and pointed, was tangled, the bags under the eyes seemed a kind of wrinkled plastic, and the eyes were crossed by red lines like some detailed road map.

Gregory sipped his drink, felt it do its work.

"Feeling good this morning, Doc?" He got a grunt for answer. Gregory leaned forward. "You sonofabitch, you mangy old whoremonger."

"That's better, Greg."

"Want me to thank you?"

"Save it when I'm sober."

"I fell into your trap. I knew it was there yet I fell into it."

Dr. Knott grimaced as if from sudden pain and rubbed his brow. "Put it down on my part to senility. Anyway, I like you. You're—"

"One of the family now?"

"Wish I could show shame. But I'm never ashamed when hung over."

"Excuses. Afraid I'll hit a drunk?"

"Want to?"

"What's the good of that now?" Gregory took another swallow of his drink. "It's not fair to Sarah, that's all. Not fair at all. Me? I'm expendable."

"Don't be so obviously noble so early in the day. What difference does it make by what foul trick it happened? You were in no better state than she was when I picked you out. A lost little lamb yourself, weren't you? With a sore tail to which someone had tied tin cans. Think of it this way, I did you both a favor."

"You don't seem so very happy about it, you rummy."

"So you and Sarah spent the night together. Not an earthshaking event."

"Both of us over the age of consent and free to mind our own business, right?"

Dr. Knott lifted his head, turned it toward the bar. "Juan, double Scotch." He set down the pick-me-up. "Mr. Beck, I wonder, have I done a bad thing?"

"You going moral, Doc?"

"I'm never moral. I'm logical, scientific . . . Thank you, Juan . . . No. Her history is such . . . Christ! Let me tell you some fundamental truths now it's happened."

"I'm not interested in her medical history. Not from you. Or what—"

"Don't interrupt me. I have some talking to do and I don't feel well. Listen."

"Who the hell are you to talk that way to me?"

"I'm Sarah Pedlock's doctor."

"So keep your patient-doctor relationship to yourself."

"You don't seem to grasp the idea that I'm her psychiatrist, and of long standing, *not* her family's old lovable family doctor."

"Some doctor. You've betrayed every ethic of your profession. Senility is no excuse, you old fart."

"She's very sick." He tapped his brow. "I'll be goddamned if I'm going into technical explanations. No, no psychological texts here, just—"

"She's neurotic? Who isn't?"

"She's been deep in manic-depressive cycles for a couple of years. She's getting worse all the time. Her family and myself, we've been making a good fight of it. And then—"

"Your stupid idea. Trap her a stud."

"Right. So, are you good or bad for her? Now are you a time bomb or—"

Gregory put down his drink. "So at times Sarah had an erratic sensitivity, wandering maybe between the improbable and the delicate. But what the devil are you saying— manic-depressive, getting worse!"

"I've scared you now." Dr. Knott gave a feeble smile, more like a grimace.

"Scared? I don't believe all you shrinks pass out as psychoneurotic states. It's in all artists, isn't it—apprehension, agitation?"

"So you think you know my disgraced trade? Listen. Open your ears. Sarah Pedlock is at times deep in a paranoid state, often she is shutting out the present, the past, locking it out indefinitely. Sloughing off the essential conditions of existence. Trying to reach something she calls God."

"Who isn't these days? Doc, I think you've lost your marbles."

"Frankly, do either of us believe in God? Either the old boy with the whiskers, or do we bend to a system ruling cause and effect with reason and logic? Can you bow to a great mysterious force, without shape or voice? Come on, tell me."

"I believe, yes, in *something*."

Dr. Knott was mellowing with the Scotch. He gave a short barking laugh. "Well maybe you can live with that ball of mist, but Sarah can't. She wants faith in the full rituals, the candles on the Sabbath, the door open Passover night and the glass of wine out for Elijah—for him to come through the door left open. Oh, I know unsubtle, fifty-dollars-an-hour psychology has easy answers. I haven't. Now, because I'm an old dog, you've got her using her body again. You've got her down on the earth, on her back. Homeopathic doses of sex delivered at regular intervals, eh?"

"Doc, your fancy talk stinks."

"You don't get past my scar tissue with that kind of insult, Greg. I want you to understand we've been fighting for months trying to keep Sarah from completely losing her mind."

"No."

"Yes."

Gregory wanted to leave, wanted to smash the old man in the face, knock his dental work out of his mouth. But he just sat. It was all like a bad wound he once got in a prison yard fight; it didn't become a bad pain until after the fight. So far no pain, just a great gnawing under his breast bone.

"You feel she talks, she walks, she eats, she smiles? She's marvelous in lovemaking. So you think, why should she appear to be gradually losing touch with reality, sanity?"

Greg nodded. "It's you doctors who are sick. Why do you go into psychoanalytical work in the first place—because—"

"The old stale argument of the thickheaded." Dr. Knott exhaled loudly through his mouth, pressed Gregory's shoulder with a strong set of fingers. "It looked bad from the start. She gave up concerts—she thinks God desired that. Why? Ask God. She retreated behind big sunglasses to some damn California colony of hallucinating creeps at Big Sur. I had hopes, maybe I could get her back on the tracks. I had retired, time on my hands, perhaps would sum up the dented souvenirs of a life in a final book. The book didn't jell—so there was Sarah. Maybe I could do something, I felt, for the recurring grayness of her *angst*. I'm not given to fancy jargon in talking to people outside the profession. So plain facts: beyond her hallucinations, tremors, I felt I could stop her deterioration."

"She's in love. Perhaps that's madness to you?"

"All courting, mating practices are not, frankly, states of calm sanity."

"Sanity, insanity are legal terms, *not* medical ones, Doc."

Dr. Knott sat back, eyes half closed. "You learned that during your trial for murder, didn't you?"

"Now you're getting your whacks in at me."

(The pain was starting, the horror too, the whole dreadful horror, and he wanted to howl, to cry out. He didn't. He sat, his breathing hard . . . What a discovery. What fears gripped?)

"When you came to your senses you wanted me to get off the ship at Lisbon and stay off?"

Juan came and picked up the glasses, Dr. Knott shook his head at the idea of refills.

"I wouldn't leave her now," Gregory said. "I don't really believe in your mumbo jumbo. It's all a theory, not a science, that psychiatrist's patter."

"Love will conquer all, eh, Greg?"

"You don't have any other choice, Doc."

"No, I haven't. Judith, of course, the wise old bag, she

saw that at once. You're in the family now the deed is done." The old man made a vague gesture with both hands in the air.

"You could have said that right away, instead of playing Jehovah in Freud's overcoat."

"Oh, could I?"

Gregory stood, suddenly angry. "I'm not sure either one of us, you or I, is adding things up properly, you creaky old sonofabitch."

Dr. Knott didn't answer. He rose from his chair as if with effort, wanted to say more, didn't, and walked slowly away. No strut left in him, just walked off. Perhaps, Gregory suspected, the old bastard, he's making himself a little more shambling than he is. What the hell, he's only a very old man, addled, a walking bag of old lecture notes from past cases. And he isn't adding up things right anymore.

But Gregory was not fully convincing himself. He walked out to the lea rail and looked down at the churning hop skip of the waves, waves indifferent to his thoughts, as the ship moved through glass-green water. Now the grip of horror on him was growing, now he could feel his entrails twitch like a basketful of electric eels. He touched his brow and it was damp. His teeth seemed to click together and there was a faint sound of chattering. It was all like being stripped in that steel gray room and being finger printed again in the prison—hung with a number like the price for butcher's meat—having his picture taken, being tossed some washed-out denims. He had felt then no man not a born criminal could go down in this destroying darkness of clanging iron doors and survive. When he fell into the prison routine, he decided never again, once I'm out, will I ever have this dreadful weight of agony.

And now he knew he would have to bring back the discipline of those dank years.

CHAPTER

23

She came awake but didn't open her eyes. That was the secret—not to open your eyes. Because if you did open them the other world would come rushing in and capture you. And it was good to tease yourself and hold it out as long as you could. It was much the best idea, Sarah knew, to keep your eyes closed in the better world that looked like the world most people had, but wasn't, no. A world that they, too, could have. If they knew. The true world was folded in so close with the outer world—like two paper fans—a world she didn't understand, folded together yet separate. But you could hardly pry them apart once you opened your eyes, *unless* you had the secret.

It was too bad most people didn't know of this double world—two-world plan. But then most people were so busy rushing around, bollixing up their lives, they didn't have time to discover the better of the two worlds, even suspect it could be possible.

She spread-eagled herself on the bed, flexed her arms, wriggled her spine, made the muscles of her slim calves hard, wriggled her long thin toes. She was happy, overwhelmingly happy. Busting out all over with joy. She wondered if Gregory had last night come all the way over into her best of two worlds. Was the inn, its private dining room in her world or a mere replica of what people called reality? She felt the ship roll left and roll back right. Heard the people outside shuffle past the window of her cabin as they walked by, and was aware of the faint smell of furniture polish, ship's cooking, fuel oil, rusting iron that all make up a ship's personal odor. Enough of dreaming eyes closed. Ahead was the daily adventuring into the world of the others. You might even say at times the enemy camp. Yes, but there was also Aunt Judith, and Dr. Knott, and, of course, Greg, even if they lived among the enemy, unaware of their peril.

Greg understood her. Greg loved her. She loved Greg. It was just like an early first-grade primer: *John Loves Spot. Spot Loves John. They Love Each Other.* She opened her eyes, laughing. It was a sunny day, all "yallery," as Tessie, the family cook, used to say. The throbbing of engines someplace far below was a pleasant sensation, like heart beats of the great steel whale. It wasn't a bad world if you were wary and always kept a wall at your back (Wild Bill Hickok forgot that). It was part of her morning game: there was no other world—or was there? Why did she deny it at times?

There would be lunch—that always was real on a ship. Overfeeding. There would be Greg, and they would make love again in leisure and in detail. This time she'd let him take the initiative. She went to the bathroom, very amused about something, and it was hard for her to stop laughing long enough to get a loaded toothbrush into her mouth. Greg had certainly been surprised at the inn when she came out of the bathroom there in the buff. It seemed so right, so natural. And he was so good about it. After that first look on his face.

She calmed down as she dressed. (Down, girl, *Heel!*) Very serious as she picked out the dainty shoes to go with the yellow linen dress, so plain but so well cut. It was like the dress she had worn the first afternoon at the Pittsfield Music Festival that summer when she gave four concerts in one week. That famous summer when she was *the* musical event for all people who went to summer festivals. As she brushed back her hair into taffy-colored curls, she decided she would go back to the piano. Play again. Having found Greg, being able to live in both worlds, peace and grace would come to her. For God had sent a sign. She wasn't sure what the sign was, but she'd decipher it in time. God willing.

CHAPTER

24

[From the journal of Edward Knott]

JUNE 1:

At 8 A.M. we sighted the Rock of Gibraltar but didn't land. Sarah, much overelated these days, said, "It's so close we could swim over." Greg is less hostile. But he's lost his respect for me. But then I lost that for myself long ago. (No self-pity, please.)

Judith, who has kept to her bed, says we are all encased in a kind of plastic bubble filled with USA, and might just as well be back with the vistas of home. Maybe we Americans are doomed travelers. Flying Dutchmen in a Time Machine. Having locked out the past as slow and dirty, we skim over the surface of the earth with not even one toe dragging in reality. We are part of an age that discovered gods die just like the rest of us.

Record of a talk with Judith: "Doc, I feel terrible. In my fever, I keep seeing abstract art."

"In the ninth century in China, Judith, they had a

fantasist who sat bare-assed in a pan of ink. Then he sat down on paper five times. He called the result 'Five Peaches.'"

"Very amusing. Tell me, have you seen Sarah?"

"She's on deck looking at the Rock."

"With him?"

"With Greg."

OFF GIBRALTAR

Have just passed the Rock of Gibraltar.

Sarah and Greg have no need for anyone but each other. They are like newly mated birds trying to find a comfortable nest and a private one on a busy street.

The ship rolls magnificently on—steady, easy, and as if run by robots. This morning they launched a motor lifeboat to take three passengers ashore to the east of Spanish Gibraltar. It took a crew of four a bruising hour, and a hysterical mechanical expert was brought from below to start the lifeboat engine. A victory for them. I had an idea the tin lifeboats were rusting into the position they occupy until Judgment Day.

Majorca tomorrow according to the ship's newspaper. I shall not call on the poet Robert Graves and recall our youth together. The steward for a five-dollar note tells me Greg has moved into Sarah's cabin. "Verra narrow beds, but—" with that Italian overdone shrug and a roll of eyeballs. Judith is convalescing on soup, champagne and chicken breasts. Is still in bed, but tomorrow she will take a tour ashore.

JUNE 2, PALMA DI MAJORCA

At 6 A.M. we slid into Palma, now a huge busy port like San Diego, with over a hundred new modern hotels in sight, looking as romantic as a bug in the soup. Day overcast. A tour to leave at eight is herded ("like escapees from a midnight fire," Judith) into huge buses, to be informed the island population is about 150,000, and that four million tourists a year pour in around and over the place. Went with Judith on the tour, she, pale but game, carries a cologne bottle of vodka.

Am writing this in a waiting bus outside the "largest Gothic church in the world." Certainly the most ugly. Judith and I did not take the half-mile climb up to it, in deep mud, a path over the old city wall. So far it's been a big sales drive for native business by the bus drivers. "Ten percent if you show thisa card in all shops." Every romantic Spaniard in sight has some angle to skin a tourist for himself.

Judith passed me the bottle and asked, Don't you envy them? Back on the boat in bed together? I said, No, one had to be there, and young.

"He looked so sad."

"I didn't get that impression. He gobbled his food."

"He always overeats when he's sad. No sense of consequences."

"Maybe has worms."

"Sean doesn't have worms," said Sarah, prone on the bed, then turning on her side to stroke Gregory's naked torso with the palm of her hand. She went to tapping her fingers on the body as if running between his ribs an arabesque of a fanciful piano piece. "He gets a tick in his ear sometimes and he howls. Howls." She put her face to his ear and bit the lobe lightly. "Oh, I love you, mister, love you."

The bed in her cabin was narrow, but not *too* narrow. They had not yet bathed or eaten, had only dimly heard the tour parties leaving for shore, the high-pitched whines of the vacuum cleaners as the clean-up crews worked the corridors and cabins. They were on a personal voyage of discovery, not merely violent physical stimuli to each other, although there had been a great deal of that; but as Sarah put it, "We're wanting to seize each other's personality, darling, don't you think?"

"Are we?"

"You'll never, never leave me."

He had noticed Sarah liked to repeat a statement or a word to make it stronger; he was aware of the rhythmic flow of his blood as it beat on his eardrums.

"Never, never," he said, fondling her breasts, old-rose nipples that grew hard to his dialing fingers, tips that went watermelon pink. It was not mere exploring, much more he hoped; a trying to grasp her verve and gaiety, even if a bit keyed up, in uninhibited gratification. Sensation begins at the end of our nerve buds.

"I want to get off the boat, Greg. Want to go away with you, alone."

"Don't see why not, Sarah."

"Call me Dedee."

"Dedee. Don't see why we can't get off, go where?"

"Capri? Too many tourists and English swishes. Rome?"

"Cold in winter. Greece is not bad, only the cooking is oily."

"They've spoiled California." Her eyes had a glowing topaz shine as she outlined a map of the United States on his stomach, made his sex serve as Florida. "Even Carmel is now for shoppers. Big Sur? Huh?"

How elegant she is, he thought, in all her slim body proportions. "It's still wild, Big Sur, here and there. Something simple in a shack set solid over sea rocks, Dedee, and seals barking in the kelp beds, otters breaking clams open on their chests with stones held in their front paws. Clever of nature—huh?"

"All that? Really?"

"Would I lie to you?" (Would I? Yes, I would.)

They began to kiss each other. Press close; aroused, thrash about in unthwarted instincts. After which, both sated, he more than she, he held her hand in his and whispered, "Dedee, you are a Cracker Jack prize," and fell into an enveloping sleep.

Sarah lay close to the sleeping man on the narrow bed. The room smelled of lovemaking and smelled of the funky air; even the air conditioning had given up on them. Out loud she said in satisfaction, "I flow. I am a glass of water without the glass."

Her mind was filled with garden images, of crocuses and pussy willow. And of the very thin Nabiscos that her parents brought for her on their trips to New York to attend a lawyers' convention or to see the new plays. What a splendid badgering intimacy those happy family times were, or weren't?

Now here she was in love, truly in love. She had been ill and she would be well again. *En avant, soldat!* She would make of their love a flourishing domesticity. They would have children. A boy. A girl. A boy first, then the girl. Maybe two of each. Oh? Yes, keep an admirable sense of proportion. She would make a home like her mother did for Daddy. Lace frills on the kitchen curtains. And a litter box on the back porch; one had to keep a cat. A garden of herbs, she weeding under a sky of softly penciled clouds over the bay. Yes, a true truce with the world.

She heard again the scud of sea foam running high on sand, added the screams of children at play as they raced the waves in over the sand. The chicken and the lobster, the sea bass, the sweet corn in the pit Greg had dug and lined with hot stones and covered with wet seaweed and a canvas was all steaming. The pit dug deep, like the very bowels of hell. Fire and brimstone, ruthless, where souls crisped like bacon frying and charred. She saw the omnivorous burning pit . . .

She was unaware she had sat up in bed and screamed in her vulnerability to her imagination; that Gregory had awakened and pulled her down beside him, stroking her arms, her hair. As she recovered she wondered at the malevolent forces that so often hovered over her. She gritted her teeth, closed her eyes, and soon she stopped shaking. She must have slept, for she heard Gregory in the shower singing.

"Oh, don't you remember sweet Betsy from Pike
Who crossed the big mountains with her lover Ike . . ."

They had just sat down to a late lunch when Dr. Knott, Judith and the tour party came back on board. Judith looked better; there was more color on her face (most of it her own). Dr. Knott had found on shore some Con Mil Amores, long thin cigars, which he admitted were fairly odious but smokable. "Not an H. Uppmann, of course, but we can't smoke the past."

The ship's music system was offering *Auprès de ma blonde.*

"A pot of tea, Chinese . . . Well, Sari, you didn't miss much on shore. The whole place is becoming a Spanish Coney Island. Full of American screenwriters, English actors escaping taxes, and all those skinny boy-girls who model for *Vogue* . . ."

Dr. Knott scratched himself behind an ear. "Even here on an island in a hundred years we'll all be standing on each other's shoulders."

"Not me," said Judith, accepting the tea. "I'll be dead."

Sarah was packing bits of bread into the tapped-open end of a boiled egg set in a silver egg cup. It was a habit carried over from her childhood. "Greg and me, we're thinking of Big Sur, Big Sur in California. It's not crowded."

"I know where it is, Sari," said Judith. "Cold lashings of rain; the fog doesn't clear until noon, and middle-aged hippies, once pioneer beatniks, bathing—*non importa*. No, my dear, you stay in sunlight. Why not the South of France, Sorrento? Or Israel?"

Gregory said, "There are certain problems."

Dr. Knott shook the ash off his cigar onto the dining room floor. He rarely used an ashtray. "Money? Living is costly even in Israel, and you're not fruit pickers or camel herders."

Sarah dug her spoon inside the eggshell. "Yes, yes. Israel—why not? To sing *Hatikvah*."

Gregory smiled and took her free hand. "I could build up some reputation there as a designer of the housing they need. Till then I could teach, I suppose."

"Come off it," said Judith. "The two of you would starve on what they pay teachers."

Sarah waved her spoon like a baton. "I could go back to my music—let it support us."

Dr. Knott smiled. "Giving piano lessons to nose-picking kids at a dollar-fifty an hour?"

Sarah flared up, then shouted, "No, damn it! Concerts. I've had fabulous fabulous offers, from Lincoln Center, Covent Garden, even the French . . ."

"Sarah, a little lucidity, my girl. Remember you haven't played for two years. There have been no offers for a concert for some time. Other young pianists of promise have come up and—"

"Give me two months, just sixty days, four hours a day at the keyboard." She wriggled her fingers in the air and laughed loudly. People at nearby tables turned to stare at the beautiful girl with the long Pre-Raphaelite neck who was gesturing so wildly. "I'll have it *all* back. Top concert form. Schubert's Piano Sonata in C, the Impromptu in E flat, *always* my lucky music. The Mozart Twenty-five in C. Yes, yes! And the *Rondo alla Turca.*"

Dr. Knott realized that Sarah already saw herself on stage.

"I'll finish with the Beethoven, Sonata Tenth in G. Always my best show. As for an encore, why not the Ravel Concerto in G? Yes, two months, in four months I'll be ready. And I'll let London, Paris have me. They want me. They'll pay. Yes, Israel, Greg. We'll settle in Israel. I'll tour only three months of the year, darling."

Judith said, "I'll say this for you, Sari, you move quickly. For years you threw up when someone said the words *music* or *piano* . . . and now—"

Dr. Knott mashed out his cigar. He tried not to sound facetious. "Let's just leave the air castles up in the air."

"I even want to smell different," said Sarah, rising from her chair, dropping her napkin to the floor. "Judith, let's go buy perfume."

"Yes, I better go with you. In this ship's shop they have scents to bring a dead horse back to life."

After the two women had gone off, Dr. Knott looked at Gregory with an arbitrary solemnity. "I don't think she'll ever play concerts again. You can't put a fabulous piano technique in storage and expect to thaw it out. Genius isn't a frozen TV dinner."

Gregory held up a thumb. "Doc, you need a brandy."

CHAPTER

25

The *Lucrezia Borgia* carried two pianos. A large concert grand of a scarred Steinway was in the main First Class salon, with moths in its felts, a few warped keys, and in need of a tuning. The Tourist Class small salon had a Knabe in golden oak, its many coats of spar varnish cracked into spider-web patterns, the top decorated by the white rings of damp glasses left there over many voyages. Mornings Sarah practiced on the Steinway for at least an hour while ship entertainment events were taking place on deck; skeet shooting, shuffleboard, deck hopscotch. She was often watched by the stewards as they polished furniture, tried to remove cigarette burns, emptied ashtrays. Some of them muttered, *"Benissimo, benissimo."*

Afternoons when the movie was showing, Sarah got in two hours at the Knabe. She was expressionless as she sat at the piano, in slacks, a yellow sweater, her hair bound up with a silk scarf, ballet slippers tapping the pedals. Gregory stayed out of her way. Sarah as a pianist was different from the girl he slept with and talked to about many things. This was not the creature he chatted with at meals, walked the decks led by that damn dog. She was always changeable, of course, he told Dr. Knott. "But when she goes to attack a piano it's like she were going to face some sacred lion god who could tear her limb from limb."

"And it could, Greg, it could. She's making adjustments of great delicacy. Goddamn it, who understands artists?"

"How do you think she's doing? Musically."

Dr. Knott shrugged his shoulders. "Like for Picasso, fine music is something I run out of the room from when I'm trapped by it. My tastes are rather dilapidated these days."

Truth was Gregory had admitted he did not feel himself a judge of serious music. He had difficulty telling the difference between a harpsichord and a clavichord; felt he had no ear for more than a casual acceptance of the classics. He never got into that ecstatic state he had seen some music lovers go into, the glazed eye, the cocked head, the keeping of time with a finger, nodding approval with eyes closed, inhaling some run of notes. He missed the special magic a baton brought out from a collection of banged, scraped, blown and plucked tools. When trapped for an opinion he would say, "Ask me about Georgian architecture."

It seemed to him, actually, that Sarah was noodling, taking a snatch of a tune, a scrap of a classic, fingering it. It didn't sound bad, he admitted, but was this the style that had made her a genius at the keyboard? He remembered the grimy, choking nights in prison, the wall radio playing one of her recordings—not too perfect a radio. It had helped move him from the scratchy cot into a world suspended between captivity and freedom. Not real freedom of the body, of course, but of the spirit, of the soul; whatever, wherever the soul was. It had helped recall a more ebullient self, calmed what the black cons called "bad vibes."

He tried to avoid hearing Sarah at the keyboard on the ship's pianos. It didn't help that she was doing it for him, or rather, for "us." When the morning music session ended he'd go in and find Sarah in the big salon, head down, fingers resting on the stained keys; keys like elephant's teeth in a book he owned as a small child, teeth neglected by a toothbrush. She would turn her head at his touch and smile at him, usually readjusting to the ship world, still damp with effort, tired, the smile pasted on. Her whole body seemed to sag in a kind of pulsating fatigue that he hoped was physical, not mental. In some corner of his mind Gregory felt there might be a great deal to what Dr. Knott had tried to frighten him with. He hoped he didn't have a warped perspective about her sensibilities. Or her.

"How goes it?" He kissed her damp cheek, dried her brow with the flat of a hand gently, slowly drawn against the paper-white skin.

"I'm not asking myself yet, Greg, how it's going. It's been a long time since I've really done solid practicing. Did you hear any of it?"

"Some. It sounded fine. But I don't write musical criticism."

"Good for you." She patted his arm, leaned her head against him, she still seated on the piano stool. She smelled of sweat, and of her own personal odor that he could identify in the dark, like long-stored apples, dried spices? The true Sarah odor, the girl, the woman scent that was her own private signature. At times the odor, too, of fear, of joy, of pleasure, the smell of her when she was earnest, that special aroma when she was ready for him, a woman urgent for full intimacy, for loving.

"I've been trying Scarlatti, bits of the Clavier Sonata, and Saint-Saëns' Toccata. Did you notice anything about the left hand . . . ? I mean, maybe a little slowness, just a teeny bit off?"

"Ask me about what we want for lunch."

"I'm beginning to hate food. The world is a huge stomach always filling itself. Doesn't it do anything but eat?"

She was usually pensive after a practice session, smoking, chain-smoking, standing at the rail, leaning on him. Not speaking, as if brooding, he thought, of impossible tasks. Lunch refreshed Sarah, wine helped; a glass of Au Domaine Moulin à Vent. She would become more animated, take another glass or two with Dr. Knott, between two expressos.

"In Rome there's an old house, sort of a palace, been made over into a small hotel. Harry Kaufman of Curtis recommended it to me. They have a fine piano there, he said."

"I hope it's not fixed up with a nightclub by now," said Judith. "Not that some of the pianists in hotel clubs are so bad. There's one at Grosvenor House in London, knows every bit of music Noel Coward ever wrote."

"I'm not in Coward's class," said Sarah, laughing.

Judith began to hum. " 'Some day I'll find you . . . Moonlight behind you.' Give me good schmaltzy corn to set a good mood."

"Charming," said Sarah, rising. Gregory followed Sarah out of the dining room.

Dino came over to the table carrying a tray of overpolished fruit. "Very good pears. Come from near my faddah's farm in Parma."

"Come off it, Dino." Judith took up a pear. "They're Bartletts from upstate New York."

Dino gave a happy Italian grimace, wry, not offended, hunched his shoulders. "I could be misinformed, marchesa."

Judith carefully peeled her pear, turned to Dr. Knott. "They're going to hop right into bed."

"I hope so," said Dr. Knott. "Let the steam out of Sarah's ears."

"The piano practice do her any good?"

"Only if she is good at the piano, Judith. But she isn't. She knows it, too. She has the greatest of all idiocy—hope. I heard her murder some of Tcherepnin's *Bagatelles* yesterday."

"She'll come round to it. She's a Pedlock, stubborn. At least we've made some progress. She's making love and she's working up a good sweat at the piano."

"Copulation and a failure to coordinate her perceptions musically—a hell of a combination towards progress."

Carefully, thoughtfully Judith wiped pear juice from a corner of her mouth with her napkin. "You really, Edward, you really think she sees God? I mean by hallucination or whatever, what does He look like to her?"

"I've never asked her. Jewish, I suppose, even circumcised, I wouldn't wonder."

"You don't amuse me, Doctor. You forget I think of

myself solidly a Jew. Even if I don't follow the rituals. My stepson, Rabbi Charles Pedlock, is in Italy for some rabbinical convention. He's getting the annual Maimonides Award, or is it the Martin Buber medal? He could perhaps convince her to be just a calm believing Jew, not a fanatic on the subject. Religion would be so much more comforting, Edward, if we could accept it like breathing or drinking water."

"When it is that acceptable, Judith, I'll become a convert." Dr. Knott stood up. "I'll join the Church, but they must make me Pope."

Dr. Knott went off with a swinging gait, just slightly arthritic. Judith dipped her fingers in the bowl of lemon-scented water the waiter's assistant set before her. She seriously studied her fingernails, the pearl-colored lacquer on them. What was up with Dr. Knott? He was as touchy as a cat with turpentine painted under its tail. Most of these head doctors, she suspected, were always making things appear worse than they were. Not for them *die Zeit bringt Rosen.* Part of their trade as Gloomy Gus; that professional manner, the solemn look, the deep frown, the clinical shake of the head. The hell with all that hot-shot stuff.

Judith thought of her own love affairs. People had the wrong impression; she had never kept count, but there weren't so many. For her age, well maybe more than most women of her class. She'd been a good wife to Mordecai. Better than Emma Ottinger, his first wife, who had given Mordecai two sons and a daughter. She remembered one of the sons, Charles Pedlock, as a boy. Always getting his older brother, Nathan, into trouble, and no sooner out of knee pants than he was feeling up the Polish maid on the back stairs at Norton-on-Hudson. Not a great rabbinical student, but a charmer, the best speaker at the Hebrew Seminary at the Shomaejim Shaarer Congregation, and reading Hebrew as easy as Jack Barrymore reciting Shakespeare. A bit of a womanizer, the rumors had it. But a good rabbi, a money raiser, temple builder, interfaith coordinator. Yes, Charlie, he could perhaps bring Sarah out of fantasy into a practical Jewish woman's comfortable faith; could in the chaos of events use some myself . . . Will the Messiah ever dare come to such a world?

Dear Gertrude:

I write in haste from where Columbus came; and I remember talking to Dame Margot Asquith: "What a pity when Christopher Columbus discovered America that he ever mentioned it." Her remark seemed amusing at the time.

The *Lucrezia Borgia* slid in this morning at 8:30 A.M., moving past a huge monster of a US Navy aircraft carrier, we waving to the thousand or so sailors and fliers and the technical geniuses who man the big toy. Our expanding desire, said Dr. K., to be well liked. The big fist held to people's noses, "WANT TO SMELL THIS?" Dr. Knott is unhappy at the moment over Sari, so he's hating everything.

Two heavy barges attached themselves to the aircraft carrier and a wealth of garbage begins to flow from the carrier into the first barge like a Roman at an orgy vomiting up surplus. Gleeful shouts from Italians on the barges as they begin to pick over American leavings. We were too far away to see their winnings.

We waited for the gangplank to be set, the purser to give the order to get ashore. The purser, who has an extreme aversion to facts, is a sardonic bastard, a hammered-down Nero who—Dino, our maître d' told me—gets his fat cut on every tour deal.

Sarah was in a good mood. She's practicing piano every day and she and Greg are close as octopi in a hug.

Ashore the shop people, the waiters are charming as they mulct you on the rate of exchange. They begin, said Dr. Knott, "Explaining how many local cowflops to the dollar, and when you begin to understand, they panic and start all over again. They don't give up explaining until you are totally confused, so you drop the change and run."

Genoa is one of those cities with a half made up

history. It gives me the creeps—a city of so many old graveyards—a Greek cemetery here has been traced back to the 4th century, B.C. I refused to visit more than one boneyard. Genoa was once a gung-ho sea power, galley slaves at oars fought dreadful sea battles ("in which, unfortunately, Charlton Heston always survived"). The Allies bombed the hell out of it to keep German supplies from North Africa. Now it is rebuilt and the lard-fat Germans are back as tourists plastered with nasty superior smiles and never an "excuse me" as they bump you or push you aside.

Sarah panicked at the Stagliano Graveyard where tour buses come and go in great herds and travelers rush at the armies of marble hells to snap the grotesque sculptures with their cameras. Huge macabre grave-carvings, hardly worth a look by anyone interested in art. Lord, how the old boys carved, detailed the horrors of death in remarkable, vulgar minutiae. Gregory led Sarah out of the place, she shaking and flopping about. But *why* did she go in at all?

I myself don't mind visiting graveyards; most of my friends are there on their backs in them someplace. Oh, I can see you and your sister saying, "That's Judith, begging us to answer, to protest, 'No, no, Mamma. Mamma you've got lots of life's wear and tear left in you still.' Well, I confess I feel maybe you both *might* think of me more. Aren't all Jewish mothers in fiction the curse of their children? Always demanding in begging tones for respect, adoration? Still, Sarah would not be so knotted up if her mother had been more demanding and giving of affection, closer to Sarah, instead of trying to get into the goyim's country club and being so proud of being a blonde. We sail in an hour, must rush this off to you. Love to Lazar and all the children.

Yr. Mo.
Judith

P.S. I was too late, Gertrude, to mail this letter in Genoa, so I might as well add this tail to it.

PALERMO, SICILY, JUNE 6.

By the notes on the ship's bulletin board we are at Lat. 36 18 E: long. 0407 W 23.33 knots: 63 miles in 2 hrs. 42 min. Try figure that out.

Sign on pier in Palermo harbor: *Die Stadt Palermo heisst Sie wilkommen. Polizia ride sports cars.* (Someone had added in red pencil *O, la bella puttana.*)

At breakfast Sarah said she had looked out at dawn and saw a sky flecked with blood as the ship glided down past gray islands to dock at Palermo at 8 A.M. I was here a generation or two or three ago, as I remember it, don't know it now. Hundreds of apartments, official buildings, even our rotten invention, skyscrapers. The waterfront and the main streets choked with traffic. Ancient buildings being torn down, a new dock is in work. To me at first glance the old Sicily of Mafia, Church, a landscape black, dry, sterile, seemed gone.

Must mail this double letter, so again love and greetings and fat wet kisses.

Judith

"Nothing is mine."

"Whatever you want is yours."

"You mean in the mind?"

"In a way."

"Not even Sean, he isn't mine."

"The damn dog isn't?"

They were on top deck by the kennels and Sean was gobbling up some greasy bits of sausage Sarah had brought him from the midnight buffet on the deck below. Overhead the stars were not too clear and the whole sky seemed made of a crushed grayness.

"You see, Sean really belongs to the Mandersons."

"How's that?" asked Gregory. The night seemed hardly real, he himself feeling not much aware of reality, of objects, real space, the sky, the ship with its night lights. The sound of the band below playing for the "Night Gang," as the ship's daily program called them, dancers circling the waxed circle that was the dance floor. No, tonight up here there was no reality in Sarah, just the outline of her in such grace against the kennels, and Sean a ghost dog, who, having finished the greasy meats, was now trying to chew up the soiled paper napkin on which they had been brought up to him.

Gregory took the napkin up from the deck and made a ball of it. He threw it over the side into the hissing sound of the sea, and some current of air took the ball and he saw it, a white ghost, a small ghost, of course, moving away in the grayish night, then blotted out in a patch of black.

"You see, Greg, whatever I've had, it was always on loan. Sean came to America with the Morris Mandersons when they came to visit Judith at Norton-on-Hudson. They had overlooked British law: you can't bring a dog into England without a six-month quarantine. And Sean is too highstrung to be locked up in solitary, among strangers."

"I understand solitary."

Sarah patted Sean's head and he made a cozy whining sound and put his head against her thigh. She scratched him behind the ears and he quivered with sensual delight. "So a year and a half ago they left him in my charge. The Mandersons, well the originals, I mean from Philadelphia, the American ones when they were called Manderscheid, or something like that, married some early Pedlock, so the two families still retain close ties."

"As Sean can't get back into England, he's as good as yours, Dedee."

"No, the Mandersons now have a summer villa near Naples, and he's going to be picked up on landing by Morris Manderson's valet." Sarah knelt down and kissed Sean between the eyes. "You're going to live in a fine villa, aren't you, Sean? Become an Italian dog, grow fat on pasta, and have bambinos, and sometimes when you're dreaming of the past, oh, Sean, Sean, will you think of Dedee? Will you remember, remember, huh, *huh?*"

Gregory took her by the arm and lifted her up from the kneeling position. "I feel like dancing with the Night Gang."

He put Sean back in his kennel, and Sarah put her arms

around him. "Catholics, you know, don't believe animals have souls. I wonder if animals worry about people having souls."

Gregory said it was an interesting question. They danced until the band disappeared from the platform at 1:30.

CHAPTER

26

ARIES

Symbol: The Ram. Zodiacal Element: Fire. Planetary Ruler: Mars. Favorite Gem: Diamond. Favorite Flowers: Tulip, Starthistle. Most Beneficial Day: Tuesday. Most Dynamic Number: 8. Most Cherished Hope: Victory. Most Frequent Fault: Haste.

[Victory? Haste? That bad? good?]

You may have genius for new methods of performing complex tasks; thus, you work where you have a chance to develop and expound ideas. There must be a good degree of freedom for thought and action in your work. You are talented for work with metals, sculpture.

[Sculpture? Oh, damn!]

A struggle ahead does not dismay you; you enjoy beating down obstacles. Curb aggression; be pleasant; never arrogant. Be discreet in your romantic life.

"It says be discreet in my romantic life."

"What?"

"My horoscope."

"What about it?"

"It says . . . oh, do you think it's worth the fifty dollars I laid out to Madame Perls for it?"

Gregory shut off the electric razor he had been shaving with, rubbed his jowls thoughtfully as he looked into the mirror. The Mirror Scene, he thought; no film or popular novel complete without it.

"What have you been saying?"

"It's just too general. My horoscope. I expected more, more; some marvelous revealing kick in the ass."

"Try reading tea cups."

They had made love after lunch, slept, and now were preparing for the captain's cocktail party, a ship's feature of the last night at sea, so Dino had assured them. Sarah's cabin was a mess of shed clothing from their open bags: his, hers. Confusion aided by some spoiled fruit in a wastebasket.

"I've never had much belief in those things, Dedee. You end up with a snake's nest of doubts."

"Oh, ye of little faith." Sarah lay naked on the bed but for blue silk slippers. She kicked one off at Gregory, who ducked. He was in a terry cloth robe tightly belted. For after sex he always felt a kind of shyness, introverted, self-analytical. Sarah, however, was all for boldness, full nudity, scratching and caressing, pinching and hugging whenever she came in contact with him in the small cabin space. She read more from the handwritten text on green paper: "Listen."

Your vivacious personality provides a channel through which sex appeal speaks out. Your head and every attraction about your face come into strong play when you use your sexuality wisely.

"Oh, boy," Gregory said, slapping after-shave lotion on his cheeks.

The ardor of the Aries woman makes you a marvelous lover. By nature you are able to display a shining, hearty and happy passion.

"How you like them apples, mister?"
"Get out of bed, get showered and dressed."
"Yes, master. Soon."

Aries-Taurus Cusp: You mingle vividness, forthrightness, and ability to act with the steady view and aims of Taurus. You expect to win; have great confidence backed up by solid attainments. Your personality is the most sparkling of the zodiac; you are dynamically energetic.

"Impressed with your girl?"
"Not until you get on your feet. Up! or I'll tear your horoscope." He pulled her from the bed, kissed her; she kissed back, arms around his neck.
"I'm a pushover, too. It doesn't say so in the horoscope but I am, I am. I know maybe the stars don't look down to watch us. We're just insubstantial shadows. Still, suppose the stars do rule?" She growled and continued kissing, words escaping her between the use of her mouth on his, his cheeks, neck, shoulders. "Just a pushover."
"A regular round-heels. Now shower."
"Love me?"
"Love you."
"Very much?"
"Very much. Cut the buffoonery, Dedee. Shower, dress."
"Prove how much."
"No! Remember your horoscope. Quote: put on the brakes if you are trying to attract a new love. Unquote."
"Just for that—" She bit his shoulder and ran for the bathroom. Gregory looked down at the marks of her even teeth and rubbed the area around the fresh bite. Like several other love-wounded areas, it wouldn't show with his shirt on; only twice had she broken the skin in her erratic enthusiasms. He got into fresh socks, shorts, buttoned his last clean shirt from the ship's laundry. He had no faith in

horoscopes, in omens or card readings. Since leaving prison he had tried to exist in a kind of vacuum, free of feeling, offering only a blank slate to faiths, creeds, orthodoxies. "Avoid deceitful softness" was one of his pledges. He had read too much in prison and had lost any desire to find wisdom in texts. Writers were such liars, such unexhilarating numskulls as thinkers.

So much for his once firmly held resolutions, he decided, slipping into his dark slacks; with a black bow tie it would pass for evening dress, for there was to be a gala dinner following the captain's cocktails. Admit it, he addressed the mirror—you are in love, part of a sexual partnership, very demanding. And as for Sarah (Dedee) I have arrived at a cessation of all reasoning faculties about her—well, almost all. Was it a good thing for her to try to return to the concert stage? (Grandpa had warned: "Keep your front teeth to hang on with.") Would she be able to? The practicing didn't seem to be going well, getting any place. Not that I'm a judge of music I usually think of as "high class." Sarah has courage, and courage may be the most necessary of all virtues.

He picked up the several sheets of handwritten horoscope, looked over the crude drawings of stars and crossed cosmic code lines, arrows, and shook his head in dubious wonder as the text in capitals caught his attention:

THE RIGHT MAN FOR YOU AND HOW TO CAPTURE HIM

You need to curb yourself emotionally, for impatience can defeat you; work steadily toward your sexual goals . . . You want a wonderful love life, marriage even, to feel that you have gained ideal love. You can be too emotional, expect much from a loved one. Avoid discontentment, impulsive urges to go off on a tangent. Try and let the man make a majority of the advances, but if you must, go!

"Crap!"

"*What?*" Sarah asked from the bathroom over the sound of the splashing shower.

"I said, how can you swallow this crap."

"Sorry, darling. The water's running. *What?*"

"Forget it."

"Love you, too. Greg, get out my blue evening gown and take the shoehorns out of my high-heeled slippers."

Just for a moment he felt he was still married to Agnes and they were dressing to go to the second-best country club for dinner and to spend the evening with poor contract bridge players, drinks too strong and avid gossip. It depressed him and he buried his face in the soft blue silk of the dress, and Sarah's personal odor—faint, very faint—was there.

The captain's cocktail party in the main salon was more of a fashion parade, a jewelry display rather than a drinking and nibbling event. Women smiled at each other with feline satisfaction, waiters and their helpers passed out tepid champagne and some poisonous purplish fruit drink. Trays of hors d'oeuvres, stale-looking bits of fish life—Judith insisted—sniplets of animal organs, dyed fish eggs, slices of hard-boiled eggs. And some item Dr. Knott said he didn't recognize as he waved away the offering.

At the big frosted-glass door the captain and two of his officers in full gold-braided uniform were greeting each passenger, every couple, with a white-gloved handshake, the captain holding on to the captive hand under the floodlights while the ship's apathetic photographer took a camera shot. A sailor handed out slips of paper informing the guests their pictures with the captain would be available in the morning at two dollars for each print.

Judith was in canary yellow, arms and shoulders still splendid, the ample neck's wrinkles partly hidden by real rubies set in massive silver. She again rejected a tray of bitsy sandwiches with a gesture of ordering back a lynch mob.

"Where are Sarah and Greg?"

"They'll be here. Ah, our star-crossed lovers just came in." Dr. Knott took two champagne glasses off a tray.

Sarah and Gregory by some instinct sidestepped the captain, the photographer, circled the greeting area, came toward Judith and Dr. Knott. Sarah smiled as she took an offered glass of champagne from the doctor.

"Didn't want any pictures, the way my hair looks."

Gregory sipped the drink given him. "This is lousy champagne."

Dr. Knott waved to Father Umbargo, who was standing by a modern, nonfunctional fireplace holding an untouched plate of smoked salmon sandwiches. ("I knew, Faddah, it's Friday," the waiter said.)

"It would not be proper, Greg, to serve Château des Tours Brouilly to this crowd of Doctor Pepper fans. Ah, Father, you have come to bless the product of the vine?"

The priest set the sandwich plate on a little table. "I have a feeling it doesn't apply here. A fizzed cider, no grapes in this. Oh, we are tricky people."

Judith smiled and patted the priest's sleeve. "Join us for dinner. The doctor has lined up some prime bubbly."

"Nice of you to invite me. But there is a preconfirmation party in Tourist I promised to attend."

Sarah took Father Umbargo's arm. "I may not be able to say good-bye in the disembarking mob scene tomorrow." She led him over to a table covered with used glasses half filled with puddles of yellowish liquid.

Judith watched the animated talk between the priest and the girl, nudged Gregory. "Well, at least it isn't formal confession in a booth."

Dr. Knott searched for his cigar case and discovered he had forgotten it. "Damn . . . Oh? Sarah is most likely being apologetic at not becoming a convert."

"Letting the padre down easy for *his* failure to score."

Said Dr. Knott, "Maybe."

Gregory decided against a second drink of the bad champagne. "I've just been listening to her horoscope."

Judith adjusted a finger ring. "Sari's family never went in for being Jewish, so, of course, she feels guilty. She's seeking indissoluble unity in the universe."

"She's studying up on things," said Gregory, "like the Diaspora. Did you know, Doc, that Rosh Hashanah means 'the birthday of the world'?"

"I'm always being surprised," said Dr. Knott, as the orchestra under plastic palm trees began the pursuit of something from *High Button Shoes*. There was no dancing, just standing groups and crowded sofas.

Gregory stood, hands in pockets, the bow tie, a snap-on job, cutting him cruelly under his chin. He saw Sarah was gesturing at the priest, and he wondered was she pleading, explaining, or doing some missionary work of her own? He said to himself: Ramadan, Hanukkah, Good Friday, Year of the Tiger—pay your money and take your choice of any of them.

"It's not, Father, that I expected any prophetic utterances."

"I wouldn't have accepted you into the faith, Miss Pedlock, so—"

"I have a soul. From your point of view it needs salvation."

"Come on, have you cut free of all your past, repudiated the skepticism for the spiritual gratification you say you want? What will you give up for it?" He made a gesture as if he didn't want to put something more, perhaps crueller, into words.

"You mean Greg?"

"Oh, I'm not going to quote St. Paul on marriage."

"Well, Father, Catholics shack, too, shack up and you confess them, and they're back in a state of grace."

"No, one must meet certain conditions to receive grace. They must be convinced they will not commit the sin again."

"Admit you Church folk are human and you've worked out a way to keep the sinners with you."

"You're short-circuiting yourself on faith. I am merely the . . . But it's no use going into dogma—you're leaving the boat in the morning. I wish you the hope of finding yourself. May you be happy and in peace."

"I feel I could kiss you, Father. But I won't, if you'll have a drink with me. Please?"

" 'I say that we are wound/With mercy round and round . . .' That's not mine," said the priest.

Sarah recited, " 'With mercy round and round as if with air . . .' Gerald Manley Hopkins. What good taste we *both* have."

But later on deck, with a sudden onrush of a headache, Sarah stood at the rail, and in the bloody boiling of a Turner sunset at sea she recited some of the 103rd Psalm:

" 'Bless the Lord . . . who forgiveth all thine iniquities; who healeth all thine deceivers, who redeemeth thy life from destruction, who crowneth thee with loving kindness and tender mercies . . .' "

And she felt sure the solitary seabird racing into the night was a messenger from Him whose-name-must-not-be-mentioned.

BOOK FIVE

Old Cities

Of God's judgment no one is spared, but no one is excluded either. The key is the enigma of being given life; to this we have yet to find a lock to open. Viewing the world as I have for so many years I have learned how not to use my knowledge, for the true seer knows how to refrain from working miracles . . .

JACOB ELLENBOGEN
Waiting for the Messiah

CHAPTER

27

Disembarking at Naples turned out to be pure chaos accompanied on all sides by a vocabulary of inept Italian gestures. The ship people with incompetent torpor made feeble arrangements to get hundreds of passengers and their luggage ashore. Gregory and Dr. Knott had to find porters on the dock and bribe them to come up and get the bags from the cabins. Signs on the dock read: DO *NOT* TIP.

The parting from Sean at the dock, to Gregory's surprise, was simple and without visible emotions. The Morris Manderson valet, Malcolm, a plump, cheerful Scotsman in a gray topcoat and a bowler, had accepted Sean's leash in his gloved hand.

"So you're back, you galavantin' creature, eh, Sean?"

Sean wagged his tail and sat on his haunches looking up at the valet. Sarah handed over a package of worm medicine and dog pills of some kind. "He's been bathed and he's free of fleas. He takes these vitamins twice a week, and he has a habit of getting burrs in his ears."

"Miss Pedlock, Sean has been with us since he were

pupped. I'm sure he'll be happy with us at the villa . . .
Heel, Sean, heel."

Gregory watched the cheerful valet walk off with the dog,
Sean trotting along, not looking back, his head lifted to one
side trying to attract Malcolm's attention, almost as if
begging for approval.

Said Sarah, "Not even one glance back. But it's all right.
It's the way I want it. A clean break. It's the way I've
wanted it every time, everything."

Gregory took her arm. "He'll miss us, later."

"No, no. I want things final when they are final. Always
when a thing is over with me, it's over." She made two short
chopping motions with a hand.

There was a barking, and ahead of them about forty feet,
beside a yellow van, the figure of a red setter was launching
himself against a leash held up short by a bulky man, the
dog trying to break free to come back to them.

Sarah turned away and pulled Gregory behind a mound
of baggage. "*No.* A final end. Final."

They became the prey of a fat driver with a German
Opel. Name of Cato, who said, "So ten dollars to the hotel?"

"The Excelsior," said Judith.

"The Excelsior is a grand old hotel. I have powerful
friendship with Excelsior."

Dr. Knott watched the traffic. "Cato, you're an ex-fascist,
I'll bet on it."

"A man does not fight what is best for himself."

There was the usual hargle-bargle with the desk clerk,
much flinging about of Italian and English as Judith insisted
upon the reservations as promised. At last Judith got the
suite she wanted and Dr. Knott accepted what was given
him. Gregory and Sarah had a good room on the third floor
after the clerk and the assistant manager had compared the
two passports and shrugged.

Sarah was keyed up. Her legs, she told Greg, were a bit
rubbery. In the room she hugged him to her after the
elderly man had brought in their bags, pocketed some
money and departed.

"Oh, Greg, Greg, we're standing in Italy. Italy!"

"If Naples is still part of Italy."

"I mean we're free of the ship and all that is left behind us in America."

"What?"

She kissed him and shivered, not given to restraint. He felt her body quiver, not with fear but with the delight in being there and being with him. Gregory was feeling a bit of a skin-tingling himself. He had come to Europe to find some kind of work, to stress the qualities in which he excelled; come from a past that seemed like a greasy black blot, huge and menacing. In his dreams he actually saw such a sooty mass cutting part of the images he held in fear. The empty marriage, the crime, the trial, the prison years, the half-contemptuous faces of those who had turned away from him.

Now here with Sarah—first plans a bit upset—he could dream on a different cloud, one light and airy with clean white light coming through it, light that was of a prurient curiosity and yet kind.

Sarah said, "Order drinks. And how about black crepe-de-chine sheets?" She laughed. "Only kidding, darling."

"No, we've having drinks with your aunt and Doc in an hour."

"Oh, all right. Darling, you're not worrying over money?"

Greg was hunting in his luggage for a clean white shirt he didn't have. "Not worrying. Wondering. I had enough to last a year here. I mean—"

"If you were alone. Don't worry. I have some stocks and some City of San Francisco bonds. I was an earner, Greg. Real big earner. I mean like Van Cliburn, Casals. Of course it mostly went, all the money. Expenses, doctor bills, handouts to artistic free loaders. Poof. Gone."

"I've got some letters to the American Planning Foundation for Europe in Rome. Working on mass housing. I'm sure they'll find something for me to do."

"I'll cable Leon Solly, my agent, to get me a concert in the fall. In London to begin with? Yes, London."

"Will you be ready?"

Sarah pulled away from him, spun around and looked out of the window at the Bay of Naples. "Ready? I'll *will* myself ready. After all it's all still inside me, isn't it?" She held up her hands, wriggled her fingers to make chicken-shooing gestures. "These are just tools. I'm a tool-handler. Capish?"

"I capish. Now shower and we'll go have cocktails with Judith and Doc."

"I'm going to soak up a bath, Greg. I want to leave Judith and Dr. Knott here and go on to Rome with you. You alone. I'm still kind of spooked with those two ancients around, looking at me as if I were a personal catastrophe. You understand?"

"Understand. But—"

She slipped up her dress, all limbs in motion, and he felt she looked like a goddess trapped in a net. She got out of her slip, stood in bra, panties, stockings, thighs flexed. "No buts. You mean can I go it alone without old Doctor Shrink? Continue the ability to love decently, naturally? I'll not be alone. I'll be with you."

"I don't know much more about the human condition than offering two aspirins in a glass of water."

"Ha." Sarah was naked, an armature of skin, tissue and bone hugging him. "The best kind of medicine. Um, *um*, nice."

"Stop *that*, Dedee."

"Hold me."

"Go take your bath. You're—"

"Shameless."

Gregory laughed and felt his own body in appetite respond incredibly fast. "You're shameless and I'm human. So go take that *bath*."

She stuck out a little length of tongue and left him; pink flanks, long torso, splendid legs.

The grand suite to Nora was a bit too grand, "All those erratic purples and yellow." And not enough dress hangers in the closets, which smelled of mice, mothballs and other Eyetalian crud. There was a great deal of gilt in the suite, Louis Seize, some Biedermeier, much marble. A mural of the Bay of Naples in some sixteenth-century confusion with a battle of men in iron going on along the shore. Horsemen and pikemen merrily engaged in a great slaughter of each other, the volcano smoking pleasantly in the background.

Judith announced, "Well, here I am in Europe again—both feet solidly planted in the air."

Once off the ship Judith seemed revitalized. Her stomach noises did not bother her. She felt a vitality that she had felt when in the nineteen twenties and thirties she had been in Naples with parties of friends, or if not friends at least fine partygivers and high and fast livers. She always regretted she had not had a butterfly tattooed on her ankle as some of the others did.

"People, Nora, don't have as much fun as they used to."

"Oh, the young ones do. We just forget how young we were in them times." Lord, if Herself got caught up in one of them nostalgia trips, the brandy would be taken on, there would be pick-me-ups and pills in the morning, and cursing and thrashing about. "It's time you admitted it was all a lot of foolishment."

"Foolishment is a way of life. Get some trays of appetizers up and some bottles of iced mousseux, Chablis, bubbly, bubbly. We're all going to have a drink of thanksgiving for landing."

"You'll spoil yer appetite for dinner."

"You mean, I'm a glutton, Irish? Well, it's damn true. I always wanted to gobble life, chunks of it, gorge on it. You people have this idea of Heaven, Hell, purgatory and limbo after you kick the bucket, and get a salad of oil and ash built on your brow. We Jews, we don't go in much for an idea of an afterlife. No, it's all here and now."

"Don't I know it."

"So phone down for room service. And menus. We'll have dinner up here. I hope they have Three Star brandy for the doctor."

"Oh, that they'll have. It's clothes hangers they're always short of."

Gathered in Judith's suite as dusk began to infiltrate, they all had drinks, looking at each other with something like pleasure as they sipped; travelers who had come on together a far way. Sarah was keyed up and happy, holding Gregory's arm, he himself aware he was drinking a bit too quickly. Dr. Knott seemed sunk into some mood of austerity, almost of trepidation. He had made no ironic remark since arriving at the hotel. He slowly swallowed his drink and stared down at his cordovan shoes.

Judith set down her glass and waved off the tray of tidbits Nora offered. "Spoil our dinner." She took Sarah's arm. "Come see Naples, the damn beautiful bay. It always gives me an apocalyptic feeling at twilight."

"You've been reading guidebooks. What's apocalyptic about a postal card view?"

The two women stood on the balcony in a slight warm breeze, the light still good enough to make out details as if in an overexposed picture. Sarah could make out the buoys of the lobster fishermen bobbing off the shoreline, the fishermen moving about in their little high-nosed boats, rowing standing up, facing the direction of their journey, moving for a catch from bobbing buoy after bobbing buoy. It was too far for Sarah to see if they were finding lobsters in freckled stone armor. The water was silver-steel color. Freighters had come up in the afternoon and anchored near shore, their weathered sides bleeding rust. At the pier in the middle distance rode the *Lucrezia Borgia*, and there was much activity aboard, some party convention crowded in before the ship sailed back to New York. Six hundred doctors, Dino had told them, would spend two days on the *Lucrezia Borgia* in convention.

Judith stared off across the bay. "Oh, there off to the right is Capri. But no desire to visit it again. One can mislay oneself, Sari, in the past."

"In my piano music school days it was the dream of every young student to go to Capri. Most of us had read *South Wind*."

"I didn't think anyone read it anymore. I knew Norman Douglas, used to eat brioches with him. In the late nineteen twenties. It was a lot of gay times, youth times, rich doings."

"I always thought Fitzgerald overdid it."

"No, it was wild auto rides, dreadful drunks, nabobs, parvenus, artists, writers, loafers, girls. And names . . . how the names pile up on me as I stand here on the balcony. Christ, a million light years away from another time. Somerset Maugham, Michael Arlen, Beverly Nichols, Noel Coward, the Murphys; if you didn't know the Murphys you didn't matter. All such esprit. It was mostly people that mattered in those days, even the expensive whores and courtesans like Peggy Hopkins Joyce. The new young publisher with money—Julian Salt's father he was—and known as Mr. Shit; the Dolly Sisters, Josephine Baker, the Sitwells—separate or in herd."

"Julian never talked of his father to me."

"He was horny for some now-forgotten actresses: Lois Moran, the Talmadge sisters, Lillian Tashman, dozens of others . . . Oh, Sari—I forgot you and—"

"Never mind—that's been over some time."

"The Salts were *all* shits."

Fragmentary images of Julian were beginning to crystallize in Sarah's memory, and a heavy rain suddenly began to fall. The volcano, the harbor, Capri were blotted out.

Dr. Knott's voice behind them announced, "Dinner is here."

CHAPTER

28

Judith and Dr. Knott were going off to visit the London people Judith knew, the Mandersons, who summered in Positano past Sorrento on the Amalfi Drive. The Mandersons were the English branch of the original Manderscheids of Philadelphia; and had not been called Manderscheid for several generations. Some were Church of England, some Anglo-Catholics. Old Morris Manderson and his wife, Dolly (a Disraeli), spent the winters at their villa at Positano, and Morris had nailed mezuzahs on several of the door frames.

"Now, Irish," said Judith, before she and Dr. Knott left for the visit, "you keep an eye on Sari and Mr. Beck. You phone us there late afternoon—if we're late returning—as to what's what . . ."

"I'll keep my eye peeled."

"Any sign they've made any plans to go on alone to Rome, you ring me up at the Villa Manderson. Here's the number."

"Eyetalian numbers I can't be reading."

"The hotel clerk will get it for you. How do you like the hat?" Judith was maneuvering herself in front of a pier glass.

"It's becoming but it needs a veil."

"Too chintzy. No one wears veils anymore."

No, Nora thought, handing Judith gloves, a handbag, they didn't for sure, or wear much on the beaches, and even the good old-fashioned drawers her mother (rest her soul) had always insisted on; they all had been replaced by a bit of fluff across what her husband in the long-ago time of their marriage had called a "beaver pie." Well, he was one for getting his jollies wherever he could.

Nora had the day to herself to do some errands. Sarah and the Beck man had gone off in the fat sod's car to visit that buried Roman city of sin and carrying-on; would be back for an early dinner. It wasn't her place to judge them, but at least they'd be no problem to her. They'd be in bed early, you could make a bet on that, and so? So I'll have a good read in some books from Ireland picked up at the mail desk, a book the housekeeper at Norton-on-Hudson had the kindness to forward, according to the itinerary Herself had left for the forwarding of all important-looking mail. Would be good to hear from Aunt Ella in Cork, her hot gossipy rhetoric, but Auntie must be having the misery in her writing hand again.

The road to Pompeii had a good amount of traffic and indifferent drivers. Cato told them of the old days when they hunted down the socialists and liberals and fed them a pint or two of castor oil. "They had not the stamina . . . so many of them they just die—*scusi*—of the straining of the gut."

Cato smiled into his rear-view mirror. "I was never a politico, always practical."

Sarah inhaled gasoline and jasmine fumes. "How much to drive us to Rome?"

"No Pompeii?"

"Pompeii first. Then back to pick up our luggage."

"Sixty dollars."

"We'll talk price later."

"We can't do this, Dedee."

(*221*)

"We can. Fifty, Cato. Last offer."

"It's not enough, but I take."

In Pompeii they were engulfed by peddlers and Gregory accepted a guidebook from a street vendor who first tried to sell Sarah a twenty-two-jewel Swiss watch for twenty dollars. It was a Gladiator, a brand no one had ever heard of. He came down to nine dollars, and when Sarah showed she had a watch, he offered to trade her even, his for hers. In the end Gregory bought the *Little Pompeii Guidebook* for ten lire because of its original idea of the English language.

Sarah read from it as they entered Pompeii: " 'This guide to sad city of Pompeii is revised edition of old one which appears many year agos that went soonest out of print. Our good price is assurance that book will be the enjoyment and will turn greatly useful . . .' I like a native publisher who has the courage to hire a translator unafraid to face the English language and fail."

"It's such a dead city," Gregory said, looking over the old stone and bricks, dark arches.

"Oh, I don't mind. They're gone, we're *here*. Hold my hand, Greg."

Sarah felt she had only to blink her eyes a bit out of focus to see the ruins whole as they once were, in good strong color now faded to ash tones; to hear the chatter of long-cremated citizens strolling by, the waiting stance of shopkeepers smelling of garlic, the pompous passage of the litters of scented whores and bored ladies. She could hear the grind of chariot wheels that echoed on the rutted stones she and Gregory were standing on. Even the slaves; lazy, doing maybe the ancient yessuh, yes*suh*, the Roman cake-walk shuffle. And in the background there was still Vesuvius smoking.

Cato said, "It was actually not the Vesuvius that destroy the city. It was companion volcano, the one alonside it."

Sarah said, "Spoilsport. Go away, Cato. Meet us at the gate."

The mood of the long-gone past was also broken by a guard who offered for five dollars to open locked gates to the interior of some of the houses.

"Everything is keyed for bribes, *la mancia*," Gregory said. The houses were fenced off by modern gates, and each guard had keys to let visitors into his section, for a filled palm.

"Damn them, Greg. We'll just walk around and get back early. Take off for Rome."

"Judith would blame me."

"You chicken? We'd be alone. *Alone.*"

"I'll think about it."

"Let's go to the Villa of the Mysteries; the first time I saw it I knew *I* had been part of the Mysteries."

He looked at her in wonder. "What an imagination."

"The fresco paintings are in one of the rooms and show the mysteries of Dionysus. The villa belonged to Zosimus Istacidius and got its name from these paintings."

"They porno?"

"Oh, shut up . . . Oh, guide, the Villa of Mysteries?"

They entered the house by a veranda leading into a tablinum with walls painted in sooty black. Gregory said, "Coney Island House of Haunts."

They followed a thin little talkative guide, he with a limp reed tail of a beard. "This is very large atrium, no? And beautiful style with tufo columns, yes? In corner of this peristyle nice statue of Livia, wife of Emperor Augustus. But most beautiful is room with decoration of big figures of priests, great ladies intending to accomplishing sacred mystery. I was a professor once. Gambling ruined me. Please let me continue."

Gregory watched Sarah's face as the guide moved on.

"The several phases of rites begin by north side wall near small door. Don' touch, lady. Here is reading ritual by child in presence of seated priestess. Now the sacrifice accomplished by young woman holding plate with sacred offerings. *Non ogni giorno è festa.* Ah—Silenus he sing while playing on lute, and look at Bacchus and Ariadne painted on the opposite wall . . . Please, *lady!* Frightened woman on wall is much scared, no? The woman, see? preparing sacrifice recedes on the vision of winged goddess, who flagellates one of her companions. Much whipping on naked arse, yes? . . . Now group of some satyrs and Silenus. He give a drink to young satyr—well, you know lustful life of satyrs—while other satyr hold awful tragic mask. Here the wedding of Bacchus and Ariadne, meaning offer of heavenly felicity to the doing of the sexing that the initiates can attain. Here the discovery of the phallus—the man's sex part—seen by young girl. More flagellation, good whipping of expiation. A dancing naked bacchante—much excitement, no? seen near the flagellated woman. The woman get ready for celebration of the mystery. Seated woman, who is already a bride and a priestess, most calm."

Gregory frowned. "A bunch of cock-crazy Roman Junior Leaguers playing around with a big phallus."

Sarah whispered, "It makes the women seem so real . . . I remember the whippings. It hurt me. I couldn't sit for a week."

"It just exaggerated nasty pretensions, Dedee."

The little guide was looking at Sarah in a wall-eyed way, staring then at Gregory. Gregory felt some unguarded impulsiveness loose in Sarah. A strange atmosphere affecting her; all those large, fleshy women painted with such dignity and marvelous skill, observed by some genius in paint at their obscene rituals. Did Romans think them obscene? Or merely some harmless cult? The red areas were still strong, the gestures of limbs and bodies not just out of some long-gone century. No. But of very serious people in a heightened catatonic sensitivity giving way to something he hardly dared express. Lear's line came to him: "Humanity must perforce prey upon itself. Like monsters of the deep."

Sarah had closed her eyes under some continuing odd stimuli. "I was young and they undressed me and they used oils and scents on my naked body. I was whipped! Then came the burning purification over this smashed city."

He shook her, but Sarah turned away and stood, arms at her side, held in some saturation of a past that was for her the present. She hardly seemed to breathe. The little guide—eyes wide open—motioned they were to leave. Sarah began to mutter, and Gregory, moving to seize her arm, recognized the words as Latin.

"Dedee. Sarah. Damn it, no games!"

"Abluat unda pedes puer et detergeat udos.
Mappa torum veiet, lintes nostra cave.
Lascivos veitus et biandos aufer oceilos
Coniuge ab alterius; sit tibi in ora pudor
. . . iis, odiosaque iurgia differ.
Si potes, aut gressus ad tua tecta refer."

He tried to recall his prep school Latin: he translated to
himself as if he, too, were an accomplice: *The servant shall*
dry the feet of the guest after washing them a napkin shall
cover the cushions he shall take care of our linen. Do not
cast dirty [lascivious?] *glances at another's wife; be chaste in*
speaking. Stay away from quarreling and abusing and if not,
go back to your own home.

He took her arm and led her out of the villa. In the strong
sunlight among a dozen other tourists the little guide
pocketed his fee, shook his head, and went off in a hurry on
his worn-down heels. Sarah leaned against a stone column.
Her eyes seemed glazed. She shook her head like a wet dog,
Gregory thought, a dog shaking himself free of water after
coming out of a stream. She smiled. "Shall we go in and see
the pictures in the Villa of the Mysteries?"
"We just did. You certainly pulled some ham stunt."
"What? We've been inside? What stunt?"
"That you were part of the ritual, got your tail flogged."
She took his arm to walk on. "What have you been
smoking, Greg?"
"You pulling a put-on?" He stopped her and took her by
the shoulders. "You did a damn good reciting in old Latin in
there."
"I don't know Latin, new or old. I flunked high school
Latin twice."
"You did it pretty good in there. *Abluat unda . . .*"
"Did I?" She seemed confused. "I didn't think I could
have remembered. I mean I don't know four words in Latin
besides the stuff they have on coins. Oh, come on, Greg,
don't spoil the day. Let's go find the graffiti. You translate
them for me."
"But you just . . . oh, I suppose so." After all, he thought

Sarah had these virtuoso flashes. He felt better as they moved from scratched wall to scratched wall where ancient screwballs and exhibitionists had amused themselves. Sarah was delighted as he struggled to recapture his once prep school skill in translation.

"It's not in modern Latin."

"Give it a try."

" '*Amantes ut apes vitam melitam exigunt.*' 'Lovers live a honeyed life as bees do.' "

"That's good—very good. Oh, this one."

" '*Stercorari, ad murum progredere. Si presus fueris, poena patiare necesse est. Cave.*' "

"Yes-yes, translation, please."

" 'Shitter do your stuff near the wall. If they catch you crapping here, you'll get your lumps.' "

"No-no, let's go find one about love."

"Let's go back to Naples."

"Never going back unless we leave for Rome. Oh, these dead, dead people, they once were like us, did as we do. It's so sad. It's over for them. Soon for us."

Gregory decided he would find some more graffiti.

" '*Amoris ignes si sentires, mulio, magis, properares ut videres Venerem: diligo iuvenem venustum; rogo, punge, iamus, bibisti, iamus, prende lora et excute, Pompeiie aufer ubi dulcis est amor meus.*' "

"The English subtitle?"

"It's gay. 'O chariot driver, if you felt passion's flames, you must hurry to the Temple of Venus. I love a very beautiful young man. Please, drive your horse, let us go, you've already drunk; let's go. Take the reins and fly. Take me to Pompeii where is my sweet love.' "

Sarah put her head on Gregory's shoulder. "Oh, God, I can't stand it. All of them dead, gone, dust, dust! Darling, they were so alive—so alive—" She screamed, "It's so unfair! Damn it! To give us all of life only on loan! Tease us with this feeling, these emotions, the bodies, the minds! And then—then—nothing, *nothing* at all . . ."

Gregory found people staring at them, particularly a large group of lumpy workers from some communist country with their own guides, staring at Sarah; they on a rewarding holiday in their ill-fitting clothes, the women in sandals; such dirty feet, horribly deformed toenails. Gregory led Sarah away to find Cato and the car. What a damn silly place for this kooky angst and agony of Sarah's disturbing little drama.

CHAPTER

29

Nora at noon had a lunch of Gaelic properness, a kind of local kippered herring, a thick farm soup, some white bread with butter she smelled with suspicion, and a good tea, Nora went up to open the mail package with the return label of the *Gaeltacht Ring Society*, forwarded from Norton-on-Hudson. It was a new book club she had joined, having gotten a nice green folder from Galway City, explaining that the Ring was organized to use its profits to help "the Fenian Fun Boys—Go Raibh Maith Agat." Nora had raised her two nephews in the church shadow of St. Lawrence O'Toole with a respect for Fenian ideals.

In her room in the hotel suite she tore open the package and there were two books: *School for Lusty Whipping,* and *Confessions of a Leather Queen.* The jackets were rather gaudy, crude, but effective illustrations. One was of a large nude woman selecting a favorite from a wall hung with whips, and the other was of a wide-arsed girl clad only in high black boots and dark cuffed gloves. She was holding up some long links of chains studded with steel thorns.

Oh, Jesus of the Sacred Heart, thought Nora—oh, the days of the Kerry dancin'—*what* have they sent me? It hardly seemed fit for friends of "the Fenian Fun Boys"—or was it? Somehow the folder asking her to send ten pounds for a year's selection had seemed simple as to its wording: "Amaze yourself by the tickling nature some of us have for the best treats in life." The two books didn't seem to indicate the nature of the *Gaeltacht Ring Society* book club. Or did they? "The best bedtime reading you'll ever find," the folder had said.

She began with a wry grimace the Leather Queen's confession, pop-eyed at first, and she read steadily into the afternoon, mouth dropped open at times, and herself feeling flushed and as dizzy as from dancing the cawsy. What with the nature of the games of the queen—an undeniably persuasive monster—the torture and the unique bits of undignified play that went on, Nora had no idea of how the afternoon went. She was unaware across the hall of Sarah and Gregory's return from Pompeii, or their sending down their baggage, even if they were just across the way. She heard nothing, her eyes on the pages. The queen had now been laboring at her pleasures for hours—you wouldn't believe how—and the two bound victims were whimpering and begging for more of the same, well laid on—as it were, a slice of the best holiday roast. The Leather Queen, dedicated, insatiable, with her silver spurs advanced to give them a bit of the rough she had been saving for them, she said, crying out in Gaelic, *"Ach magairle Annraoi, Ri . . . !"*

It was near teatime when Judith and Dr. Knott came back to the hotel, and Nora O'Hara came out of her trance and seemed to have no idea what day or year it was as Judith called out, "Irish, Irish!"

Nora flung the books under the cushion of a sofa, and feeling as if encased in aspic, came out into the living room.

"You're back early?"

Herself was waving her hands in the air. "They're gone, gone—"

"I was catchin' up with my darnin' . . ."

"Gone to Rome! Where were your eyes, Irish?"

Dr. Knott was reading from a note written on a sheet of hotel stationery. ". . . so we shall be in Rome together, just the two of us. Alone, *capish?* We'll be in touch with you soon. And so be darlings about this, Judith, Doc. Both of you. Greg joins me in regards . . ."

Judith addressed the ceiling: *"Das ist ein ganzer Kerl!* I didn't like that Mr. Beck from the start. Oh, Irish, you were there to watch them."

"I couldn't put salt on their tail, now could I, if they wanted to scamper off, could I?"

Cato on the road between Naples and Rome drove with audacity and verve but no mercy on car or his passengers. "If I get to Rome before eight tonight, I pick up passengers for trip back."

As they neared Rome, it began to rain. Sarah had been very still most of the ride, kissing Gregory's cheek from time to time, and he pressing her hand in reassurance. They saw the outskirts of the city as rows of apartment houses. More were being built, but both the new and the old already appeared to be in decay. Sarah leaned forward as a church dome in the distance dared to force its patinaed head above the silver of the rain. They passed Mussolini's sports city. "Very large," said Gregory, "and in such bad taste. A sort of wedding cake modern with classical columns of too lean legs." Then rows of modern-style new buildings, all flat surface and bronze. At last the center of old Rome. Gregory explained the ruins: Roman, Papal, nineteenth century, the vulgar Victor Emmanuel monument.

"Don't sleep now, Dedee—wait till we get to the hotel."

"Rome, darling," said Sarah, hugging Gregory. "Alone."

Brutal traffic with raffish disregard of life or fenders. It never lets up for a minute, pouring in every direction; beyond control, an insistent chronic crawling on the streets. Small German, Italian, non-American, buglike cars, yelling drivers honking horns and often charging out of their cars to wave fists. As Cato drove into alleys that spared his car only an inch or so on each side, Sarah felt as if trapped in the brownstone entrails of a mad monster. Like going through some giant's intestines, she told Greg, "One who has only half-digested cars, people, shopfronts, doorways." Cato driving madly barely missed a tourist, who cried out, *"Herr Jesus Gott!"*

Sarah said, "I've been advised by friends to avoid the big hotels."

"What's the place we wired for reservations?"

"There is this out-of-the-way place called the Hotel Fausto off behind the Piazza Navona."

It took Cato a long time to find it. When at last he did see it down an alley that seemed paved with listless cats, he shook his head. "Because one-way street, closed off Navona Square. I not get to it direct. *Must* circle."

Sarah read from a folder: " 'The Hotel Fausto, small, intimate, private, tucked away in the heart of the city.' "

Gregory said, "Let's go on to the Hassler Villa Medici."

"No, Judith has reservations there."

After many detours Cato found the intimate place set in a sea of parked motor scooters.

The Fausto, Gregory suspected, was once an old brothel or a private prison in its original classic form. Inside they saw it had been gutted and done over as a lobby in ice cream parlor marble, its floors carved up into cubbyholes. With Marco, "Manager, Desk Director," an inspection of the rooms followed. There seemed no busy season for the Fausto. The rooms were all alike, small with little furniture. They decided on one with two narrow beds just like the others with sparse lighting, but with vines growing over the high-set windows. The drains were "sensitive," Marco said, showing them a sad smile, so please, *attenzione*, it took time to empty the wash basin. *Che cosa vuole.* He promised to find bed lamps and put back bigger bathroom bulbs: 50 watts.

They didn't unpack. Sarah insisted the closets smelled of

goat cheese and attending mice. She put her arms around Gregory in an exuberance that was also introspective. "Alone, alone. Me. Thee."

"Alone." He held her close to him, and they didn't hear the scooters barking outside and the flushing of water someplace in the historic walls. Gregory was aware of a great change in himself, almost psychological nuances. The thing was a miracle, perhaps. He was different, no longer chafed by gnawing crosscurrents or unbearable feelings. He had come out of prison marinated in self-pity. Now he was an entirely different person, here in this scabby hotel in an alley off Navona Square in Rome. With this petulant girl in his arms. Where were his once-hard reasons, the dry serious logic to go it alone? To wear protective armor against all outside adversities, ignore public duties, friendships? Well, reason is always addled by feeling and chance.

"We'll take a nap, Dedee. That auto ride has driven my spine right up into my skull like a spear."

"Unpack?"

"Just what we need. Now, first the nap, then shower, dress, and there are some eating places I remember from my student days."

"I have a list Solly, my manager, gave me. Must cable Solly to set a concert date."

"Easy, easy." He kissed Sarah's closed eyelids and she shivered and laughed. As she lay quiet, he tried again to see her as she really was. Closed-in at times, adamant *and*, he suspected, often cruel and destructive to herself. Kooky, of course, moods of despondency, an exasperating inner intelligence. In other words "a woman," as his grandfather would have said.

"Better let your aunt know where we are."

"Not just yet, darling. It's a good room to make love in."

"After dinner."

"Vanilla soufflé, grilled partridge, huh?"

"Sounds terrible. And not Roman."

They undressed and got into dressing gowns, lay on the two beds pushed together, listened to the city, the footsteps in the hallway. They faced each other and whispered casual banalities until Sarah dropped off to sleep.

For some time Gregory watched her sleep, searched her face, traced the good bone beauty under the fine skin. A rather high forehead, pawky wrinkles in the corners of the eyes, a bit of a frown etched on the brow. A face of delicate sensibilities—and something else, a benign presence of fears?

It was good to be here, he thought, to love, not to think about it too much. Too many understandings, too many Dr. Strangeloves of everything already exists . . . Now, all I need is money. But don't open *that* can of worms tonight. I'll cash my last two traveler's checks, try and touch the textbook publishers by air mail; they want me to do a textbook on early American frame houses. Some such nonsense. I really don't worry over anything anymore. So just bear up under new feelings. Avoid needless and tangling dialogues with myself. I've lived too much with some damn selfish integrity, never daring to get away from the past.

Sarah stirred in her sleep and her fingers gripped his shoulders. She muttered something that sounded like "pinpricks, pinpricks of summer rain."

He had a supreme confidence all would go well. Only in the night, the deep dark of night when waking, hearing her breathing, did he think of that fool doctor's talk of the progressive deterioration of nervous systems. In daylight, at lovemaking, in intimate embrace it could not be true. In Sarah it was just the mesh of reflexes any artist carried, the creative urge escaping from reality—whatever the hell "reality" was. So in the elliptical round of dozing and thinking he, too, slept.

They came awake to the night sounds, the baritone mewing of cats somewhere, and still the scooter sounds and the hum of traffic a block away from the hotel's alley.

"Yes, Greg," she said and reached.

Their first lovemaking in Rome was good. Not the best one, Sarah agreed, but goodo. The shower was a problem.

There was no shower pan and a lot of water drained into the room, but they built a dam of towels to soak it up. They dressed; Sarah in simple dark blue somewhat wrinkled, he in slacks, white shirt, maroon tie.

"Ready, Dedee?" They could see only sections of themselves in a slice of clouded mirror. They looked at each other with admiration, feeling their youth, sensing time flowing and the ultimate nature of things . . . and their hunger for food—the healthy hunger after a shared pleasure.

First to hunt a cab. Already the Roman night traffic was heavy. "Mounting each other like cattle in a stampede," Sarah said. "All human decency is lost in Rome when driving."

They finally got a Volkswagen cab.

Gregory thought the taxi driver drove like a fast-working surgeon tracing a diseased vein, dodging, swerving in narrow alleys, tunneling through humanity and sidewalk cafés. Sarah was delighted. He pointed out to her the sacred *merde* on all the older buildings as they ran by little squares, narrow alleys, the Largo Febo, Via di Santa Maria dell Anima. All packed with humanity and little cars going in all directions. "No American autos," Sarah said. "But once I saw a full-sized car here, a new Lincoln belonging to a cardinal being driven past the Piazza Colonna, his holy grace smoking a cigar *this* long."

The eating place, Battista Premolio, was a series of small gloomy rooms, no Inglese-speaking waiters. "Solly said he ate here every day for three months."

"They must have hot pastrami."

Sarah ordered, usually by guess. "Let's take a chance. Peppers Ligurias, zucchini, fritters, Bacala Nero, some sort of fish? A white wine. To finish off, two brandies."

As if out of a De Sica film, three old men appeared carrying two violins and a bass. They stood over Sarah and Gregory and softly played some popular Italian music. Sarah asked, *"La Bohème?"* The musicians tackled a bit of Verdi. Gregory suggested they go away. They stayed on, attempting an Italianized version of Irving Berlin. The waiter said,

(234)

"*Senta,* they no leave unless you pay." Gregory held up ten lire. The waiter said, "*Non basta.* More lire?"

"Like hell," said Sarah. She stood up tall and waved her arms. "Shoo fly, shoo."

The men played on. Gregory dropped money on the table and some coins into a music-maker's hat. They ran out, very pleased with each other and with Rome.

For a week they wandered over Rome, two lovers alone in the damp hot city, oblivious to the weather. Gregory got to thinking the sacred merde of Rome had a quality all its own. It ran in color from mustard-yellow to milk-chocolate brown. The buildings also had some ancient color of their own, deep reds faded to sun-killed velvet, gamboge tints sunken to vague greens. From the Via del Corso to the Fountain of Trevi the sacred merde was in evidence, touched on the surface by chemical action, the wind and rain, the aging and merging. Gregory called it patina history. He found Rome impressive, built for size except for its alleys and dead-end squares, everything in a wainscoting of dust and stain.

Two hours in the morning, two in the afternoon Sarah practiced on the old piano in the small room off the lobby. She worked hard and was surly after practice. And hard-faced. Gregory went out while she practiced, loafed, visited dusty museums, sat in cafés and drank caffè expresso, Frascati and Valpolicella, and watched the traffic.

For them, together, Rome lifted itself from what were once seven hills but now borne down by the weight of stone.

"Nothing seems to have been painted since they crucified St. Peter standing on his head."

"Or Michelangelo threw Irving Stone down from the ceiling of the Sistine Chapel."

No money came from the textbook publisher. No cable from Leon Solly, the concert booking agent. Yet they were very happy, and ate too much, a different *ristorante* every night.

They wanted to be alone, but did meet an Englishman next door to them at the Fausto. His fair hair was slicked back, his teeth bucky and twice life size. He wore a stitched linen hat, carried a furled umbrella. He seemed to keep his sang-froid in full view. His name, he said, was Charles (Chalky) Nembow-Charters, as Gregory found out when both reached for a three-day-old copy of the *Rome American* in the Hotel Fausto lobby. Gregory was waiting for Sarah to return from a beauty parlor.

"Sorry, old chap."

"That's all right, take it," Gregory said.

"No damn news in it. All imbecility, flaming strikes."

"Not much news," Gregory agreed.

"You have one of those bloody rooms here?"

"Next to yours."

"Ruddy ruin. Bad flooring. Dry rot, I'm sure. Damn near broke my bloody leg first night going to use the loo. The flaming beer, you know, does flush the kidneys all night."

He pulled an old-fashioned watch from his knit waistcoat of yellow with blue-and-red flower pattern. "I say, time for the first today. Join me in knocking back a pink gin?"

Gregory said fine, and they went back to a little bar made of old harpsichords by the look of it, and Charters said to the barman, "Two ginos, pronto. Very dryo—righto?"

Gregory said, *"Barista, vorrei qualche cosa da bere."*

Charters said, "Don't bother translating. Got on to the bloody natives' talk right away. Just add an *O* to every word if you can, gesture and glare. Only real Italian you need is *quanto* and *troppo*. The buggers catch on after a while. Really charming people. Love 'em."

"Gasosa?" asked the barman.

"Soda," Gregory said.

"Been here two weeks. Have to hop it some day. Run a bloody antique shop for musical instruments in Mayfair with a partner. Any fiddler's junk I pick up here gets five times what it's worth from you bloody American colonials."

The gins were fine. Gregory treated a round. *"Prendiamo un altro."* Charters smiled, leaned his chin on his umbrella.

"Bought a marvelous woman last night. Right by the Pincio Terrace. A mare, rump *this* wide. Talked all the time, felt like stuffing a sock into it—her mouth. Five thousand lire—don't pay a bob more. They can be haggled down."

"Do you rent out pianos?"

"Town's bursting with them—whores, I mean. Jolly fine. Best kip workers stand outside the Pantheon. On Navona Square the girls are mostly art students, what you call hippies there. Bints, sad-looking bitches picking up a few shillings for their boy friends. Want to make a night of it? We'll buy a couple of women. No? I say, forgive me—you're not gay?"

"No."

"Of course. Remember now—that girl in with you. You want a piano for her?"

"In London—she may give a concert."

Charters said, "Lucky chap . . . purity, devotion and all that . . . Of course," ordering another drink and a plate of antipasto. "Concert grand? Big bastard of a Steinway on hand. Another, gino, pronto. More dryo—*what?*" To which he added a calligraphic series of gestures with his furled umbrella.

"Of course, we're not sure yet about the concert—but a practice piano—"

"Just phone the shop—here's my card."

"Thanks."

"Not married to the bird, are you? I mean if not, *don't.* Never marry an *artiste*—drive you up the bloody pole. My father did—a rope dancer from the music halls—never had a sane moment from then on. These antipastos give one a thirst . . . Gino! pronto. Of course, I don't know if lady piano players are Delilahs or Jezebels . . ."

CHAPTER

30

Out of respect for his step-mother, Rabbi Charles Shaphan Pedlock stood in his jockey shorts in front of a mirror in his room at the Bernini Bristol, undecided between the neat brown-and-gray tie or the rather sporting bow tie with the blue polka dots. With Judith, intention didn't do as well as performance. Charles was a portly man in his fifties—handsome, a receding salt-and-rust hairline but a good brow. A thickening middle but very fine legs. "A striking figure of a man," as some of the widows of his congregation, the Reform Conservative Temple Oheb Sholom in Los Angeles, would sometimes remark over their cocktails at the Zion High Club, or at their parties in Beverly Hills, Holmby Estates, Bel Air.

He decided on the bow tie, did it up with meticulous exactness—and set himself at ease in the charcoal-gray silk suit. He had always admired Judith Pedlock, his stepmother, the old biddy must be getting way along in years. Now it seemed she needed his help. That Sarah Pedlock girl was in trouble; a dubious daydreamer. Whatever else people said of Charles—the popular California rabbi; that he was an Uncle Tomashafsky, kissing the ass of the powerful goyim, a seeker of social status by his TV appearances, and interfaith cookouts with Cardinal Drood and the Reverend Golamighty—still he was a force for good and a rallying point for the Jewish film and television makers, bankers, bottlers, food processors, tax lawyers, that made up the clout of the congregation of the better Jewish temples in what Charles Pedlock called "the Southland Shtetl." People liked his sense of humor, his admitting he was a bit flamboyant and not above human vanity, even a healthy hint of the weakness of the flesh. But a mighty fund-raiser for the Lord, a champion of the UJA, ORT. His counseling of the emotional, the sexual and marital problems of decent people was highly rated (edited) on his television program: "A Sense of Goodness and a Sense of Godliness."

It was good to think Judith was in town now that the World Rabbinical League International was meeting in Rome, and he (solid rumors had it) was to be given the Martin Buber Award, and also the Maimonides Plaque. Yes, in a way, they were honoring his stepmother, for she had raised him.

Oh, God, I try to be humble and I am thankful, he thought as he finished dressing, brushed a wet-finger order into his eyebrows. He went down to find the hired Bentley the Rabbinical League publicity girl, Netta Rosegold, had arranged for him, waiting. He had refused a 440 Mercedes, "and a Rolls, Netta, my dear, is too, just too much." For a good Jew the center of gravity is the Mosaic law, not the eight-cylinder special. Rabbi Moses Isserles, the Ashkenazi seer, had said ride in dignity in a carriage, and behind one horse. No more, times changed.

The desk clerk at the Hassler above the Spanish Steps welcomed Rabbi Pedlock and said Madame Pedlock was up on the roof terrace for lunch. There was a good view there over the city—St. Peter's dome, as was only proper, dominating the city—the smog of civilization making a golden belt on the horizon.

Judith in jade earrings, an expanse of yellow silk, took Charles' kiss on her right cheek and patted his waistcoat.

"Getting a paunch, Charlie, a bit of a bread basket, *nicht wahr?*"

"Too much social flummery. But I'm still—nearly—the same weight I was at the Yeshiva Seminary. Oh, a few pounds extra baggage—now and then I get after it with handball. Judith, like the text of the Pentateuch, you don't change."

"Martini?"

"With Beefeater's, if they have it."

"They have it." She was aware of how much a garrulous politician a modern rabbi had to be.

"Rabbi, how long are you in Rome?"

"Just the rest of the week. I'm dedicating the Warsaw Ghetto Memorial next week, Vav-yod raysh aleph, and there's an honorary degree in Liverpool. I'm speaking on Genesis and Teilhard de Chardin. Getting old, being covered with honors instead of working."

"Don't try to charm me. I know your good and bad sides. I want to talk about Sari."

"Sari?"

"The pianist, the Pedlock girl, you know . . . Hungry? Have the Segliele alla marinara."

"Genius, you hear, produces strange qualities."

They both ate with relish and Judith talked. Charles nodded, and decided against a second martini and the zabaglione. He felt good about watching his weight and asked if he could smoke a cigar.

"So there it is. She's here in Rome, Charlie. Doctor Knott has tracked her down to some place off Navona Square. With this man."

"He's Jewish, this Peck?"

"Beck, Gregory Beck. So what if he's Jewish? We're not hiring a *shochet*. Pay attention, Charlie."

"They could get married."

Judith wondered if Charlie was really so square.

"Charlie, you were always making out you didn't understand me. When you were a kid, you'd always try and tell me how to find a street I wasn't looking for. But always willing to help." She patted his head and there was almost a tear in his eye.

"I always said, Judith, the stories about stepmothers were not true, not in my case. Anyway, I suppose if the girl is that far out, well, a swinger, even nervous, it is better I have a good talk with her. Oh, nothing to pressure her. Believe me, Judith, the work I do does help the *neshome*—the soul." He made a gesture of a man put upon but willing. "The shrinks admit I'm almost operating on the same level."

"Don't go upsetting Sari. Try to calm her idea that being Jewish is a special gift and she has to be something remarkable to a part of Judaism. Right now, she is thinking she is going back to the concert stage. That's what worries Doctor Knott."

"Edward Knott? I once was on the same platform with him, an Arts and Humanities evening at UCLA. Wasn't too sober, but brilliant."

"He's at the Rothschild Hospital this week, lecturing, but I'll have him meet you. Sari used to trust him."

"*Yiddishkeit* has its problems with so many American Jews trying to find integrity *and* materialism in the same God. Moses Mendelssohn used to say—"

Judith stood up, brushed some crumbs away as if batting flies, tossed her napkin down on the table. "I'm going shopping, come to a tea I'm giving tomorrow at about five in my suite. Kiss me, Charles."

They exchanged affectionate good-byes.

He had a four o'clock appointment next day with Netta Rosegold—publicity director of the rabbinical conference—just the two of them and some charts at his hotel. Netta, "a smart handmaiden out of the Old Testament and Madison Avenue," someone had called her . . . It would have to be set aside. Judith and her *shailas* came first. Judith had brought him through a sticky, sickly childhood, a baffling adolescence (once he even had the gun in his mouth), had gotten him out of a jam with his first congregation. (Another handmaiden.) He honestly respected the old biddy, and there had been a tear in his eye when he kissed her good-bye. He had a busy day ahead, the interview with the *London Times* man, a taping of a short film for the Fund Drive for the Hadassah ladies. He had gotten the ORT

Scroll of Honor last year. Somehow the Pedlock girl, "the piano player," seemed the least of his schedule at the moment.

Of course he hadn't been too truthful about his reaction to Dr. Knott, with his stepmother. A free thinker, a free liver without any sense of guilt. Lord, how I envy him that—the hedonist and drunk. And Knott had dared to call Judaism "the humorless godhead of wandering primitive shepherds and desert illiterates." As if Genesis had not said: *Va-yemer Elehim Yehy Awr Ve-yehy Awr* . . . And God said let there be light and there was light—for *all* mankind. Let the damn shrink learn the Aleph, Bayt and Ghimel of the greatness of God, before he brought in those rotten atheists, Freud, Marx, Mailer. Charles Pedlock wasn't sure about Wittgenstein or Sartre. Must check and see if they too are Jewish dropouts.

The service at the Hotel Fausto didn't improve, but it didn't get worse. And Leon Solly called early one morning from New York; the phone service was nearly perfect, just a bit of buzzing mixed with small thuds. Solly began simply:

"So, you want to go back to concertizing, Sadie?"

Sarah winked at Gregory. They were still not dressed, the bed unmade. She held the phone close to her ear. "You're damn right, Solly. In four to six months, anyway the fall season."

"Listen, maybe a first tryout in an exclusive girls' school in Switzerland? A little show work in Israel for the armed forces? I think, nicely, nicely, we can make it for next season, the one after this, but . . ."

"No school or desert benefits. I want a real sixteen-jewel sellout concert. How about the Albert Hall, Solly?"

"How about the Grand Canyon? You haven't played in public two, three years, and all the gossip about your, well, face it—'retirement.' The critics, they'll murderize you. Listen to old Uncle Sol, and . . ."

"No, you listen. I'm doing four hours a day at the keyboard—with clarity, quality. It's like I've never been away . . . There are several good concert nights open in

London. Maybe some Soviet dance group will all defect. Book me in their place."

There was a pause from across the world; she could hear Solly sniff and cough a bit. He suffered from a bad nasal drip, after two years as one of Patton's tank commanders. "Sadie, who had faith in you? Who smeared you-know-who to get you Carnegie Hall? Who? Me, Solly the *swantz*. So believe me, I want nothing better but you should be knocking them dead. You, who showed them how to properly play Bach, Mozart. You. So, God forgive me my foolishness—listen close. You know Vittorio Crivelli? runs a music school in Rome. Just a few special pupils?"

"I know, I know."

"I'll get him to work with you a month. A test run? Agreed? If he says to me, 'Solomon, she is ready for concert!' I'll go along. Is that fair? But it's gotta be Crivelli. No schmuck out to bamboozle you, me."

"Crivelli, he's musically clairvoyant, and honest. Oh, Sol, I'm so happy. I'm playing Bach *una buona parte*, lots of Bach. And, Sol, I'm in love, I mean no, no, don't think of Julian, or, or . . . Just now, here." She blew Gregory a kiss. "I'll write you a letter."

The phone line filled with the harsh crackle of crows.

"Love, eh, Sadie? Maybe you better strain that out of your system. Look what that writer broad did to Chopin. Just joking . . . in love? *Mit Glick*."

"Sol, I'm so sure of the concert, you can send me a thousand-dollar advance on my fee."

"Ut, ut, utt! Solly the easy touch. I'll send it from my own personal account, mind you, not the firm's, and against your next recording check—five hundred. And I'll phone Crivelli—we'll see what you got, little lady."

Sarah sent a kissing sound over the phone and hung up. She seemed in a truculent self-immersion of joy. Gregory put down the copy of *Réalités* he had been thumbing through.

"You don't have to borrow. My textbook publisher will come through."

"Didn't borrow. It's an advance on my future earning,

recordings. You know, Greg, what I used to get paid? Cliburn was the only young pianist who could match me. As much as Lennie. Thousands, and the recordings used to sell, too. I feel good, Greg. I feel fine. You ever feel the world is made *just* for you? and what you do for the world is a great good done for everybody!"

"When I do I stay in bed and don't get up. There's a delicate distinction between feeling and fact."

"We'll call Judith and Doc, spread the good news."

Gregory saw Sarah was driven by perception, but was also a compulsory lemming. "Judith knows where we are, Dedee. Don't ask me how. Maybe she just had Nora call every hotel in Rome. Spoke to your aunt yesterday, while you were at the piano. She shouted at me that she isn't angry at us."

"Why the hell should she be?" Sarah was burrowing through dozens of music scores kept in torn brown envelopes. "Damn it, where is the *Kreutzer* Sonata? I had it just yesterday, or the day before."

"Let's go get breakfast."

Living at the Fausto was adventuring. The two towels usually provided consisted of one thin gray square (the hemmed remains of some flag of truce used in the late war, Gregory insisted) and a terry cloth towel which, if one used one corner a day, would provide a few days' clean dry spots. At first, Sarah was phoning down violent protests. But Marco's calm, kindly Italian took the edge off barbaric American anger by whispering "*Non capisco*," then "*Non parlo Inglese*." Actually, Marco understood at least six languages.

Ordering breakfast sent to the room proved the hotel usually ran out of supplies near the end of the week. The milk often curdled, the yogurt became a hissing pot of acid, having gone through, Sarah insisted, some amazing chemical changes. The rolls and bread remained delicious, no matter if hard as a crusader's mace. The coffee, Gregory agreed, no one has yet described. "Musk and rust stains, water from a Roman well into which enemies once were flung."

The Hotel Fausto has a basement dining room, well

decorated, untidy, restful. It has three waiters, not all often on duty. The headwaiter was a student and spoke English. Also a fourteen-year-old motor-scooter rider with an over-sized head, grinning all the time, who never spoke. And Stupido—Marco's, the manager's, name for him. Stupido was bald, rail-thin, suffered some secret sorrow. Sarah and Gregory were unlucky enough to get him, and the meal became a contest, a ritual of error and fumbles.

"Never mind, dear, think of my concert."

Gregory ordered hors d'oeuvres. Stupido brought a nearly empty plate containing razor-thin shreds of ham, four fragments of pickles. Gregory shook his head, "No tuna, sardines, anchovies, hard-boiled egg?"

The headwaiter came over. He shrugged. "We are, sir, all out of sardines, tuna, anchovies. It is end of week."

"Open fresh cans," Sarah said.

"Is the end of week. We cannot do so. Hotel rule."

"Why?" Sarah rose, her voice too.

"Is—is—the tradition here at the Fausto."

Gregory became worried: Sarah needed hours to recover from one of her rages. "No sweat, Dedee—we'll try again, something else."

Sarah was smiling. "Crivelli always liked my playing."

Gregory smiled: a crisis was past.

Sarah left after breakfast to work on the Hotel Fausto piano in the writing room. Gregory, reading in their room, heard a knock on the door, and opened it to Chalky Charters, the Englishman. He was certainly being friendly, Gregory felt—a guest wearing only long drawers and a tattered bathrobe. He appeared to have hammer-locked toes. Chalky looked in pain, his eyes slightly out of focus.

"I say, old chum, have you some Eno salts?"

"No. Will an Alka-Seltzer do?"

"Do bloody well. Had too much strip-and-go-naked. Huh? Oh, that's what we called gin at school."

He swallowed two big tablets, a glass of Fiuggi water.

"Heard the piano going below. Your girl?"

"I'm afraid so."

"Good, damn good. Let you use one of our pianos free—in London, of course."

"Of course."

"Just charge you cartage to wherever you're staying."

"We can afford a rental fee."

"Never refuse a free offer. You sure you're not married to her?"

"I'm sure."

"It's not good doing the town alone, lonely. If you want to stray, I know these sales birds at Gucci's. Give me two more of those tablets." Chalky swallowed, burped and sat down. "Made a hell of a night of it. Some black studs and American college quiff. Odd action; I suppose they're punishing their fathers with a black dong? You wouldn't have a hair of the dog?"

Gregory gave him a slug of brandy in a toothbrush glass.

"Ah, mother's milk, as the Cockneys say. Be careful what you drink here. Poison, absolutely poison, lot of these Eyetal mixtures made in a tomb cellar. For aperitifs, stick to straight vermouth—the dry. My father taught me—was a gourmet. Keep away from Bitter Campari. Cling to wines, Valpolicella Balla, Chianti Brollo, or the Ruffino. With fish, the white, of course."

"Of course."

"Red meat, Castel Bracciano and . . ."

There was the sound of heavy cursing in Italian from across the hall.

Chalky said, "Righto." He cocked an ear to the cursing. "That's Irena. Salesgirl in the leather shop near the Spanish Steps. Great little sport. Needs an espresso." He yelled, "Shutupo, you effing sluto." He held a hand to his head. "Oh, really—been a murdering vacation."

The cursing continued. It was deep, profound and obscene, ending with "*Vorrei aver un medico.*"

Chalky Charters rose and yelled, "There are gentlemeno in here, you bitcho." He excused himself. "Sorry, old chap, they need a tight rein, a touch of the spur. Oh, could your girl not go at the piano so early?"

CHAPTER

31

Rabbi Charles Pedlock phoned twice to the Hotel Fausto, missing Sarah Pedlock, leaving messages for her to call him, but she didn't. And he was a busy man: committees, interviews and a little recreation with Torah comrades, and with Netta Rosegold. Also he had promised *Commentary* a story on *The Great Synagogue of Rome*.

His secretary, Miss Mandelbaum, back in California, had sent on some notes on the article for him to "polish!" He read: "The street crowds used to yell '*Evviva Il Papa!*' It is usually heard now from the throats of pilgrims coming to Rome in the Holy Year. The Roman is cynical about priests; his women do most of the pious crossing and bowing to the clergy. It is hard to believe in Rome that other religions exist. Protestant groups have hard problems in getting space, building permits, placing of signs and advertising of their faiths. And they lack—for Italians—the show of Il Papa in brilliant color and laces being carried high on his litter, called the *sedia gestatoria*."

The Jews, the notes read, used to be locked up every

night in Rome, and forced to listen to Catholic sermons. But in what was called the Ghetto Section of the city there was the magnificent Main Synagogue. Miss Mandelbaum, back in Los Angeles, had noted: "It is old, splendid, with a fine Ark for its Torahs. Its fittings as good as any of the best churches in the city. It escaped Fascismo, the German killer squads, and is now in good repair. But 40,000 Italian Jews no longer exist."

He set aside the notes, recited *We-yotsey harishon admoni* in their memory. He could not face details of operations, accidents, historic massacres. He once gave away a prize gift cat rather than castrate it.

The doorman of the hotel told Charles Pedlock that to find the synagogue you cross the Tiber over the Ponte Fabricio going toward the Trastevere section. There was an island in the river, the Isola Tiberina . . . From the taxi Charles saw a mass of jade-green gardens, tall feathery trees. Just beyond, on the river bank, he caught the first view of the great dome of the synagogue. He wondered what pledges had been forced from the Jews of Rome to build it. As he went up the steps, he saw there was some activity going on in the place.

A little guide, speaking in Yiddish—a Litvak accent—offered to show Charles around, skipping ahead. The vast Hall of the Torahs was empty but for an old man puttering around some candlesticks. Charles felt close to tears. The place smelled of good wood polish, soft warm candles and lamps, old velvet, the fabrics of curtains embossed with ritual decor of lions and ancient Hebrew lettering. The *bema*, the platform where the Ark of the Torahs stood, was dimly lit. Somehow he felt, even to unbelievers, the incandescent glow of this old faith came through to us American Jews.

The little guide said, "There's a wedding in one of the halls. A fine proper affair."

"Would they mind—if I?"

"No, no—"

The big room was well lit: The men were all wearing black Homburg hats and sunglasses. Charles thought: like a meeting of the Mafia bosses in an old Warner Brothers movie. He must have said it out loud for a man at his side said in English, "It's the black Homburgs and the sunglasses."

It made a strange contrast: the noble room, the dark handsome Italian Jews in their mode of finery. A proper ritual wedding among the well-dressed men and women, the overactive children. The bride and groom were calm and smiling. Charles felt a sense of happiness as the Italian rabbi spoke up and sang out under the *chuppah* to that herd of dark-hatted males in sunglasses.

A girl, with the man who had overheard Charles, asked, "Why the wine glass wrapped in a napkin, placed on the floor?" The bridegroom shattered it with a bang of his heel. There were loud cries of relief and pleasure that the bridegroom had not failed to smash the glass.

Charles said to the girl, "It's the ritual at Jewish weddings. There are several explanations. One rabbi claims it is to remember the destruction of the Temple in Jerusalem; others say it is a symbol—pardon me—of the breaking of the bride's maidenhead on the wedding night."

The girl grinned. "Who has time to think of temples at a time like that?"

Honey cakes and brandy and Moscato for the women were passed out and people began to wish the couple *mazel tov*—good fortune.

Charles Pedlock was staring at the girl joining in at the cries of *mazel*. Deep feeling there—no naïve gullibility. He said to her, "You're Sarah Pedlock."

She turned, smiled, made a grimace; mistaking him for a tourist?

"No autographs, please." And offered him a cup of wine. Didn't at all seem to be in any extreme predicament.

"I think we are sort of cousins, in some way. I'm Rabbi Charles Pedlock."

"Oh," with no surprise, "Judith's son?"

"Stepson. I've been trying to contact you. Left messages with the hotel clerk."

The man said, "Sorry—really sorry, rabbi. Marco's writing of English isn't too good. To us your message read *Pet*

Shop. Oh, I'm Gregory Beck. Miss Pedlock is a student of Jewish rites, and we're making the tour of Hebrew settings in Rome."

"Yes," said Sarah. "Sorry we read the message wrong."

Charles smiled. "No need to, Miss Pedlock. Judith had been keen I talk to you two. Not that I'm an old-fashioned busybody, or one to talk a *shidach*." He was rather proud of his use of the Yiddish vernacular. In a jesting way—to use on the film and TV producers, gentlemen tailors, tomato paste converters of the board of the Oheb Sholom Temple back in Los Angeles. "Could I buy a lunch?"

Sarah took his arm. A beautiful handmaiden, he thought, and the gold *mezzach* on a chain on her neck. (Ah, how good of God to make Eve, even out of that rib.) "Lunch?"

"Only, rabbi, if you promise to tell me all about the state of faith among Jews today, and why it seems so settled, so placid, almost a permanent convalescent."

"All of that?"

"All of it," said Gregory. "She's on this faith kick."

"You don't understand, rabbi . . . While I'm simpatico, I'm also puzzled."

"Call me Charles." The wedding party was making a clatter; kissing, shaking hands, all talking at once.

"Charles, I was raised as a goy, but knew I was mostly Jewish by genes. And yet I wasn't, wasn't a Jew either. I hate the word Jewess, don't you?"

"It had an ancient harem sound, Sarah. A King David concubine."

"I mean I was neither one or the other. Half an ass in each camp. When I know you better, Charles." He patted her arm. "I'll tell you of some baffling mystic experiences. So—"

The little old guide was, with desperate audacity, pulling on one of Charles' jacket buttons. "One hundred lire, balbos. An alter mench has to live also."

Charles handed the little old man a lesser sum. "Also, I don't want to spoil you."

The little old man muttered, frowned, said, *"Mit Gazint,"* and went off.

The wedding guests were trailed by children—laughing, pushing. The men, their Homburgs and dark glasses still in place, were reaching for cigars and listening and talking of business—other weddings.

"So," said Charles, taking Sarah and Gregory each by an elbow, "let us go feed our faces."

A wedding guest said to someone, *"L'ultima che si perde è la chutzpah."*

Sarah talked while they had a good lunch at the Palazzo, the fine villa that once housed, or so their waiter whispered, Clara Petacci, Mussolini's mistress. It overlooked all of Rome, and Sarah sipped black coffee, enjoying the view in a bittersweet, detached mood. The way she liked to absorb scenes. She muttered in a kind of serene senescence.

"The sacred candlesticks from the Temple were brought here. You can still see it represented on one of the victory arches. The candlesticks were melted down. I suppose to make earrings for some of Nero's favorites."

Charles smiled at Gregory. "If I had the time, I'd write a history of the Jews of Rome. You write, Gregory?"

"Only on the art of buildings. I wouldn't know how to begin anything else."

"Who does?" Charles signaled the waiter to pour him another cup of coffee. "We've been talking, Sarah, all through lunch. You ask my advice on your feeling of not belonging, and your doubts. I'm no moral bluenose spoil-sport. But it seems to me you have another problem to solve first. There *is* a permissive freedom in our times. To be sure, I can't always agree with all its facets. But I'm a broad-minded man. Still, why don't you two marry? At this point, frankly, it would please Judith."

Sarah shook her head. "That thinking is out of gear with our times. Not that I agree with those libbers—dogs and dykes mostly—that talk of liberation as if castrating the studs. I mean, an artist doesn't like the strait jacket of holy matrimony. I haven't seen in it the deep-seated world of true human response."

"That's a Gentile phrase—holy matrimony. We Jews

observe the stronger rules of a great closeness to making for full human response. And our tradition is giving in marriage and begetting and begetting."

"I take the Pill."

"The rich potentialities of Jewish married life are the reasons for our survival. Look, here in Rome we've survived the Etruscans, Greeks, Romans, the Fascists, the Germans. Only because of what? What we saw this morning in that synagogue. What were they without their faith? Junk dealers, fashion designers, smugglers, art experts, taxi drivers. What else—who knows? But Jews, we are sure of that. Sorry if I'm preaching. I wonder do they have a Dom Pérignon on ice here?"

"All right." Sarah stood up and spun around in a dance step, coffee cup in hand. "Uncle Charles, convert me. I mean, you know the whole ritual. The *mikva*, the sacred dipping, all that, and I'll get married after the first concert."

Gregory signaled for the check to the waiter. "Who are you going to marry?"

"You, you goon. I meant *we*." She bent over and kissed Gregory's neck. Charles Pedlock tried to reach for the check on the metal tray set down on the table. In the end of a brisk few moments, he agreed to let Gregory out-wrestle him for it. "Let me at least leave the tip. It's been a very successful lunch. Now, Sarah, you will promise to call Judith. She likes to feel she runs the families."

"And does she?" asked Gregory as they went down to get a taxi.

"Does she? I'd say she does, Gregory," Charles said. "In a way Judith is the only member of the families that has the old vitality, the drive and the sense of the founder of the two lines in America."

"Two lines?"

"The old Joseph Pedlock line, Sarah's side of the family, and the Elijah Pedlock branch that founded the stores. Someday when I retire, I'd like to write a history of the Pedlocks."

"You'd have to leave out a lot," Sarah said. "Hanky-panky, the razzle-dazzle, furtive privacies and the gonifs?"

"Oh, that would be the best part. The second, third,

fourth generations aren't as interesting, not 'with it,' as the expression is today. Not one—but for Judith, and she's only a Pedlock by marriage. And perhaps my brother Nathan, who runs the stores, there isn't much vitality in most that's left, a solid Judaism. Not as to the faith, as to pride. Not enough as to an awareness of the dangers of slipping away into the gray placid mass of assimilation."

"Sounds like one of your sermons, Uncle Charles," Sarah said.

"Touché. Yes. One of the best I ever gave. But to talk about Judith. Isn't it terrible to speak so well of a stepmother? You have to pause and wonder why she isn't flabby, have our faults. Oh, yes, I know my faults, my weaknesses."

In the taxi the young unshaved driver, his head shaggy, smiled, a proper figure from an Italian realistic film, who said, "*Lantzleid.* Where to?"

Solly, as a top concert agent, made it clear that there were those who thought Vittorio Crivelli was the greatest teacher of the piano in Rome. Some felt in all of Italy, even Europe. There were also those—Solly said he had letters to prove it—who merely insisted that "no teacher in the entire world knew as much about bringing out the best in young prodigies and budding maestros of the keyboard than Vittorio."

Crivelli himself ignored praise. "Rewards increase as taste declines." He lived and taught in an old house that appeared in danger of collapsing, a house with shaky staircases. Hidden away behind the Capuchin Chapel on Via Veneto. Vittorio was an old man, vastly fat, nearly three hundred pounds, bald but for white floating hair around his ears, up his nose and producing rather frightening eyebrows. The face was plain, usually calm, his voice thin, and words seemed half gargled. He moved slowly, with a stiff hip, balance aided by a beautiful long stick like a ballet master's baton. A good pianist in his youth, his fingers now were veal sausages: short, fat and seemed worthless for music. He had no pronounced idiosyncrasies.

Crivelli had never been a great star himself, being too shy

to appear as a soloist, only as an accompanist to violinists in his youth. Those who heard him play in private long ago insisted a Liszt, a Rubinstein was lost in Vittorio's inability to face an audience on his own.

He said to Sarah in the wan sunlight of a Roman morning, the two of them in the huge studio lacking drapes at the windows and a cleaning in the corners:

"Now, miss, we begin."

He spoke English carefully, having in his middle years "done time," as he expressed it, at Curtis. "Now, my dear, so you have begun again. I give you my candor, perception. The last hour you have played badly, all the faults of a bad student but one; *you* are a genius. Here and there, I catched [he failed at times to grasp the proper form of word], I heard something no one else could do. Of course I remember your 'La filla aux cheveux de lin . . .' " He kissed his fat fingertips . . . "What more is to be said?"

"I must give a concert this fall."

"Must? Must in this life is we must all die, miss. All the rest is, is . . . [he hunted a word] is expectancy. So first the discipline of the wrists. Try the 'Barcarolle in F sharp.' There is the music."

"I know it," said Sarah, seating herself at the big rosewood piano.

"You know nothing. You read the music. Now play Chopin." He tried to raise his voice, but he was not a stern man. He had yet to rap a pupil's knuckles with his stick as he had once seen done, to his horror, in a film. Sarah, without any coquetry, turned to the keys. Crivelli sat down in a huge chair that protested a bit and wiped his brow with a silk handkerchief. He listened to her playing, he expressionless as Sarah's fingers seemed to have a life of their own. What a gift, he thought, and how badly warped. He had had a long life of many sorrows, small successes, until he became the great teacher. He had molded so many talents, precious talents. Some that had become masters. But none like this tainted wizardry at the keys he now listened to. For all its off timing and too loose phrasing here and there, *this* was his one solid golden talent. Yes, he would even rap her on the knuckles if he had to.

CHAPTER

32

[From the journal of Edward Knott]

JULY 11, PENSIONE SANTA CATERINA, ROME
I am beginning to sense the perceptible loss of time.
Today a call from Judith—with no subtle nuances—saying
all seems well, "hunky-dory" is her expression. Sarah is
preparing for a concert under a man named Crivelli. And
that her son (or stepson), some rabbi from California, is
counseling Sarah, in what I don't know; chicken plucking or
matzo baking? I have no respect for any clergy. I see them as
extreme cases of pathological states.
I can look back, here in Rome, to some two weeks of
pleasant lecturing on the philosophy of Wittgenstein at the
summer session of the university here. I seem to come back
to his Tractus Legice-Philesephicus. *I remember Wittgen-*
stein at the Technische Hochschule in Berlin-Charlettens-
burg. How much like Sarah he was then, sometimes, of
course, in reverse. Refusing to admit he was a Jew, and she
trying to prove she is. The same escape in both from reality,
when at their prime. She giving up her recitals, concerts, he
refusing for three years to teach a batch of nose-picking
yokels in some remote Austrian villages.

I remember visiting him in Vienna—he not yet famous—
and our going down to Maxergasse and the Sepheinbruke to
the parkland of the Prater. Here he would pick up the rough
homosexual trade, and stand them treats in the Sirk Ecke in
the Kartnerstarabe in some sad perversity and need, riddled
with after guilt.

At least Sarah's sexuality, as raging at times as Wittgenstein's, has, so far, been directed towards the "normal" male.
Wittgenstein was always talking suicide and I expected for
years to hear of the final event. Sarah, too, has these periods
of what's the use and get it over with. But then Wittgenstein
didn't kill himself after all, did he? Are they both, he, Sarah,
messianic pretenders?

It is amazing how much the two think alike. Not that
Sarah has ever read him. His leitmotifs are hers as a way of
life. The abandonment of the world and its comforts, an
interest in the meek, the poor, the peace lovers and the
persecuted, the healing of the sick. He perhaps wanted a
band of disciples, handsome young males most likely, and
working some kind of miracles? What did Oskar Fuchs say
to me of W? "Such men, Herr Knott, are taken to be crazy,
but one just ought not to measure them by ordinary
standards."

Certainly those who measured Sarah by ordinary standards got a shock.

JULY 12, ROME

This afternoon I'm going to meet Sarah for the first time in
Rome. The Contessa de L. is giving a tea for Judith. Sarah
will be there and Greg, and the rabbi stepson, I suppose.

I have been going over my notes on Sarah. As a
personality is it through experience rather than heredity that
she is so paranoiac? Does she, deep down, hug a distrust of
her great talent? Does the overcompensation, the impulse at
times to dominate, the assertion of the will, make her what
she is? I must agree with the old fart who said, "Chaos is the
reality, order the illusion." What can turn one to extremes in
the extending of a personality? An extension that can at
times prop up the ability to bear the burden of self-destruct?
But it does increase the anxiety . . .

There is a once very exclusive, very small world of Rome that few visitors ever see. Now made up mostly of very old people of fine manners and tradition—with some angst and melancholy—the last of the salons of a vanishing class. The palace of the Contessa de L. is in sight of the Borghese Gardens. The palace is not what it was years ago. Has a dusty archaic tone today . . . Tried not to think of what had been sold of the de L.'s paintings, furniture, manuscripts. The Contessa met me in the grand room facing the umbrella pines grouping dramatically beyond her walls.

"We are dying on our feet, our kind of people," she said, leaning on a gold-headed cane, she still with a grace, a perceptive sensibility in her greeting. (Damn, what nature and time does to beautiful women.)

Kissed her hand, and she, slowly sitting down in a high-backed chair, introduced me to her guests. I nodded to Judith, Sarah, Greg. I had known the Contessa years ago in New York when I was interning at Bellevue. She had come over to sell a small Ingres drawing. We had become very good friends in an atmosphere of Irving Berlin, Czerny etudes, hand-holding walks in Central Park, dark-cornered Greek eating places, and that foolish yet exquisite anguish of early friendships. Why should Judith's, Sarah's world intrude here?

Seeing the Contessa again, it seemed an afternoon of another world far from disturbed pianists. Her mother had known Henry James; the Contessa had helped Santayana find his last agnostic shelter with the Blue Nuns in Rome. It was, I saw, besides us Americans, a tea for old bones, cross-hatched faces, other eras. Two Papal knights, a fat painter of too green gardens, an old English fury—Lady Cocksedge, I think, as I caught her name—with a marvelous head, who had a vineyard in Sicily. ("Château Rothschild? horse piss!") All around on chairs old ladies in black lace, who had, it seemed, to lean on gold-headed canes.

I nodded to a red-headed American baroness who was a convert to the Church. I sipped a brandy (avoiding the tea). Most of the guests seemed to create a self-indulgent conspiracy against today, as if life outside the windows would go away if they ignored it. Several old-young men were present—men who dyed their wigs black and tried to act they were still under fifty. I talked to a fascist flier poet; only one eye and one leg. The blind eye held a black monocle. The Contessa took me aside: "Occhi miei, occhi non gala ma forti. Do I seem as foolish as my guests?" A fool would have reassured her. I stood mute.

"This Sarah—is fey?"

"Who knows, any of us?"

The only emotion I really had was amazement at how quickly historic time had moved. I could see the once-solid core of old Rome casting only faint shadows at the Contessa's tea. Jesus, what an attack of the Old Nostalgia. I think it was in the brandy.

So buried in the aspic of memory where everything turns to false gold, I was aware of Sarah at my elbow. Looking damn marvelous in jade green, hair caught behind one ear in a knot, very Grecian, and large carved lapis lazuli earrings.

(Let me see if I recall the dialogue.)

"See, maître, I come to you."

"Damn sure of yourself, my girl, aren't you?"

"Oh, come on, Doc, I'm feeling fit, I'm playing better than ever. Greg is going to get a job with the American Rebuilding Commission and we're looking for an apartment for three, four months."

"Gaily, gaily, gaily. Haven't I warned you against these elated, these overelated periods? When your emotional elevator is up, up in the penthouse."

"Prognosis, therapy and cure? Ha, you think my elation is overcompensation—it drops down to the basement next? Nothing like that. I've my work. I'm in love. And—"

I avoided several passing trays of glasses.

"You've made your peace as a Jew?"

"Doc, you're marvelously dense at times. Not a full peace yet. Judith's stepson, a very clever rabbi, not stuffy at all, is talking to me. I mean, oh, hell, don't frown, Doc." She kissed my cheek, put an arm around me. Smelled wonderfully scented. I thought, like the Contessa long ago in New York. Subtle bitches, women, I used to think, all living flesh, scents and body odors; and (like male moths who can fly five miles

to a detected female scent) set up also in a collector's trap to capture the horny male.

"I'd like to have a long talk with you, Sarah. Any time you're free for a few hours."

"Have a heart, Doc. I do four hours a day at the keyboard. But I promise I'll fit you in. You having fun? Rome, I mean."

"An enormous abundance, but I'm not tempted. Call me at the Pensione Santa Caterina."

Sarah spread her fingers, entwined them with mine in a too strong grip, and went off. At least she hadn't seen God lately. I hope not. The third time she sees God, I don't think she'll come back without her being—at which point in my brooding, Gregory patted me on the back.

"Don't like to see you drink alone, Doc."

"Doesn't spoil the drink, no matter how you guzzle it. You've gained weight, Greg."

"Too much eating in fancy places. Judith is really the Jewish hostess under all the veneer of cosmopolitan finish. She thinks the more she feeds us, the happier we'll be."

(Yes, I recall the dialogue fairly honestly.)

"You're working, Greg?"

"Hoping to. These bastards at American Rebuilding suddenly find they don't like my prison record. They knew of it when I applied back in the States. Now it's a hassle. But Senator Silverthorn promises me it will be fine."

"Big scandals blowing up in Washington . . . Greg, you think Sarah can give a recital?"

"Hell, I'm no expert. Crivelli, he doesn't say no, doesn't say yes. You think he's anything but a greedy con man taking Judith's money?"

"Greg, my field in treating women used to be hormones and menstrual cycles. I don't know music that well. Will you make Sarah call me? She's in a very dangerous state of ecstatic elation."

"I can try. She's damn stubborn. She isn't at all as on the boat. Sometimes I feel frozen out after practice hours."

"Greg, gratitude is harder to find than love."

(I know I'm giving myself the best dialogue.)

"I'll remember that."

"Like railroad time-tables, as a prince I once knew said: 'Women are liable to sudden changes.' Pardon me, the Contessa is signaling to me."

I walked away. Poor bastard. He had changed to a more vital, interesting person than the numb loner I had first met on the boat. Rather colorless then, a clod really. Now loaded with problems, duties, affections, thinking of the welfare of someone else; is he better off? Well, a little suffering will move him into more affection, more suffering, change him so in a year or so, nothing will be left, not much anyway of the characterless passenger I first approached.

The mood at the Contessa's remained sustained. At dusk a cardinal came in, also people who were back from the south of France ("È troppo caro") and were going that night al ballet, then ad un cabaret. One had to make small talk in several languages. I didn't think they'd last the night.

"Butterflies," said the Contessa to me. "At their age they should cambiare le lenzuola [change the sheets] of their lives. You are going?"

I kissed her cheek. "A domani."

She said, "No, it is addio."

I added, "Was there ever for us New York, the parks, the walks, that music?"

Outside on the street, I tried to thumb my nose at the past and return to the second half of the twentieth century. A taxi driver called me an obscene name as I nearly got run down.

I have the usual banal thought about the past. Shame on me. As one gets older, the poignant sense of all things passing becomes clearer and nearer. In youth, death is something for strangers in another country, and time seems made of rubber and can be stretched and stretched.

(Still July 12—near midnight—can't stop writing.)

The Contessa had found life very enchanting, endearing, emotionally filling. She would stay, I hoped, to the very end on her feet, leaning on her gold-headed cane.

Long ago I had discovered that the Prince—who had

given her a letter of introduction to me—had been her first lover, and I was young enough then to feel that kind of great outgushing of pleasure that people—I've been told—no longer feel about love affairs.

She had said to me in bed near dawn one night, "The Prince was a vulgar man, you know, your Prince. An awkward lover. Only interested in his three ugly daughters."

"Hell, no," I told her. "He's a charming man, a sensitive, great grace, wit."

She said she found him foolish and greedy. Always the talk about the grapes in Sicily, and the repairs to the old palazzo. He carried bits of paper in his pockets scribbled with rows of figures. He argued with cab drivers over five francs in Paris. And his gifts, pinchpenny knickknacks. Vulgar really. So Jewish. I mean, she added, with a Jewish lover there is always that damn sense of duty to his family first.

(Near dawn—still writing. Damn!)

I'm old enough now to know we don't see people as others see them. How could the Prince have been vulgar, greedy, frugal? And as a lover, awkward? Keyserling, he told me, had once said to him: "Whoever profoundly understands a superficial part of life, Prince, necessarily gains metaphysical insight along with it." But the Prince and the Contessa, weren't they only a superficial part of my life? There was no way to make them a permanent part of my existence without giving up my work. And I didn't really want to do that; wear a Borsalino hat and coat. I have remained Duty's Child. Greg, Judith, Sarah, are right. I'm a cruel, a cold, cruel sonofabitch, always wanting things my way, greedy but only outgiving when it's to my advantage, or for my work.

Sarah phoned as I was still writing in this journal, she in a voice with too flexible a range. "Doc, I depend on you. You know how much. I'm on my ass without you. If I'm staying away, it's a testing of thin ice. To see if I can walk on it, walk on it safely. If I break through, stand by. Love you."

(Thank God, I've about run out of ink.)

I did tell her I loved her too . . . It has just begun to rain.

I listen to the pizzicato drumming of it on the roof overhead. I find I am thinking of some ancient Greek who at ninety, desire for sex gone, felt "as if set free by a furious master." And—

CHAPTER

33

For all the acute fluidity of his musical mind, Vittorio Crivelli was getting discouraged. There were sessions at the rosewood piano when Sarah played as she had played at her best. But there were, too, many hours when he wondered if she knew how she had wandered away from her gifts. After some hard practicing, she would sit and sweat and pant, flex her fingers and then start again, go back to the attack. Or sit and just touch the keys, even merely hover above them. When he spoke to her, there were moments when he was sure she had no idea what he was saying, but was lost in some disembodied reflections.

But it was during what he called those golden moments that he believed in her; when all was right and the tone and the pacing, the bringing of some chord to perfection, put the smile on his plain fat face. "Yes, yes, Missy, how can one savor music without biting." He would lift one of her hands and with rubbery lips kiss it. "Ah, you and me—we know just what music is, and just how it should sound, and doesn't with so many, so many." At such times, Crivelli was no longer an essentially fat farcical figure.

In the third month he had to admit Sarah was making progress. He no longer scolded her so much, or cried out, "*Basta! Basta d'un pazzo per casa.*" More and more, he would repeat loudly, "*Chiarezza*, clearness, brightness, ah, purity as if in a prayer."

Sarah seemed indifferent to his reactions, good or bad. She, seeking an intricate refraction of herself, felt she could force her talents through some dark tunnel of effort into the light: could not fail herself. All else seemed locked out, blurred. Even with Gregory, at times, she wondered *who* was this stranger—and with recognition came lust hard to satisfy. She had not called Dr. Knott, she didn't return Rabbi Charles Pedlock's phone calls. Forgot to thank Judith for some Thai silk outfits. Her world was the keyboard, the true sound of her world was not Rome's, but Liszt's *Valse Oubliée*, Falla's *Ritual Dance* from *El Amor Brujo*.

Vittorio Crivelli under tension grew fatter, not leaner— he lived alone over the big practice studio in which he taught. A widower of many years, copulation a mere ancient memory, he kept two finches in cages, and a broom handy to whack the noses of cats that tried to come in through the balcony to attempt to feed on the birds. He cooked for himself indifferent messes; when he felt a need to be alone and not go out to sit and drink Chianti or Frascati with other musical people. Men with bass viols, unemployed timpani players, a tenor who had lost his voice, someone willing to sell a family musical treasure, a violin, perhaps a Stradivarius, most likely not.

"La Pedlock," he said to Sarah when he stopped calling her Missy, "I had the despairs, but also I have a great deal of faith. Yes, yes, I know faith moves mountains, but faith doesn't give recitals. Now join me in coffee, and let us talk. Forget the fingers shaking. You take milk? The cream here is not good. Sugar? no. So sip it. Very good. Two things I know—the piano, and making coffee. I am a genius about both." He looked over the whitewashed walls of the studio gone grimy, on which hung photographs, drawings, posters, newspaper clippings of the most famous musical names going back three generations. All inscribed to him with lavish, overripe praise. And newer faces, too, but not so many. "You see I am getting old and I am taking less pupils. Money I don't want. I have an orchard up near Perugia. And while I look like a gross feeder—no?—all I need are a few black olives, the head of a fish boiled with basil—pasta, not too much. Still I'm a prisoner of my fat. Now my little birds sing to me with *abilita*—Vittorio, Vittorio, they sing; why fuss, they ask, with La Pedlock?"

"You're very kind, Maestro. I knew I'd come through— but I was so drag-ass. You have been a great help."

"More coffee? So. I don't lie to you. Your playing is still uneven. More discipline, more nearness to what only you and perhaps Rubinstein can do. And between us two—we know, eh? he slides a bit too cleverly here and there. Why not with your recital wait?"

"I must have a concert this season. You understand, my life has been a hell of a mess—so I don't know what will happen to me if I relapse as I once did. I've had a nightmare in my mind."

"Ah, what artist doesn't? So. Enough coffee. The Schumann Romance in F sharp, let us take it phase by phase. And remember, when we dream, the moment of awakening is at hand. Play."

For Gregory it was a time of tautness, of having too much time alone. It was clear to him that unless some political pressure was put on in Washington, he would not get work with the American Rebuilding group. He waited. The textbook publisher wrote asking for a new outline. Gregory drifted around while Sarah practiced. She slept deep-drugged with fatigue, long practice hours in the late afternoon. He felt he was encroaching, for the room at the Fausto was too small for him to be present and awake when she wanted sleep. He walked about in Rome, that typical solitary figure of overserious writers' texts—a stranger in a strange city. He visited the Capitoline Museum, its long hallways flattened his feet. And the three basilicas, no use missing one; St. Maria Maggiore, St. John Lateran, St. Paul Outside-the-Walls. But his interest was not in church art, or the drama of the Spanish Steps crowded with camera snapping tourists, or aging studs dressed as Marlon Brando or Lennie Bernstein, and all the offers of porno cards outside the Baths of Caracalla.

Gregory in the end liked it best when he had nothing much to do, to sit in the big modern railroad station, enjoy the peasants arriving with rope-tied bundles, or some film star, silicone-inflated, and entourage, enjoying a staged entrance. He studied odd-looking furtive men hunting through waste and litter containers, picking up cigarette butts, sliding with wet glances into the lavatories, as if already committing some sin.

Chalky, the Englishman, in the London antique piano business, took Gregory along twice for a pub crawl. Chalky Charters had one major object in life he admitted. "Women are, you know, about all there is, with money, without money. Oh, it's hard tittie without the ready, I admit. Drink, it's something too, and if you need a friend, buy a dog. But forget all that art and collecting of art business. You know, you wonder in the end what of it? Art is for ball-less wonders."

One morning when Gregory was to go with Chalky to the Café Doney on the Via Veneto, Chalky came down from his room accompanied by a long-haired blonde, she heavily curved, long plump legs on high heels. They were laughing and leaning on each other. She kept demanding *"un paio di occhiali di oro."*

"Shut up, Bianca—very respectable hotelo. English people live hero. Oh, Greg—sorry—must get this bird back. Spare me a fiver till Thomas Cook opens?"

The last Gregory saw of them, Chalky was pushing her into one of the bug-sized taxis, banging fists into her rump. Marco, the hotel manager, said to Gregory softly, *"Mi scusi,* but that gentleman is not the good for you. He is *si*—a type. We do not cater at the Fausto to the wild *divertimenti* seekers. He is our cross. A perfect gentleman when he comes to us from London. Then a few weeks of his *strada malsicura* . . ." he raised his eyes to the lobby ceiling. "You will forgive me—he is not for you. He will borrow lotsa money, your clothes. *Mi dispiace di disturbaria,* and it will hurt your reputation to be seen with him."

"Grazie tanto. Why do you permit him to stay here?"

"Ah, he comes from a much fine family. His father, the late major, saved this hotel during the war when a Russian mission wanted to move in. Those filthy pigs! The bidets they use for . . . We owe the family of Signor Charters much thanks. A cousin is a member of parliament; another cousin is with the embassy in Rome. It would cause much embarrassment if we turned him away, *mi pare.*"

Gregory said he understood perfectly, and that he had no interest in his own reputation.

That night in the lobby, Chalky Charters asked him for a 10,000 lire loan, and Gregory had to admit he was low in funds. So Chalky lent Gregory 4,000 lire.

Dr. Knott made no more effort to contact Sarah when in the next few weeks she didn't call. At first, her indifference hurt his professional pride, then he felt guilty to an unfinished commitment. In the end, he became interested in a series of demonstrations at the Salvator Mundi International Hospital of new ways of reading brain waves through computer-controlled implants of special metal under the scalp. He tried to think he had done what he could with Sarah, and he no longer cared for the highly strung nerves of all artists.

His attending the demonstrations was also a good excuse not to be writing his great book, or putting into some practical form the dog-eared packets of notes and photocopies of some texts of best years that lay on the bottom of his battered Gladstone bag.

Dr. Knott did get one long letter from Sarah's father, A. Lincoln Pedlock—there had been two before that—a letter which he wondered how to answer.

The last paragraph was a cry of pain . . .

her mother and myself have, as you asked us, for the last year and a half had no contact with our daughter, but for simple birthday greetings and some small family gossip on postal cards. But now Fran is really worried and we both wonder if perhaps we should come over and see her. Even take her back with us. If nothing can be done for her nervous condition [*hysteri-*

cal ways had been crossed out], wouldn't it be better she be here with us on the Eastern Shore? With her family, her own room . . . This is nothing against your treatment, or your methods. It's just our heartbreak (not a medical term, we know) for our daughter. And isolating her from us, and us from her, for whatever you think we did, or did not do, to bring on her nervous condition—the separation is unbearable. What would be the danger to her of us coming over to Italy now?

> Cordially,
> A. Lincoln Pedlock.

(He remembered Sarah telling of when she was ten, asking her mother, "What is a French kiss?" and being told, "It's what gives people a sore throat.")

Dr. Knott sat at a table in a small trattoria off the Piazza Colonna, one hand on his beard as he twisted it to more of a point. He cursed softly. He wondered what to write back. That he wasn't really attending Sarah now? That while he felt the damn concert idea was all wrong and dangerous, she seemed less hypersensitive? That Sarah was a goddamn mean and stubborn girl? As all the Pedlocks seemed to be? After all, wasn't it a case of conflict between will and ability, artistic drive and capacity? Damn all creative personalities.

He was tempted to cable: *Come and be damned. Come and do your worst.* Instead of which, Dr. Knott took out his old-fashioned fat Waterman fountain pen and slowly wrote on the onionskin stationery of the Pensione Santa Caterina.

Dear Mr. and Mrs. Pedlock,

I have read your letter with great interest, and much feeling, if you can believe a doctor in my field of endeavor can feel. And I do. I think it wrong just now for you to come to Italy. There is the pressure of practicing for the concert which she hopes will be given this fall. Great pressures there. She is in love with a rather decent young man. I'm trying to put this damn delicately—she is going through a physically elating experience, I suppose. But also demanding of her nervous system. There are some precarious intangibles in any affair. I hope none here.

Give her three months more. Two months, if you want to, come over for the recital. I gather it is to be in London. No final arrangements have been made, for all of your daughter's fervor. It all depends on a dreary hulk of a music teacher preparing her for the concert. Come then to the event, if you must. But take my advice, *not* now. If you do, I shall withdraw from the whole matter. No, forget that last sentence, the last part. I suppose I'm as profoundly insecure as the next person. I would feel I had failed, Sarah had failed, if now you were suddenly to appear. I am not going into the matter of her childhood traumas, wondering *who* was she, *was* she Jewish? *was* she Christian? was she *nothing* among other things?—for her a chaotic world . . . Just have a little more faith [he scratched out *faith* and wrote in *patience*]. All may come out well.

Truly,
Dr. Edward Knott.

Not a good letter. Ludicrous in part. He prided himself on having a sense of style, a use of words. But he never could write with ease to relatives of cases. Something excessively spurious crept in. It was why he had never gone into general practice, or specialized for any length of time in female disorders; no bedside manner. He also left surgery. The human plumbing and wiring was too pathetic, patched together by the Great Bungler. With a little more thought, a better nervous system and much less digestive gut, less whacked up glands could have been worked out. So here he was, at the tail end of a career, exploring the habits and games of the cortex, the mind. It called for a fresh drink. Thank God, anyway, for booze.

Nora O'Hara hurried down the Via Frattina with a flask of face lotion she had bought for Herself at the Lido profumiere. She was hunting a taxi among priests in cassock and biretta. There was to be a cocktail party at the hotel suite at five, and there were the horrible little ghinny cakes to set out, and to be sure the ice was there, and lots of it. She pushed forward into the crowd.

> Pay them back woe for woe
> Make way for the Bold Fenian Men.

Nora looked around her, clear of the mob. Down an alley like a little street, there was a bookshop of one dirty window and some hand-done signs: LASTIST BEST ZELLERS and ANGLISH BOOKS. Here, two days ago, in the window, she had side glanced at some paperback volumes. *Fanny from Behind, Sadists' Abbey, Torture Tower.* And a very strange one indeed, if one could judge by the cover painting, *The Perverted Vampire.*

She hadn't the courage that day to go into the shop. Today she saw the *Torture Tower* was gone. No picture of a woman hung naked in chains with bats flying around her parts (poor gurl if they got into her bush). To one side was a hunchbacked figure heating wicked-looking irons over cherry-red charcoal.

Nora scampered off and got a taxi, sat back, breathing hard. Ever since the first books sent her by the Gaeltacht Ring Reading Club, Nora had been carried along against her will—her *amour-propre*, as Herself might say—with a drive to read more of the sinful silly stuff. Nasty it might be and sinful. Oh, sinful for sure. She couldn't resist it. It was a self-indulgent harassment. Lord, give me strength not to go back to that bookshop and buy those bits of evil. You can just imagine what that horrid little hunchybacked creature with his swollen crotch would be doing with red-hot irons to that girl hung up there like a fried cod in a fishmonger's on O'Connor Street.

There was nothing for it, Nora O'Hara, but to resist, to find a wop priest and confess the reading and the games— and be put back into a state of grace and let herself alone. Was it wrong in her misery to be muttering the Litany?

"Blessed be God, Blessed be His Holy name . . . Blessed be His angels and His saints . . ."

Back at the suite in the Hassler, Nora set her senses right with a neat three fingers of Jameson's and no chaser. She went skillfully to work with two of the hotel's waiters; they always ready to play noughts and crosses on the maids' behinds. The antipastos, the other hors d'oeuvres seemed properly non-garlicky. The ice? "More, more. Ice. Ice." For drinks? "Soda, soda!"

They nodded as if they knew but that was the daft Eyetalian way. Smile, nod, shrug it off. No wonder they never won a war. The trays of mixed nuts. The bottle of Strega, Buton Vecchia, the Sarti. Most important, the House of Lords gin. "Napkins? napkins!"

Good thing Herself was soaking in the tub, or she'd be yelling "Irish!" and asking for self-indulgent tidbits the natives didn't have. Time to change, so Nora nodded to Vlad and Tony, "That will be all, lads," and moved to change. Then did, *or* did not, Vlad thumb her arse? Did he, or didn't he? Or was her mind a mush dissolving from all her reading and rereading those books. Lord, why did I ever leave Russell Street, North Circular Road, Dublin, a pure gurl, Lord (there he goes *again*) and come to this?

"You there, stop your natting. More clean glasses."

CHAPTER

34

He was a dainty, darling little man in perfect proportion. Judith saw that at once, after Charles Pedlock introduced him to her at lunch on the terrace of the Hassler; her place always reserved for her—Marchesa Pedlock's table.

"Judith, this is Jacob Ellenbogen," said Charles, "whom I met at a rabbinical tour this morning. He's just what you have been asking for."

The charming, handsome little man, a healthy El Greco face, a reddish moustache and a tuft of chin beard like Napoleon III, just smiled and made a gesture of why ask for me? He said in a singsong English: "Jacob Katzenellenbogen is the whole name. But for the Amerikaner, Ellenbogen is more than enough, thank you, as Job cried out when the Lord added boils."

Judith: "You'll have a drink, Reb Ellenbogen?"

"A little bronfin . . ." He sat down, a slim biblical patriarch, Judith thought, in an old alpaca jacket, frayed but clean cuffs.

Judith ordered brandy, smiled, rattled her bracelets. "You

see, it's like this, I have a sort of niece with a current dilemma."

"A genius," said Charles Pedlock, helping himself from the tray of antipasto, avoiding the thin rolled bits of Piedmont ham he was so fond of, and the wedges of mouth-watering lobster. For he respected Jacob Ellenbogen, a cabalist, a seer among Hasidim. Feared him, too, a bit. Jacob didn't seem to take American rabbis seriously. He had, on meeting a group of them that very morning at a rabbinical gathering, looked over their shaven faces, their splendid tailoring, flowing ties, and had whispered to Charles, "Tell me, they're all circumcised?"

Judith leaned forward, her still magnificent bust over-hanging the serving of blue Alpine trout with almonds. "I must know, tell me, can people still be inhabited by a dybbuk?"

"Shana, lady," Jacob spoke up—amused, somewhat troubled with his Vs and Ws, in an English learned in Buchenwald concentration camp from a Polish dentist from Lvow, who had practiced twenty years in Liverpool. "Shana, one, I could be living proof. If not, what saved my life was that I was entered by a dybbuk in 1942. A demon wise as Solomon, and what can I say, did he lead me to survive with his cunning when so many died? You feel that in modern times such a thing is not possible?"

"A folk myth," said Charles. "Of course, Reb Ellenbogen, I don't say a faith doesn't need such things. I respect everything that has that certain quality of a spiritual legend."

"Oh, shut up, Charles," said Judith. "Rabbi . . ."

"Call me Josof, or Jacob, as they say in America." He sipped his brandy with the relish of a man deserving it. Big sips, and smiled at Judith. "You are not thinking it's all a bobbe-myseh—grandmother's gossip?"

"Oh, of course not—you'll eat something? Now this girl, Sari, has great beauty, much wit, and yet for all her great skill—she is a concert pianist, or was—I'm beginning to think she is possessed. She talks of expiation, penitence."

"You've tried one of the meshugana who talk this Freud nonsense? There has been this lying down on a couch and talking nonsense—like asking who's taken too soon off the potty?"

Judith nodded and motioned a busboy to refill her coffee cup. "It's all been tried, Jacob. All, everything. A great doctor of the mind says it's artistic nerves gone taut. She's no better. He's given up, I think."

"Withered like Jonah's gourd? A Jewish doktor?"

Charles said, "No, a founder of a great mental health clinic."

"Ah, a goyische kop. A little more bronfin? Or do they have a slivovitz? No, thank you, I ate a big breakfast as a guest of your son here. It's a small belly, I have."

Charles looked at his butter-gold hunter's watch, snapping up the lid. "Reb Ellenbogen once was chief rabbi of Warsaw, Judith. I must hurry away, forgive me. You two have so much to talk about." He pressed the watch shut, stood up and kissed Judith's cheek. "I'm delivering a paper to visiting rabbis on Jeduda Halevi's *Kuzari*, and the heretic text of Solomon Mainon."

"Pleasant *kockerye*," said Jacob cheerfully.

Charles departed, nodding to some people at a corner table—strangers, it turned out to be. Jacob smiled at Judith. "At first, Shana, I couldn't believe your son that he was a rabbi. Not at all an idyutt, you understand. Just all of them this season in Rome so optimistic and happy. I could feel *antehsemiten* have yet to yell *Vli Zmir* at them."

"Stepson, Jacob, but I raised him. Not a bad man—but not the lucidity of crystal either."

"So, kind lady, let us take up serious matters. A dybbuk is an incubus, the soul of a dead person that enters a living person on whom the dead one has some claim. Mine never told me why I was honored."

"It must be a claim?" Judith was fascinated as she reached for a cigarette. Offered one to Jacob.

"No. There are still mysteries we don't know, even if I say so. When I was dying in a concentration camp and my mind was water, reality gone, I knew only so much of dybbuks, even if one took up board and bed—as the saying is—in my body."

She lit their cigarettes with her lighter.

"Fascinating, Jacob." They sat smoking at their ease with each other.

"King Solomon had a dybbuk who dethroned him for some years. It was the demon Ashmeddai. But tell me, how does a handsome figure of a woman like yourself travel alone?"

"Do you always ask direct questions? I'm a widow of long standing."

"Standing, sitting," Jacob laughed and closed his eyes to enjoy his little joke, pulled on his tuft of beard. He had not been drinking so much of late, and he was feeling his drink, pleasantly. He had been having hard times. Did a bit of typesetting for a little Hebrew newspaper, a weekly newspaper in Florence, wrote a sermon now and again for a fashionable rabbi in Hamburg. But in all, his *mazel* had been bad until the weekly sent him to Rome to cover the *chozzerai*, the chatter strange Jews, who called themselves rabbis, were involved in.

"Always people ask *me* question. Now it's my turn. What *mazel* to have met your stepson. He's reading papers at meetings and asked me about amulets and incantations to protect Jewish women in childbirth from an incubus. One thing led to another, to talk of a *tzaddik* who had the ability to exorcise a dybbuk from a modern person. And so here I am, a bit drunk, full of two days of too much food."

And was he really—he thought—holding the hand of this large beauty with *tsitskes* of—*Gottenyu*—of a mature goddess. Jacob Ellenbogen was a wise deep student of old texts. "I am," he said, "an observer of modern life. Not in disapproval."

"No, of course not."

He delighted her—the ironic twist of his body, even sitting there, it was almost in a Hasidic dance, when excited on some subject close to his heart.

They talked. He was, he said, a survivor who had not become rich, or been repaid by the Bonn Germans. He was a survivor who never had anything but a wife once, and some children. "They had all gone into the gas chambers and the ovens that became Mercedes and Volkswagens for the postwar Jews." He never thought much of the dead anymore, for he had been mad for a long time, he explained, or so he suspected, during those ferocious years. Living, existing, had taken all his efforts. He stopped talking, remembering his efforts just to have a bed in some corner, a bit of braided bread on the Sabbath, and a herring, the wing of a chicken on holidays. Why bring all this to the surface, or the fact he was not a sad man really. He loved the volumes of the Cabala, wine, sunlight, green growing things, the sight of beautiful women walking, all limbs involved, bodies like limber cedars of Lebanon. The fire might be low, but the ashes he often thought were warm, hiding burning coke. He looked up; why not a few good sparks? But she was a stranger—and soon this meeting would end. Yes, he was drunk.

"I'm not a believer," said Judith. "You understand, I've reached the age when blissful assurances about life don't fool me. So if I've come to you, or you to me, Jacob, as it seems, I've reached that point with this girl where a terminal patient goes to a witch doctor, or for goofer-dust as a cure for a problem. Not that I see you as a witch doctor."

"Don't give it a thought, Shana. Call me what you want. Still and all, you find something puzzling in this girl?"

"Sari, or Sarah as she calls herself."

"Surah in Yiddish. Ah! It could take time, and I have other duties—a job, and a corner of a room. Call it a job? call it a room? Still—"

"I'll pay you well for your time."

"No charity. Just enough for a good belch after a meal."

"I think you'd better have some coffee and cream, on all that brandy." She was smiling.

"Just, please, black. Yes. It's a challenge. First, of course, to make sure there is a dybbuk. I am admittedly not a fully holy *tzaddik*. But I am a Baal Shem who can preside over a minyan of pious true Orthodox Jews. None of these Yankee-panky rabbis. To drive out the demon, I read over the invaded person the Ninety-first Psalm. Very loud, then in a voice raised very high, order the dybbuk to go from the body of the possessed. In God's name I command it to go to

its own eternal rest. It's a poor misguided soul like the rest
of us."

"And it goes?"

"There are, ta, ta, stubborn cases. Then the Baal Shem
orders the ram's horn, the shofar, to be blown. A blasting
sound, loud and dreadful. That sends the demon away. A
guarantee."

"How can you be sure?"

Yes, his head was screwed on wrong, but she was still
smiling.

"There are, kind lady, two signs. Either one will do. A
tiny spot of blood appears on the saved person—no more
bigger than the head of a pin—shows itself on the little toe
of the right foot. Or a window close by develops suddenly a
small crack. You believe?"

"I am simpatico. I wish I could believe it. I mean no
disrespect, Jacob. If I did, would I be telling you Sari's
problems?"

"You haven't told me any of them. Just said you
suspected a dybbuk."

"Would you like some cakes with your coffee?" She
motioned to the waiter.

"I am given to strong desires for sweets. I have, you may
have noticed, all my teeth. Yet there was a time when I ate
sweets, day and night, had a silk top hat, smoked Dimitri-
nos, owned a golden soup ladle, and red leather slippers
with tassels. A house, too, a family. A fool's paradise, and
then"—he banged the side of his slender hand down on the
tablecloth—"done with. Over."

Judith, tears in her eyes, motioned for the cake tray to be
brought over.

He reached for a cigarillo. She pushed the gold case at
him. "Here, take them, the case too." He refused firmly.

Sarah had fallen into a mood of depression, and for the
best of reasons, Gregory thought. Vittorio Crivelli had a
doubt. He waited for a miracle—a sudden crystallization of
her performances in the studio sessions. When would it
come, could it? A recovery, almost over night, of that near

perfection to her playing that had first amazed the musical critics? The flaccid innocuousness of the return to the piano gone.

There had been nagging weeks of Crivelli reprimanding her, the agony of his browbeating when she made the most simple of mistakes. "When is the thin pale flame to blaze up again?" Those late afternoons when Crivelli came around to thinking that it would never be again; La Pedlock in a public performance as she had once played.

In the days of his disappointment, feeding his finches, opening the window wide to try and find some breeze in the hot Roman summer, Crivelli would mutter to himself: Old fool dreaming, a fool who doesn't hear well anymore, a fat old man ready to slobber his way to a home for the senile. I must tell her tomorrow not to come back anymore. It's over. Lost. To go take up hooking rugs, or raising small smelly dogs. But never again, never will she be what she was. He would put on an old recording of hers on the German turntable, and listen to her play Bach, Brahms, do wonders with Chopin, Mozart. Then his courage, his madness, as he called it, would come back. One more day, one more time. There were half hours of her practicing as good as her early best.

When Sarah's playing, in longer and longer sessions, became what he had hoped for, he had flung himself against the piano and smiled, wiping his moon of a face with the back of his hands. "That is better than any time you have played it before on stage. So we must expand these good periods to be the whole. Work!"

And when she did just that in extravagant, overextended strength, with piece after piece, he pointed a finger at his rain-stained ceiling and said, "I send cable to Solly. You can be ready for a concert."

It was this "coming to flower," as Crivelli called it, that surprisingly lowered Sarah into a pit of melancholy. The next step meant facing the public, the people—go back to herd values, success ethics, in the music world.

In their room at the Fausto, Sarah lay in Gregory's arms, a small brass fan blowing with little success on them, as it

moved from side to side, doing little more than stir the red
ribbon tied to it.

"Don't you see, Greg darling, what's next? A shaking
stage fright. My whacked-out anticipation of the coming
concert. This dream I used to have is back. In it I'm sitting
at the concert grand on stage, facing a couple of thousand
people, white shirt fronts, family jewels in place on patrons
of the arts, all waiting for me to make a mistake, fumble a
chord . . . And me in this dream, I can't reach the damn
keys, see? My fingers are all bloated and rigid, can't bend
them. I sit and the people begin to jeer, shout, laugh . . ."

He patted her damp back, set in order the shoulder straps
of her slip down over her arms. "Don't you see, Dedee, by
becoming good again, you've not painted yourself into a
corner. You're free."

"Oh, sure. I know, I know." She burrowed her head
between his chin and shoulder. "But I had to prove I could
do it again . . . Play well. Now there's the concert, then
more concerts. The timetables, the planes that leave late,
never on time, stacked up over smoking cities. And hotel
rooms, with stale odors of food, stale cigars, sexual cruelties
. . . Yes, I can smell pain and weeping. To always be living
from a suitcase, always the tasteless food not being digested
. . . And faces, faces . . . faces of managers and reporters
and the mincing faggot critics, and just always the shirt
fronts, the family jewels. I get mean enough to kick flowers.
God, *why* did You invent music?"

He felt her shiver in his arms, smelled fear.

"It's what you wanted, Dedee. You damn well know this
mood is just a kind of stage fright, buck fever, my
grandfather used to call it. When I went on my first deer
hunt with him. Great actors have it before every performance. Matisse used to shake a bit when facing a fresh
canvas. Performers are all such lousy, egocentric bundles of
jumpy nerves."

"You'll not leave me, Greg? You'll see me through? Get
me a Miltown. I'll sleep a couple of hours, and bushy-tailed
and toe-tapping, we'll go out for dinner. The Biblioteca del

Valle, or George's. Something epicurean, but no chrome or plastic, huh?"

"The Osteria del'Orso. They claim Dante ate there."

Sarah rolled away from him and laughed. "I hope they've changed the chef since then. I'm such a jerk. Don't I know Vittorio wouldn't let me play a recital if I were not really up to snuff? And Solly, that kosher fox, he wouldn't be working out a concert tour unless he was convinced."

"Now, Dedee, Solly, he didn't say a tour. He said one concert to begin with. To test the air, his own words on the phone."

"Solly is a greedy bastard—I know him—and he's smelling a world tour at top fees. You ever been to Australia? They're mad about musical women Down Under. Melba came from there, Sutherland, too, you know. Let's dress. I'm hungry."

Sarah was as elated as she had been depressed a few minutes before. The change in moods in her, Gregory had noticed, was now quicker, more frequent. He had tried to outguess her, to be able to chart her changes from gloom to joy, from brooding to exhilaration he had to hold down. "Christ, you're like a balloon, overcharged with lifting power. Simmer down." He was aware of his own feeling of being needed, and didn't know if he liked it. A change in his attitudes toward the world. He had become a protector, even a sort of manager, guide, adviser, arranger and, yes, victim. No longer the wary crouching antagonist to society. He admitted to himself he enjoyed it, liked the whole new atmosphere in which he now lived. But for the drag-ass hours he spent in cafés or museums while Sarah practiced. Even waiting gave him a sense of being needed, ready to serve. Would Grandpa have approved? He hadn't been thinking much about his grandfather of late. Perhaps he no longer needed the hovering of a comforting ghost, as when he was a penitentiary bleached number (420670) waiting for a parole board meeting.

Still the old man would have shaken his head at this business of Sarah—and repeated one of his favorite lines as the whiskey was purring in his veins. "When you take a woman in your arms, *yingel*, remember to be careful you

don't fall into her hands." And most likely he'd sing a verse
or so of a favorite song, "The Old Chisholm Trail."

> I'll sell my horse and I'll sell my saddle
> You can go to hell with your longhorn cattle.

> Goin' back to town to draw my money,
> Goin' back to town to see my honey.

BOOK SIX

On Route

Tanchelin was a twelfth-century heretic who sold himself to Adrammeleck, grand chancellor of hell.

This Tanchelin was given such awesome powers that pious Jewish husbands begged him to sleep with their wives. Before a year was up he preferred honeycake to women, and begged a minyan of rabbis to rid him of his dybbuk. In the end he became a happy shoemaker.

JACOB ELLENBOGEN
Waiting for the Messiah

CHAPTER

35

Dear Gertrude:

How are you and Saul and all the brood? I'm growing sentimental in the youth of my old age.

Rome is really like a dead whale cast up on a too small beach, and the sea worms crawl in and out on bus tours, but soon even they will find this great corpse of a city not fit to visit, as it chokes on the crowds it cannot handle. This image is not mine, but by a marvelous Hasidic mystic I've found. It agrees with my impression of last night's clotting of faces, people, Fiats, Volkswagens, Porsches, outcries, auto horns, when we all went out to dinner—it attacks my nerve ends. I came back to the hotel with two ideas: I had gone off the edge into incipient madness, or I was in shock from a flare of hautboys and auto trumpets. And what is called "reality" had been misplaced. No one who has never spent a night trying to cross the Piazza di Tor Sanguingna knows what I am writing of—the motorized barbarians. A city unresisting before the gasoline engine and the jet planes. Jacob—that's my

Tzaddik's name—is a great help, and he's going to counsel Sari too.

Our group, Dr. Knott, Sari, Beck and myself, hired a car to visit the Holy See in St. Peter's Square, day before yesterday. It had begun to rain as we neared the huge square. There were few pilgrims, art lovers or camera fiends around. The square is impressive in its almost, well, phlegmatic dignity, with the semicircle of columns, and the saints. Sari said, standing on their stone toes above us on the façade of the church "as if on a hot stove."

Sari and I went off alone to inspect the cathedral's façade. One of the peddlers came over to Sari at an easy pace, as if reading her character. Looked like one of the cherubs on a holy picture, a cherub turned fat and middle-aged, weathered curls showing a bald center spot. He held up a tray of his offerings [the letter breaks off here] . . .

"*Buon giorno*, a holy medal, blessed by a Pope?"

"No, thank you," Sari said.

"*E libero*; look at a set of fine art pictures, all bright colors, of Roman churches?"

"No."

"Buy somethin'—I am in *cattivo stato*. Here is a little statue of the Virgin? A set of beads—real coral. Look, I bite them—they don't break."

"No room in my luggage."

He moved closer. "You got jus' one American cigarette?"

Sari smiled, handed him a cigarette. He lit up carefully, inhaled, sighed, gave a short catarrhal bark. "I miss American cigarettes. I smoke two pack a day when I was prisoner of war in Texas."

"Texas?"

"I was on ship with many 'talians, prisoner of war sent to Texas when captured in Noor Africa. Very fine place, United Stated. I lead a band—make music."

"How long were you there?" Sari showed great interest.

He set down his tray. "Two hull years. I make two, three bambini there with fine Texas women. Musta be bigga childs by now. Very fine black girls there—zigzag alla time. *Ero pronto* for love then. They send me home. But I miss Texas."

"What kind of music you play?"

"All kind. Violin, piano."

"Classical, popular?"

"I play the jazz . . . When I coma back to Roma, I marry—Cattolica. No can play here—get work."

"I'm sorry. Maybe I'll buy a holy medal. What kind of jazz you play?"

"*Mi è molto simpatico, Lei.* This one of St. John, two thousand lire."

"You're a thief, jazzman."

He held up five fingers. *"Bene?* I play hunky-tonk piano. St. James Infirmary, St. Louie Woman."

She gave him some paper money, took the cheap pot metal item.

He held the last half inch of the cigarette carefully, puffed. "You from Texas?"

"Maryland. Keep playing music."

"They don' unnerstan' us here. We peepul who come from America."

"Addio."

Sarah was weeping as she rejoined the group. "Musicians have a hard life of it."

How is Sari? Judith wondered. God knows and He isn't sending down any answers. Ready to give concerts. After visiting St. Peter's, Judith's feet were swelling from all the walking. Back at the hotel, Jacob was in the lobby waiting for her and she introduced him. She hoped Sari never tumbled to the fact it had all been done for her, getting him into the group. After dinner they all went up to Judith's suite, all but Dr. Knott, who insisted he couldn't stand the credibility of any oldtime religion.

Judith took Beck out on the balcony. He looked harassed but happy. He pointed out to her what building was what—even if she knew them long before he was born. They could hear Sari and Jacob at it in the drawing room, like a rabbinical college. They were discussing the Haskala, the Enlightenment, and how Franz Liszt went to hear schul cantors sing in Vienna. She wanted to read original texts on the Talmud.

"You don't know Hebrew, my dear girl?" Jacob asked. "Yiddish is an Ashkenazic invention. You have time for lessons from me?"

So Sari, among a dozen other things, began taking an hour a day of Hebrew lessons after lunch, insisting she was going to be converted to Judaism, at which Jacob laughed. "It's like being converted to breathing."

"Borchu es adonoy hamvoroch. Boruch adonoy hamvoroch l'olom voed."

"A Talmudic prodigy—the way you repeat it," said Jacob Ellenbogen. He and Sari were sitting on a stone bench in the Piazza di Spagna above the Spanish Steps. It was noontime and tourists were moving in the direction of the old church of the Holy Trinity of the Hills. Sari and Jacob were eating sandwiches out of a wicker basket, sipping wine from metal cups.

"You think I'll make progress after I learn the letters?"

"Who wants to make progress? Just right now enjoy the sounds. What the goyim and the shaved Jews think of as progress today is just *bykocktah* speed."

Sari was chewing on a sandwich and writing with a pencil stub in a neat notebook. It was a sliced hard-boiled egg sandwich with a creamy dressing over smoked salmon. She tried to capture the spelling of the Hebrew she had just recited.

"What, dear child," asked Jacob Ellenbogen, "if it wasn't God but the Devil who said to you once to give up the concerts?"

"What?"

"There was a cult called Gnostics that expressed the idea that the best of what we think is good is *really* bad. The true God, the Gnostics said, could not have created so despicable a material world. So they said there is one who is absolute truth and light and rules a heavenly realm. The lowest being is a woman, Sophia, who offended by producing a child without a man. A malevolent god, Yaldabaoth, and he created our world. He is a bad copy of the Old Testament creator revered by Jews and Christians."

"And you think he, *not* God, is what I had visions of?"

"The Gnostics see the serpent of the Garden of Eden as a hero; he helped reveal the secrets of the Tree of Knowledge that Yaldabaoth hid from Adam and Eve. Yaldabaoth, working with Noah, tried to drown the knowledge-hunting Gnostics with a flood. He attacked them later with brimstone in Sodom and Gomorrah. The Gnostics say a speck of divine light is in some bodies. Redemption is through possession of the mystical gnosis, and redemption long before death. Their text says Jesus did *not* die on the cross. No, Simon of Cyrene carried the cross to Golgotha and was crucified in Christ's place, while Jesus looked down from Heaven and laughed."

"So my visions were what? God's, or the—?"

"Think. So, back to our lessons."

"Been thinking too much. Now, how goes the chanting of the *chahzan?*"

Jacob chewed slowly, he fed daintily like a cat, took a sip of wine, picked up an apple and hefted it in his hand. *"U'tahhair libanu l'avd choh be-ehrvess . . ."*

"What does it mean?"

Jacob took out a small pocketknife with a mother-of-pearl back, opened the remaining unbroken blade and began to peel the apple. "Translated from the Hebrew it means: 'Purify our hearts to serve Thee in truth.' When a real chahzan puts his cantor's voice to it, the sound is enough to shake the candlesticks. Now! *Yehy awr Va-Yehyour*—Let there be light and there was light. But you must start with the letters first."

He was cutting a long peel; a narrow apple peel coming from his pocketknife, he working the apple around in his long thin fingers as he cut.

"My father," said Sarah, "used to peel an apple like that."

"He ever do it with an orange, Surah?"

"No, I never saw that."

"Ah." He held up the long, long peel, and a few passers-by took notice of the feat. "An orange, now, that's sophisticated peeling." He put aside the peel and cut the apple into segments, gave one to Sarah. The bench faced the street and was near Judith's hotel.

Dr. Knott came out of the Hassler and looked about him and saw them on the bench—came over, walking briskly swinging his cane. He wore a jacket of hound's-tooth pattern, a cloth tweed hat. He lifted the Malacca cane in salute to them.

"Judith said you two would be out here picnicking."

"You've met Jacob Ellenbogen. Jacob, Doctor Knott."

"Met Mr. Ellenbogen at Judith's. How are you, rabbi?"

"It's been a long time since I was rabbi, Herr Doktor."

"It's been a hell of a time since I was a practicing medical man."

Jacob motioned to the wicker basket on the bench. "Have a sandwich, a fruit?"

"I'm gaining weight. Judith is giving too many dinners. Well, Sarah, the recital is set for December, I hear."

"In London—The Thames Hall."

Dr. Knott smiled at Jacob. "I'm the last to know these days. Any more wine in that bottle?"

"Enough, enough. I don't want you to feel I'm doing anything, Doktor, but teaching a little Hebrew, a little inquiry into Talmud."

"It's no contest, Ellenbogen, I'm no longer Miss Pedlock's, how shall I put it? adviser."

"Who puts it?" said Jacob as they sat sipping wine and a wide Japanese tourist took their pictures with two cameras. "You mustn't think, Doktor, I don't know the sophisticated games of getting into the modern mind. I don't eat oysters, but it must be like opening one—needs a special skill."

Sarah refilled the cups with the last of the bottle. "There are enough neurotics around for both of you. And paranoiacs by the ton. So don't fight over method." She laughed. "Cast your nets in any crowd."

Dr. Knott was amused, "You have patients, Ellenbogen?"

"Patients, no, people, yes. I talk, they listen, they talk, I listen."

"In my trade, only they talk. It's easier and I'm a lazy man."

"There was this little old candy store owner, Seidenbaum,

I knew in New York, some years ago—who wanted to talk: to a mind doktor. He had this problem, and his son, an allrightnic, a *shiksa* wife, two children, Anthony and Brad, yes. He sent his old father to this Park Avenue psychiatrist's office. Leather wallpaper, he told me, a nurse with so short a skirt he almost saw her pupik."

Dr. Knott smiled. "Pupik—navel—yes?"

"Yes. The Herr Doktor asked, 'What is the problem?' And my old Jew said, 'I have this terrible thing happening. Don't think I'm crazy, but under my bed all night little people dance—three, four inches tall—and other little people play music—a band. The little people play loud music and dance.' So the doktor says, 'No, no, Mr. Seidenbaum—don't think you are mad. It's a complex syndrome based on some trauma that creates hallucinatory periods at night that are congenitally self-destructive and—' "

Dr. Knott nodded. "You know the shrink lingo, Ellenbogen."

"I know nothing. A crumb here and there picked up. So the doktor says, 'Come and see me three times a week, a one-hour session, in two, three years, with analytical scrutiny, I am sure we'll get rid of the little people dancing and playing music under your bed.' So my old Jew says, 'How much this cost?' And the doktor says, 'My fee is fifty dollars an hour.' Seidenbaum shakes his head, says, 'Thanks, can't afford such terms.' And he comes to see me."

Sari leaned forward as Jacob handed her and Dr. Knott a slice each of the apple. "What happened?"

Dr. Knott laughed and chewed on a bit of apple. "What happened, Sarah. Why, Rabbi Ellenbogen cured him with one line of advice. Am I right?"

Jacob just grinned, chewed apple.

"But how?" asked Sarah.

Dr. Knott rubbed his fingers to dry them of apple juice. "He told his old Jew Seidenbaum to go home and saw the legs off his bed."

Sari opened her mouth in amused surprise. Jacob shut his pocketknife with a snap. He held out his hand. "Doktor Knott, I'm going to like you."

Sari said, "Is that, Jacob, what you advised—saw the legs off the bed?"

"What else?"

"And was he cured?"

"What else?" said Dr. Knott. "I'll stand treat across the way to caffè expresso, all round."

"I'm meeting Greg," said Sarah, "and then to Crivelli for two hours of Bach. Have fun, you two wizards."

Dr. Knott watched her go, running, moving he thought, like a deer running away from something.

"Well, rabbi?"

"I don't answer for God's way with people. He had trouble even with his angels, and people are worse than angels."

"And he can't order *them* to saw off their legs."

Judith insisted they all go—she, Sarah, Gregory, and Dr. Knott—to see the Sistine Chapel. Sarah hoped she would not have another vision of God there. She did not feel ready.

As for Michelangelo, he was to her, she told Gregory, the prophet of every audacity, neary conquered.

The Michelangelo frescos were on view from about 9:30 A.M. to noon, and they joined a huge army of visitors paying about thirty-eight cents each, Gregory figured, to pound their feet along the long, long halls.

She held Gregory's hand tightly, feeling a tennis ball of fear fill her throat. "Why can't one get into the chapel directly?"

The day was warm, the mob moved slowly forward, mellow and a bit rank with, she sensed, the sad futility of mobs. I feel swallowed up, she thought. Ahead and behind me various groups move under leaders carrying special banners to identify the tours they represent. *Columbia, Liberty, Star, Explorers.* The spiel of guides never ending; comes from all sides in several languages. I almost panic, turn and run, but retreat is cut off by more people.

Feet shuffle, shoe leather hisses on worn marble floors, we inch forward as the crowd seems to thicken. Oh, Greg, hold my hand tightly. Here and there we jam up as postal card and picture stands appear. Will God talk to me in front of all the people? In Hebrew? Dr. Knott looks bored.

The entrance to the chapel comes at last, a sort of narrow marble tunnel with several right angle turns, room only for two Indian files—one shuffling in, one shuffling out. Greg goes in front of me. The chapel itself is packed like a subway at rush hour. I'm in. Can't step back and focus on the ceiling. Can only arch back my head and look.

"*Ach, Gott, wunderschön,*" someone says in my ear.

"You're trembling, Dedee."

"Just warm."

"Want to go?"

"No—No. Just hold my hand, Greg."

People push me. The ceiling, oh so damaged. But nothing less than the Bomb can really destroy it. The air is getting thick. I must make haste to get the hell out. More people come in than leave. There is God—in paint, up there on the ceiling. Jewish whiskers—he flying in a bed made of a cloud of angels. He is coming down, *down;* the finger points, not at Adam, but at me. He's zooming in, he's aimed right at me. I feel the heat of his vitality like sacred steam, and now the belligerent finger, the finger of God, is pointed right at me, the sinner, the one who still does not fully recognize Him as Jehovah, the one true God. And why is Dr. Knott pushing close to me? *Halevai she'ani ma'amin—would that I could believe* . . . the majesty of the beard, the awful grandeur fills the chapel, the world, the universe . . . *Achhhh!*

"She just fainted in there," said Gregory.

"Broiling in there." Judith held a handkerchief, wet at a street stand, to Sarah's forehead.

Dr. Knott looked about for a taxi, but there were only a herd of reeking buses packed together outside the Sistine Chapel, unburdening themselves of more tourists, more collective groups under banners reading: HOLY SEE TOUR: TH. COOKS: AM. EXPRESS.

Sarah opened her eyes, found a wall against her back. Gregory was looking at her earnestly. She said, "Okay, okay. Just too damn crowded back there."

"You screamed something." Gregory felt her cheeks. She held his hand against her face.

"Who wouldn't scream," said Judith. "Somebody go find a taxi."

"I don't remember screaming. I'm all right." She tried to walk toward the curb, felt as if her legs were those of a limp Raggedy Ann doll, or an escaping scarecrow. Dr. Knott was watching her . . . The old bastard, he knew that as she fell she had shouted, "The devil is the other face of God."

CHAPTER

36

[From the journal of Edward Knott]

JULY 22, ROME

What to make of Sarah's performance in the Sistine? An exhibitionist act, a lapse of her nervous system brought on by heat, or the crowd, or just seeing the remarkable paint smearings on the ceiling by another genius? Strange are the reactions of saints, sinners, the insane and the mystics. I must have a long session with her before the Hasidic clown sends her down into pious paranoia. Of course artists encourage the psychopath in themselves, perhaps with the hope to be able to probe deeper the possibilities of creation— going beyond the security of everyday health. So that in self-induced sickness they face the enormous yet unmarked blank of the unknown to work with. They seek beyond solid intentions or conventions, want not already well traveled roads. But Sarah is a pianist—not a composer. Still—I must have that session with her before she and Gregory go off together alone, for those few weeks before that first concert. If there is to be a recital with Sarah's sensibilities swinging like a pendulum between hyperactivity and depressive fears.

This noon I was on my way to have lunch with Charles Pedlock (another one of God's classmates). I kept thinking of the old-fashioned delights of the early Freudian soothsayers in that total answer, the death wish. I must admit that Sarah has the death fear. Hemingway had it the last time I talked to him, this fear of natural death. So he committed fellatio with a loaded shotgun. Did the trees sway? Well, as the old medical school joke had it—none of us shall leave this world alive.

Yesterday Sarah and I saw a middle-class burial party gathering on a poor Roman street. There was the most marvelous hearse, dark green with age and verdigris. It had once been a burial coach pulled by four horses, but had now—sad to say—been motorized—a huge blackish ornate ship with sides of plate glass, the drama carved with all the dreadful details of skulls and crosses, tormented religious images, flowers, sadists' symbols of saints and holy land-scapes. All dark wood and polished with symbols of final, worm-riddled, irrefutable death. On the four corners of the coach were huge silver shapes, oil or candle lamps, from which hung fluffy black plumes and yards of black net flowing loose and ties in intricate bows like hanging nooses. A strange-shaped casket (strange to me), wedge-shaped, was being pushed into the hearse's interior, crushing a great mound of flowers, shoved in by a crew of professional mourners, or undertakers in training, who wore gray gloves, and claw-hammer coats. Mourners sobbed, watched, then took to howling. Sorrow, or social patterns made mourning audacious rather than cautious. I wished Judith were with me—we both enjoy the trappings of popular rites. People were patient as they waited—yet vibrant with anxiety, crying out, "Dio vi benedica!"

Sarah hung on my arm.

The violinlike sobbing of women dressed in soot black with veils, black lumps of hats set on heads, made a sad composition. Their sound rose to a wailing outcry as the women collected in groups and held each other up along the curb as they sobbed, "Peccato, peccato." Children also in black wept or silently stared. The men, overshaved yet swarthy, merely stood in their ill-fitting black, or wore black armbands, and waited, expressionless. The hearse rolled off, under a threat of a delayed rain hanging over the rooftops, creaking like a ship at sea, and the apprentice undertakers ran after it, hurling flowers on to its top as if offering hasty benedictions. A priest droned some Latin, and pulling up his skirts, hopped into a following car. Three other cars were packed with sobbing people. A fat man, coming up late, waved a furled umbrella at a passing taxi, while a few overlooked mourners stood waiting for delayed transportation, crushing under foot shreds of discarded flowers.

Sarah said she sensed a true feeling of death here, an expression of agony let loose in sobs and wails at the solitude of parting—final parting. Unlike, she said, the American burial racket at Forest Lawn or Israel Zion Park. Some indifferent minister, priest or rabbi to mutter of the merits of the dear departed—mostly lies or ignorance—of someone he usually had never met. The expensive graveside, raw earth discreetly covered with green plastic grass, the machine that sank the overpriced, casket—costly as a Caddie—into the pit to the sound of canned music leaking from loudspeakers hidden in the trees.

Standing there, we two, we became aware of a little man in an alpaca jacket, a flat-brimmed hat, watching me. It was Jacob Ellenbogen. He smiled and came toward me.

"You're collectors, Doktor?"

"Of what?" Sarah asked.

"Of what? Of body plantings of the *totentanz*. How people put away their dead, so the living can go home, wipe their eyes, eat, go on living."

"The Italians feel death is real, they don't go to spiritualists or work the Ouija board. For them, death is not the greatest perversion, the final kick in the ass."

"Each religion, Doktor, reacts differently."

We stood on the curb among the trodden flowers, black ribbons. The old man told us this story: "I once had a Hindu student in my youth, now a psychiatrist, who told me he never got used to us barbarians burying our dead underground for the worms. He said burning, cremating, was the only true respect to the body—clean fire, not slimy decay.

"Ha, in the second concentration camp I was in—German

*hospitality—there was a sailor from New Caledonia, with
filed teeth. He never forgave the efficient Germans for
burning up men, women and children in their gas ovens. In
his wild hill country, the proper honor for the dead, he said,
was to eat them. The heart for its bravery, a few savory
items of the genitalia for vitality, legs, thighs, for strength in
hunting."*

Why not? Sarah asked.

*We walked on together. When we came to the Tiber, we
leaned and looked down on the river, at some young men in
a rowing shell, a mixed collection of dead dogs, discarded
crates, here and there some bush or tree struggling to keep its
head out of the mud.*

Later when Sarah went off to practice piano, the two men
had a long talk, looking down on the river, smoking cigars.

Jacob inspected his cigar ash with respect. "Doktor, with
Miss Pedlock, I think you've come to a closed door."

Dr. Knott made a silly amused sound with his lips, almost
a sputter of mirth. "Judith has told you her crack-brain idea,
her dybbuk nonsense."

"Nonsense it may be. You or me, perhaps, we'll never
know its shape. Maybe you'll never want to know. I have so
open a mind, the wind roars through it."

"With Sarah, I've come to the conclusion that her drives
and resulting problems are the outcome of overeffort, after
she has lost sight of her real goals."

"Real goals? Ask that corpse we saw carried off what was
the meaning of real goals in its life."

"For Sarah it was to produce the music of genius. And
now she wants to make a kind of arrangement, a court
settlement with God. She's playing a concert to show Him
how good and great she is, and not just to make music. I
think she's lost her spontaneous daemonic genius in seeking
such a deal."

"No matter how you split a herring, Doktor—what
matters is that you can still eat it."

The goddamn Jews and their whacked-out folk wisdom,
Dr. Knott thought. How much more scientific it might have

been *if* Freud had been an Episcopalian! Sarah's attacks of elation or depression are classic cases. Judith called them "Vapors," such a fine Victorian word, and it has marvelous resilience. Gregory withheld any judgment, and felt he was avoiding facts, or being wise. He couldn't decide which.

Dr. Knott never had a long private talk with Sarah. Either she refused it, Judith said, or his professional pride felt bumped by her. Sarah did cut her practicing by an hour, and Vittorio Crivelli told her the first recital would be no problem for her. He wiped his huge head with his handkerchief as he said it, and mopped his neck inside his loose collar, swabbed at his jowls.

"I will not come with you to London to hear you play. No. You would use me like a backup wall—think of me listening—not of the piano. I want you free of me and at ease with yourself."

"You don't think there is too much Bach?"

"Never mind all that now. You're not weighing pasta, or measuring out pepper. So soon a great success. One bit of advice. Don't travel with the big woman, or the little Jew."

"You don't like Jews, maître?"

Crivelli showed the palm of a hand, then the back of the hand, the palm again. "Yes, no, no, yes. Does it matter? But travel slowly to London. Study the scores, find a good piano here and there. But you alone. Oh, of course the lover."

"He's more than lover."

"Don't ask for more, La Pedlock!" The old man set his bulk down into a wide chair, clasped his hands in front of him. He spoke in a low croupy voice: "There is nothing more in a partner than a good lover. If the art is going well."

"It helps the playing, to be in love."

"For the woman artist, it does no harm. For the man, it is a destroyer if prolonged—becomes a madness. I can't express it to you—only in Italian it doesn't sound indecent —I mean. But you seem to know. Take him, take yourself, travel north, travel east. Don't think of the concert. Think only of music. It must be the greatest of all the arts. Music. Or I have wasted my whole life."

He sounded strangely emphatic. She went to him and kissed the old man on the cheek, took his fat fingers in her

(299)

slim hand. Their eyes as they looked at each other were positively telepathic. "Words are worthless, maître. You know my gratitude. Let me say it, you saved my sanity . . . All those seas of faces in my audiences that wanted to test me, some to see me fail, had made me so fearful I wouldn't do my best. I fled. Yes, chickened out."

"Dante wrote, '*Non ragioniam di lor, ma guarda e passa!*' You understand? 'Speak not of them, but look, and pass them by.'"

When Sarah was gone, leaving behind a perfume he thought of as ripe lemon, the odor to him of genius, he wept for his own unquiet youth, his talent never fully tested, fears of his own making. And he wept, too, with a feeling that, *Deus det*, he had been given the gift of being able to teach others.

CHAPTER

37

They left the Hotel Fausto very early, the smell of charcoal and river in the morning air. Only Chalky Charters, coming in after a night on the town, saw them off. "Well, cheers, chums, and farewell. See you in London, and get you a fine piano . . ."

Gregory had decided they'd take the extra fare train, the *Rapido*, to Florence. Capturing a taxi, they drove to the new Rome station; the train had not yet arrived. After a short wait, it rolled in, they were off, and enjoyed the landscape. Hungry, they discovered the first lunch sitting sold out. Everything was done by writing, by buying tickets to use the seats in the diner. *("Si puo fare colazione ora?")* Sarah said, "No Italian genius has yet thought of selling space in the Ladies and Gents, but they will."

The train ran at fine wooshing speed through beautiful ochre-and-green hill towns, vineyards, umbrella pines, villas and groves. One American lady exclaimed to Sarah, "Why, it looks *just* like a Renoir painting. Once artists painted our world and its beauty. Not now . . ."

"I hope we get fed soon."

They got the late second lunch sitting at three o'clock, a hurried affair. A military-stiff waiter and one damp helper—Sarah insisted he was Oliver Twist—served a hundred passengers at the speed of a quick step drill. First he came rushing by with an armful of wine and beer and spring-water bottles, and motioned for Gregory to quickly pick his choice and hurry about it. His helper ran up with a tray of hard rolls and tossed down one to each of them, with the skill of a basketball player. By this time, the soldier waiter was back, slapping down—as if timed by a metronome—*one* slice of ham, *one* slice of salami on each plate, and his follower ran behind banging down half a stuffed egg and two olives. Then came sliced green peppers dropped in the right place on the plate. While they were still eating this, fresh plates were spun down before them.

Sarah grinned. "It's a modern ballet in rehearsal."

"Tasty too."

The waiter and his helper were both on the run as they slopped down on the plates sections of what looked like white garden hose (short-snipped into sections) and covered it with a dollop of tomato sauce. Rock-hard pasta and uneatable, Gregory insisted, except by Italians. The waiter with a melancholy lambent stare shook his head. *"Bene, bene."* Both serving personnel were now dripping wet as the train speeded up to seventy miles an hour. The diner rocked and rolled.

An Italian watching them, smiled. *"Pazienza."*

"We winning or losing?" Sarah asked.

Gregory smiled: *"Scandaloso*—who can eat at this speed?"

As they rode, trying to keep up with the mad but very expert servings, it became to Gregory a speeded up Mack Sennett comedy. After the garden hose (all the time fresh plates were being whirled up before them) came a postage-stamp-sized slice of very thin veal, string beans in a delightful sauce and something like hashed potatoes.

Sarah waved her napkin in the air. "I'm holding back the service. I can't eat fast enough."

"Chew faster. Don't let the team down."

Most passengers on the swaying train were trying not to

destroy the waiter's speeded up system. Cheese came—very good—and one of those dreadful Italian cakes—all gooey cream and, Sarah insisted, colored cement. They had the fruit instead. Coffee cups rattled down and were filled with the vile Italian drink called "coffee."

Sarah, amused and enjoying it all, asked for cold milk for her coffee and got hot milk. Gregory explained the word for "hot" in Italian sounds like "cold."

"No wonder they don't drink the stuff."

They were exhausted, a bit stained by food droppings, but smiling.

They had not let the waiter down.

The waiter was smiling and came around with a huge tin box to collect for the meal—$4.50 each.

Gregory said, "We paid for what is really only the outline sketch of a meal, rather than a meal. But a hell of an amazing performance of man against a railroad timetable."

"It was fun, wasn't it Greg? We are having fun, aren't we?" They got to Florence at 4:15. It was raining lightly, falling politely, a silver hovering in a dainty shimmering over the hills and city. The Arno River was low, no sign of the annual flood, just the high-water mark of stain on the buildings. Florence seemed to Sarah a calm, pastel city after the clatter and madness of Rome.

They waited, smoking, window gazing, arm in arm, an hour for the bus of the Park Palace hotel some few miles out of town in the hills. Those hills, Sarah recalled, where Boccaccio and wenches and friends and drink and food ran to escape the plague and to write or act out the dullest of erotic classics. Or so Dr. Knott had told them when he recommended the place.

The hotel was once "a millionaire's villa," a lobby sign noted. Their room was big, the window a huge picture frame with the city of Florence below.

"I shall have a drink (alcoholic) and rest (soft bed) and hope to digest the train's racing meal (gut growling)." Sarah plopped herself on the big bed.

She felt content—the rest of the world nebulous, elusive —and for the first time felt free of any arbitrary inscrutable power in the universe.

The Park Palace was very much a posh villa done over as a hotel, with ornate modern bathrooms; marble tile, shiny plumbing, the expected bidet, and tube lights. Sarah felt it seemed fitted out "for one of those Fellini film orgies."

The night, she felt, had been like black obsidian, the morning weather was rainy, then merely misty. The only two other guests were two old folk, an English couple by their accents, helping each other to stand upright, their joints creaking loudly. A pretty girl—she had a chipped front tooth—was at breakfast, but sped off in a hurry in a white Mercedes, her tires setting up a scream running down the driveway, a sound as if coming from a human diaphragm.

As far as Gregory could make out, they were in the Michelangelo Park, an old site still half wild, very green, with a castle out of Cesare Borgia behind them and a highway in front with a good-paced traffic busy on it, much of it half-nude girls clinging to bare-armed scooter-driving youths, full of *amore*.

The hotel swimming pool seemed full of frog spawn, the tables in the open asking for guests. Umbrellas were up for shade around those wicker chairs with enclosing sides that, to Gregory, suggested outhouses. There is no strong sun, no warmth. They stayed indoors, sending down for ice and Strega.

Sarah said love cauterized the mind. Gregory said good thinking is no credit to man's character in a place like this.

On the rare afternoon the sun shone, they went into Florence treading with care amongst the dog turds.

There were many Germans in the city. Fat, neckless, humorless. They all looked to Sarah like cartoons by George Grosz. Gregory told her his grandfather used to insist: "Every German is a dynamiter of human hope."

All Germans seemed to Sarah stereotypes. A sort of Brechtian alienation from the rest of mankind sat on them. But closer, at table eating and drinking, she had to admit they were very human.

"One wonders how they act so murderously evil at times."

"Perhaps, Dedee, they are functioning captives of a self-hatred, people seeking outré outlets."

One afternoon, while staring in a Pucci window, a tall, balding blond man came up to them and spoke in poor English, asking if he were permitted to take pictures with his camera of the bridges. He smiled, teeth outlined in gold. "One must be der goot neighbor, *nein?*"

"It's all yours," Gregory said.

All around were Germans, moving in groups, sweating in the hot Florentine sunlight as their shoes moved in frenetic rhythm toward the shopkeepers, Italians still greasy around the mouths from a late breakfast.

Sarah said, "Today—to forget the Germans—we buy sweaters—maybe three fluffy ones. Unlike Hemingway, I cannot sign a separate peace, not with Germans. You say Bach and Mann and Duer were Germans, and I'll scream."

"Duer was a Hungarian. Now everything is closing until four o'clock. Siesta time, Dedee—back to the hotel and ice for drinks."

For a week at the Park Palace they made love in leisure and in detail. Ate, drank, walked in the damp gardens, and Gregory translated for Sarah some Italian verse from a tattered anthology found in their room.

> "*In terra d'oltremare
> Ista la vita mia.*
>
> My life is there
> In a land over the sea."

"Not too good. Maybe a bit of Petrarch?"

> "*Padre del Ciel, dopo i perduti giorni
> Dopo le notte vaneggiando spese.*
>
> Father of Heaven, after my dissipated days
> All the night wasted in vanity."

"Must be getting old, poor Petrarch," said Sarah.

"Always disliked D'Annunzio as a too florid novelist. Still this bit of his poetry has some grace.

> "*A mezzo il giorno*
> *Sul mare Etrusco*
> *Pallido, verdicante*
> *Como il dissepolto*
> *Bronze degli ipogei, grava*
> *La bonaccia.*
>
> At noon
> On the Etruscan sea
> Pale and green
> Like a new-found bronze
> Lies the dead calm."

The dead calm? thought Sarah. To die spent, in debt, all breath gone. *But not just now, O Lord.*

CHAPTER

38

NOVEMBER 31, LONDON:

A circle goes nowheres, a spiral has aspirations upward. Is this trip circle or spiral? Judith, Ellenbogen and myself have been staying in Paris. The news from Sarah and Greg has been little more than three postal cards, the last one saying they have gotten to London, and she is preparing for her recital. I have promised Judith I'd stay for that, but I feel an air of fragile unreality about this public appearance, I'd rather go off, alone, to some place like Franzebad or Cap d'Antibes, and make believe I'm working on my book. Brood anyway in a low-keyed serene retrospective, near the convent where flowing nuns move about as if without body joints. Move among fluffy mimosas, olives and oleanders. A retreat, Santayana used to write me, a place for getting one's life's work over with on paper. How George used to insist the true jauntiness in men was lost when we discarded canes.

Judith is so sure all will be right with Sarah after the concert. Ellenbogen caters to the woman with his chaotic

*absurdities of his ghetto mystics scratching themselves
between bites at a herring. But he and Judith do have*
rapport. *How Judith laughed when he said, "The world may
be Sodom in our time, but there is no Lot's wife. Today to
state a problem is not to solve it by turning somebody into a
pillar of salt, eh?"*

*We took off—half an hour late—for the 45-minute flight
to London.*

*New Bond Street, a street punctuated by fine lampposts, a
busy shop-lined street, people sombre as would-be suicides
at nine o'clock, hurrying to work. Thought of Stendhal's line:
"There is nothing ridiculous about dying in the street,
providing one does not do it on purpose."*

*Judith will try and get in touch with Sarah through Leon
Solly's manager here.*

*At Buckingham Palace they were changing the guard in
front of what looked like five hundred buses and a
half-million tourists with their cameras aimed at the
mounted Horse Guards; over polished silver breast-plates,
the steeds dropping golden smoking horse apples. Lots of
sacred* merde *also—centuries of it on the Abbey.*

Judith has located Sarah—but she is practicing.

*I look out—think of the elegance of the rows of London
houses still left (but going), the Georgian symmetry of
certain streets where only yesterday* The Beggar's Opera
*was new. Pickled oranges were cried in streets lit by Negroes
in red wigs carrying torches, and the traffic was of chaises,
chariots and landaus. Someone once told me the Jamaican
golden rum was 86 proof when Hogarth and Rowlandson
drank it.*

In the afternoon's mail I got a folded poster:

PEDLOCK
A BACH RECITAL
THAMES HALL

Jacob Ellenbogen had cut himself off from the thin
lifeline of his typesetting of a Hebrew weekly in Italy,

parted from the few sons of junk dealers, shopkeepers; fathers who still insisted on a regular *Bar Mitzvah* boy coached phonetically to read a Hebrew portion from the Torah. Gave up the few lire to be made finding ancient *siddurs*—prayer volumes for some visiting rabbi. Had given it all up and come to London in the menage of Judith Pedlock. One hour a day he taught Sarah Hebrew, explained the more complex of the Sabbath and dietary laws and added some readings from the Talmud. Tea he had often, even dinner with Judith at her hotel suite. He was tracing for her the Pedlock line back to a twelfth-century Baltic merchant prince on one side, to a tax collector of a German house in the 1730s (who was publicly drawn and quartered when his protector died).

"Shana, it's all nonsense hunting a family's past. Go back far enough and we're all related to Adam and Eve. But like yourself, I like to drift back in time, find out how actually other people lived and, frankly, went to bed together, lamented, sang and died. How banal the cry of 'Vanity, vanity, all is vanity.'"

"Were they at least good Jews, these Pedlocks? Becks, Morgenstarren, Longstrasses, Godoffskis, Ben-Amirs and Hudvanies?"

"Look, here a runaway monk—there a rapist-crusader, how can any Jewish line avoid them? But it was a Pedlock, an army contractor, who fed Napoleon's army in Italy, and a grandson who brought Wagner and Ibsen to England, and another ran for parliament with a Rothschild and was refused his seat when he wouldn't take the oath on the New Testament."

"The greater fool he, Jacob. How are Sarah's lessons going?"

"Between the piano and the agony of what her local manager calls publicity, I get squeezed in."

How did Jacob manage to exist from his fees, Sarah wondered: "From air and free meals." Jacob lived somehow in Whitechapel, in some mysterious surroundings, with a cluster of extreme Hasidic families, given to earlocks and long black coats, wide hats and strong desires to argue loudly on any point of ritual and commentary. Jacob drew for them charts for the Kabala, and led happy hand-clapping orgies of dancing and chanting.

Once he invited Sarah and Dr. Knott to such an affair, and they both joined in the shouting and arm waving. He took notes for his journal, felt it needed detailed study, then decided if he was ever to write his big book, he should stay in his bed-sitter, a small room on a quiet street near the British Museum, to which he held a card. Here he would usually be found in the reading room of the museum, a pile of books at his elbow, aware he was again avoiding work under the excuse of research.

Sarah and Gregory had subleased a small flat near Grosvenor Square from an American screenwriter whose wife had insisted on returning to California supermarkets and sunshine. The furnishings were sparse and not very functional. So there was room for a piano.

On Oxford Street, a short walk from the American Embassy, was CHARTERS ANTIQUE AND MODERN PIANOS AND MUSICAL INSTRUMENTS, EST. 1812. And a small brass square: *By Appointment to H. M. Elizabeth II.*

Chalky, in a long smoke-gray coat, a well-knotted cravat, was no longer the hedonist of Rome, but in the deep wide store the proper owner of a respected and established business.

"Grand, grand to see you both again. Rome seems far away, what?"

Sarah looked over the walnut paneling, the velvet cases of instruments, several pianos and base viols set among rich, yet discreet hangings. "I'm looking for a concert grand."

"Had you in mind for a decent old hulk that used to belong to some German bigwig, shot during the Blitz; spying I suppose."

He led them into a smaller room where a huge Steinway grand dominated its surroundings. "No demand for one this bulky, everyone these days packed up in flats or studios in some mews. But it's happy as Larry—give it a tinkle."

"You'll rent it?" asked Gregory.

"Better still, just borrow it."

Sarah lifted the keyboard, tapped a few keys, sat down, tested sound and pedals. She stood, motioned for Gregory to lift up the lid while she examined the strings, plucked a few. Chalky and Gregory stood to one side smiling, as if waiting, Gregory thought, for the announcement of a birth.

Chalky must have had the same idea. "Well, Doctor, will it live?"

Sarah held up a forefinger and thumb in an O sign. "Marvelous, *if* it can be tuned. The felt is in good shape, pedal rods need oiling."

"A bag of nuts. Have one of the staff take care of that. No sweat. Cost you five quid to get it over to your flat, and hoisted up. Sorry."

"We'll rent it," Sarah insisted. "Pay for its use."

"No. Said I'd help the damn music world, didn't I? Get ours back when the recital gets publicity reviews. Run an item in the papers. *Sarah Pedlock's piano for sale, collector's item.* What say?"

"Why not?" Sarah was back at the keys doing a bit of a Bach exercise.

"A dinner then," said Gregory. "A night in Soho?"

Chalky seemed delighted. "Done. Have it delivered tomorrow afternoon. Give the tuner a half day on it. Put your poster in the window."

Leon Solly's London representative, Matthew Flagg, a brisk young man with hard bulldog face and one scarred cheek, former footballer from Liverpool, had begun to send out publicity. There were notices to the major music critics, and a two-sheet poster in blue and dark brown.

PEDLOCK
PIANO RECITAL
ALL BACH CONCERT
Thames Hall
DECEMBER 15TH
Tickets at all major ticket agencies

It had a good solid look. Nothing modern as to type or format. The poster was beginning to appear in music shops, art stores, school halls, and would soon be seen on the sides of a select number of red two-decker buses that ran into what Matthew Flagg called, "the more intellectual suburbs, and the culture-vulture enclaves . . . Now, Miss Pedlock, I'd like to set up some telly interviews."

"No. Ugh—that little red eye."

"Nothing heavy, you understand. Professional chatter with one of the long-haired, horn-rimmed Kingsley Amis Oxford types."

"It's out, Mr. Flagg."

"Could dig up old Barney Neustein, music historian, laid away some place in Kent. Be delighted to come down, expenses paid, to kick around a bit of piano history with you."

Sarah insisted, no, and *No.* She didn't want to join the television or radio forums, or be the object of the dry wit of the young men at the BBC. Matthew Flagg said if no was no, he'd think of something. Would she pose for a publicity picture for the *Picture Post?* Sarah said she'd think it over.

Two weeks before the recital, the newspapers and musical publications were given an old photograph of Sarah, retouched to change the hair style.

Sarah had become—in Judith's expression—a dedicated nun. Gregory slept on an unfolding sofa in the living room of the flat. Sarah took two sleeping pills after a hard day at Hebrew, piano practice and the turmoil of deciding *and* undeciding what pieces to finally play. Also going with Judith to an old Frenchwoman for fittings, out Bayswater way, to have a black gown made, and to Bally's for the proper shoe measurements, then a drink of hot milk and to fall into bed and into a deep sleep.

Twice in a week before the concert she woke Gregory with kisses and ardent embraces and rather incoherent words and cries for violent sessions of love-making. In the morning while he prepared her eggs (runny soft) and coffee and buttered the English muffin, she seemed to have forgotten the passion of the night.

As the concert date neared, she was neither flustered or

keyed up. Anyway on the surface, calm, professional, taking, she told Gregory, the concert as part of the routine of her life.

"A dress fitting at one, so you'll have to go get the shoes for me, darling."

"Give up Ellenbogen, at least until the concert is over."

"No, no. It's a morale booster I need. On this rock, Hebrew, I plant my church." She laughed, "No lunch today, see you at dinner at Judith's. She's taking us someplace." Sarah left unfinished the second half of the muffin, wiped her mouth absent-mindedly and seized her coat off a chair. "Must rush, Greg. Must." A hasty offer of a coffee-and-egg-scented kiss, a pat on his cheek and she was at the door. "You have things to do, I am sure."

"Oh, yes," said Gregory, lighting a cigarette. "There are the dishes, and I can carpet sweep the flat and—"

But she was gone and he heard clatter down the steep stairs. He poured himself a cup of coffee, smiled, and opened the *Times*.

CHAPTER

39

Nora O'Hara walked with a strong stride past Marble Arch gate, past where the rabble-rousers at Speakers Corner were tatting away against God *and* for God, exhorting Marx and vegetable diets and peace. A black preacher was pointing up the evils of Sexual Marxism in a dialect like no other she had ever heard. He was a powerful black man with a bushy head of hair as big as a keg of Dublin ale almost. "Oh, de divil is in the sexual aspic of air sinfold urge for de sinful lusts."

Under her arm in a brown paper sack Nora had a half pound of boiled sweets, and two books from a little newspaper shop that under the counter did a brisk trade in a lending library, a shilling for two days. She had returned to the shop copies of *The Fur-lined Virgin*, and *Miss Pussy's Wild Weekend*, and was carrying with some anticipation *Bishop Rod's Secret Room* and *The Harem Prisoner's Ordeal*. These entertainments would hold her until the book club from Ireland sent its own monthly items.

Nora had a good color, a splendid appetite for food, much improved in the last few months. She felt a vitality and strength she hadn't felt since she first left Dublin to take over the charge of an invalid lady of a good family—a patient at Bath who had marvelous fits in which she flung small objects around and ended up for a cooling off with her head in a basin full of water.

Nora, for all her improved health, eagerness for food, felt sad when not reading—about the state of her soul. She had become an addict to literature and she knew it, like some to tobacco, some to drugs, or "the gargle," as her Uncle Nick called strong drink; so she had come down the road to ruin by the way of books. The printing press and the education of the workers to letters that Father Norton had preached against: "You get the printed pages of the devil into the hands that should be putting their use to the plow, and gurls that should be bending their bodies over the wash tubs, instead are twisting their limbs in lascivious dances. Let them just read books and they will form from the reading produced by the printing press thoughts of abomination, degrading and lusting misuse of their bodies created in original sin. And to sin in thought, in action it will lead right to Purgatory! Everlasting fire!"

And there was a devil of a lot more to Father Norton's sermon—he a popular whiskey priest, a good man too—for what he didn't need for drink, he gave to the parish poor and the needy; his winter overcoat never lasted him a week but some poor sod had it in pawn himself.

Nora worried about her soul, it seemed to her a real object, like, say, a small woolly dog running around her and barking, and she ignoring its pleas to stop reading in the torrid texts. Hours at a time, when she could, she read in flushed torment—and snatching even a ten-minute hot read between duties for Herself, who was busy with that little Jew man banshee; a regular look to him of one who knew the little people. Nora had more time for her reading now that Jacob Ellenbogen was working out the Pedlock family history. Lord, if he kept it up long enough, he'd have the Jews coming from the line of the very kings of Ireland.

Judith was in a pale-blue dressing gown writing a letter to her daughter Gertrude when Nora came into the hotel suite.

"There you are, Irish, where have you been?"

"It's my top bridge—it got loose a bit—almost dropped it down the W.C. Plenty of time to order up a tea for—"

"Never mind the tea. I'm moving in as house guest, as you know, with the Mandersons on St. James Square, and I'm lending you to Sari, Miss Pedlock, for a few days until the recital."

"I was thinking during that period of going to Ireland on holiday."

"You can after the concert. What's the matter with you these days? You're always flushed and seem walking in a trance."

"It must be the change of life coming on me. Me aunts got it early."

"The menopause? Nonsense, not yet." Judith looked at Nora, sighed. "Can it be we've been together all those years. I suppose we've become too used to each other to see each other as we are. We change and no one of us sees the change. Not me in you, you in me."

"I've never contemplated the years, and you've been decent to me, most of that time."

"I'm very fond of you Ir—Nora, I hope you know that. For all my—"

"I've never been hurt by the rough side of your tongue, if that's what you mean." Nora found she had made some sobbing noises, and she turned away. Judith nodded, and servant and mistress were suspended for a few moments in silence. "You're the custodian of a ruin, so I've left you something in my will. And the necklace, the one with the rubies." Tears now—a choking sound—Herself too, dew-eyed.

"No need to talk of wills. You're the picture of health. If it weren't for the rich food, and less bulk to you—I mean, what's the Jew saying? 'till a hundred and twenty . . .' sure, now."

Judith waved off the idea of so advanced an age.

"I've been thinking over my life and Mr. Ellenbogen has been helpful in making me see the futility of human endeavor in a world of mystic happenings we'll never understand. I've taken to his ideas and . . . never mind. You see Sari is dressed properly for the concert. That she has something solid in her stomach these next few days. And cheer her up—you're full of all those Irish ghost stories and Gaelic old sod whimsy, or aren't you?"

Nora shook her head. "I never was one for that daft idea we Irish had any special charm or wit, or were addled in the head by seeing leprechauns and the hearing of voices."

"You disappoint me."

"Truth is my family, the O'Haras and Deegans, were small clerks and plumbers, house painters. Never poor and never in trouble or playing jig tunes, doing the Pat and Mike. It's Americans that made all that up about the Irish—just writing all them songs and dying to be wearing green on Saint Pat's on Fifth."

Thames Hall was large and old but still had an Edwardian dignity and a splendid ability to reflect the true sound of instruments and voices better than almost any hall in the world. Its acoustics, Sarah explained to Gregory, were the marvel of all the talk of conductors, soloists and performers who compared it to the Albert, La Scala, Salt Lake Tabernacle and above, much above Lincoln Center, the Dorothy Chandler Pavilion, the Sidney Opera and the Cow Palace. When speaking of the Thames Hall, respect was for the true sound.

Gregory in late afternoon was sitting in the third row of the empty hall, a work light on a stand on stage, and three members of a stage crew moving a concert grand around as if wrestling a torpid elephant. Matthew Flagg in a fingertip white tweed topcoat, tiny hat on his big head, was motioning them to move it back and forth.

"Just a bit now to the left. No, no, left, *left!*"

"Make your mind up, mate."

"And has the floor been waxed?"

"That's the bloody maintenance union's pitch, not oren."

"Just see it's done. I want the canvas flats in the back, a bit forward in semicircle."

"They was until you said snatch 'em back against the wall."

"Well, bring them back. And a lights man, where the hell is the lights man?"

"Out for a pint, mate. It's pass four o'clock."

"Manager! manager!" Matthew Flagg shouted. "Damn it, we haven't tried the lighting yet. Where are the baby spots and the scrim clusters?"

"Manager's gone to hospital, his missus took bad last night."

Matthew Flagg turned to Gregory, a tight smile on his face. "About as usual, mucked up a few days before a concert."

"Miss Pedlock wants to see the lighting and the flats—the sound baffles—in place, and test the acoustics."

"Oh, she will, she will, in time." Matthew Flagg sat down by Gregory's side in a seat that seemed to sag badly. He took out one cigarette from a jacket pocket, lit it, coughed, closed his eyes, inhaled and coughed again. "These things killing me. Don't worry, tell La Pedlock we'll have it all rigged by morning. Then we'll have to take it all down as some Bolshi Chinese touring troupe are here tomorrow night. But we'll be set up ginger fine for the concert. How is she?"

"No problem, you forget she's done a lot of recitals."

"Not for years of late, she hasn't." Matthew Flagg coughed again. "Old Solly had me on the trans-Atlantic blower this morning. He may fly over. I said it's all going as well as tea at Windsor Castle. How *is* it going, Mr. Beck?"

Gregory sank his neck deeper into his coat collar, the fog seemed to drift in from the street, a cold, clammy peasouper up from the river and, as he saw earlier, blotting out the tops of buildings and running along the street surfaces among the tires of cars and buses like gauze.

"It's all going just fine. But in this weather, will we get a crowd?"

"Crowd? Audience? Yes, we can always get an audience. But if the Right People talk it up as a sterling event, it's real money."

"How are tickets selling?"

Matthew Flagg rubbed the end of his nose, touched just for a second the scar on his right cheek. "Going along fine.

Could be better in the boxes, and parts of the balcony, but it's been my experience there are some people who wait until the last moment. Oh, say until they're having dinner in town and wondering where to go after."

"Not a sellout?"

"Not so far, Mr. Beck. But no loss. I mean no red ink. Solly will make a little, or lose a little, maybe break even. But he doesn't care. It's the launching pad here of the new La Pedlock concerts he's got his Yid eye on—meaning no offense, Mr. Beck. The money isn't all in the big cities— after costs—compared to what you rake in on tour after Berlin, Rome, Down Under and wherever they really want the big names."

"You think Miss Pedlock, she's still a big name?"

"Solly thinks so. I think what he thinks. Makes for harmony in our relationship." He coughed. "Solly, he's a wise old—owl."

Gregory stood up. "Yes, I suppose so. I'll be seeing you, Matthew, and be sure the lights are right, not in her eyes or reflected on the piano surface too strongly."

Gregory went out into the raw street, shapes dissolving into their own version of form as seen in Japanese prints he had once owned; all sold with the rest of his assets to pay his lawyers, his appeals, costs of court records, the hiring of "experts" on anatomy and the pathology of blood, other expenses. He would have to tell Sarah about Agnes' death, his prison years, soon. After the concert. It was becoming the world of "After the Concert" for all of them. Judith wanting to return to America, he, Gregory, wanting to get married. Sarah seeing in the concert a return to her art, to her former self, also resolving the God question through Jacob Ellenbogen. "Am I Jew or not Jew?" Even Dr. Knott was delaying his book, he had told Gregory, until after the recital.

"Just pottering with footnotes," he had said. "It isn't I don't think she can't play a concert, Greg. No, to me the more practical question is *will* she? Oh, I know you all say she is calm, professional, ready, on her toes—or is it fingertips? But first of all she isn't the player she was three years ago. No champ makes a true comeback at full strength. Also you all seem to think she's marvelously calm, just waiting to go on. It's my profession to doubt. Not that I'm consulted anymore. I suppose it's going to be a shame to bill Judith Pedlock for my services. I should split my fees with that half-assed dybbuk Ellenbogen, don't you think?"

Nora, in a shared confidence, got on well with Sarah. Or was it Sarah that got on well with Nora? It didn't matter. Nora on loan from Judith felt a release from pressure. For Herself, she admitted to Sarah, "when in soigné mood, was a handful." There was so much to do for her aunt, holding back the aging process. At least the surface. Lotions, creams, cover make-up, body massages. The laying out of vitamins, other pills that were supposed to tone up the skin, take up slack when she got into the kip.

For internal wellbeing there were other vitamins, pills, liquids. "And, Miss Sarah, twice a year Herself went to Switzerland for health." To take doses of some ground-up organs, Sarah knew, of unborn lambs, or was it goats? Dr. Orgell, a nasty piece of work. Greedy. Judith didn't ask too much or how the process worked. It did seem to help her vitality, but she was bright enough, Nora admitted, to know that expectations could fool one, and it might all be nonsense. The pills, the shots, the ground-up organs. "Hell, Irish," Judith would say when she stood in front of a mirror examining her skin, pushing back a bit of flab here, there, "for all my attitudes, cosy recriminations—in spite of years of being with the best minds, and in a brutal insensate world—I admit that what I see now is an old Jewish yenta, who should be bright enough to know you can't stop age, can't recover youth." (They both had been drinking very cold Chambery.)

"It's against God's way," Nora had said. "If he meant us to get round the wearing down of ourselves, now wouldn't he have spare parts handy? Or be able to send ourselves back for an overhaul, or a correction, like the factories recall cars to Detroit that need adjusting? Wouldn't he now?"

And Judith had sighed and turned away from the mirror. "He could if he wanted to. Jacob says he works in his own way when he wants to."

"The old Jew fella is a kind of scare-booger, meaning no offense. A kind, what do you call 'em?"

"Dybbuk. I wish I had your faith, Irish, in the supernatural. To me Jacob is just a very lovable, witty, wise little man. And to him, I'm Shana, pretty one, is that a laugh?"

Nora didn't think so, and didn't say so. If Herself was after a bit of a lark, well, the old girl still had enough fire in her for some last sparks. Sell her soul to the devil, she would, to keep licking up life. And why not? She was lonely, old, and her children had lives of their own. Were a dull lot compared to the old rip herself. Oh, very soigné. They didn't need her and Herself wasn't one to really need them. You hear this thing of Jewish mothers smothering their kids. Not Herself. She could take them or leave them alone.

When Nora had parked her suitcase and some books to go to Sari's, Judith had said, "Just keep her calm and not jumpy till the concert. My concern is humane. And don't bad-mouth Jacob to her, the way you do to me. He's '*pas si bête.*' "

"I never."

"He means a lot to Sari from the ritual side. He has several sides," Judith said with a camel-like smile. "I'm thinking of getting engaged to him."

"I never."

"You said that before. *Not* married. Just engaged."

"Well, I wish you both the best, I am sure, whatever way it is. You'll find all the pill boxes and bottles in order. Don't go stuffing yourself with rich food. The stomach drops are in the pink container, and the enema bag is hung where it always is. Just hot water and soap up the—and not too hot and nothing else."

"Get the hell out of here."

Yes, being with Sarah was a treat. Oh, the gurl was jumpy as a Tipperary cat that had mislaid its kittens. But interesting. And Mr. Beck the star boarder, as they say in Killarney and Tralee. What went on between them didn't seem too much these days. Lord, after what was in the books I've been reading, they were more like an old married couple worried over the drains and the grocery bill, than lusting after and accommodating each other's parts.

Nora had decided to taper off her reading, and when clean of her abomination, go find a strange priest, confess and be put back in a state of grace. The bite and itch was going out of the texts. It was all becoming a sameness. You would think now the writers could work out new vileness, filthier games, not the same damn whipping and pretzels coupling, fey positions, dirty little charades. In twos or groups. It was a pleasure, when Sarah was practicing piano, to go out, away from evasion and duplicity, to find a cinema where *Gone with the Wind* was playing for its tenth or twelfth time. She had seen it eight times herself and never wearied of it. That and *Sound of Music* were her favorites. She had seen *Sound* six times. But *Gone* was her love. Oh, if she could now shake off the foul pull of those books, and the solitary absurdities they drove her to, she'd be reborn.

Deep down, Nora thought of leaving Judith for good. But had she the strength for it? She in many ways liked the life they lived. The good living, like a bishop's fat ways—and the travel. She admired Judith, loved her in fact, deep down, respected her for her independent way of life. A sinner? Without grace? Maybe the Jews served a different version of God's rules—and he was more tolerant to the chosen about sinning. Insisted only on respect and ritual. Jacob was certainly an influence for good in that direction. Herself was less likely to flare up now when her hair was combed and it tangled. Certainly seemed more at ease, even comfortable. Didn't bellyache so much about life and people, and the world going to hell in a basket.

So if Judith wanted to play at love with the old Hebrew, why not? He was lively as a parish flea, always jolly and laughing and reciting some story or other. Sometimes she even got the point of one or two of his yarns. He was kind, and he didn't demand, like some that in the past had latched on to Herself, freeloaders and moochers. No, he didn't want anything but that slivovitz he knocked back like a Dublin docker, without a shiver, licking the last drop off his lips.

Life with Sarah was a vacation, and more. Sarah liked to

gossip after hard piano practicing, or sessions of reciting that Hebrew with Jacob—a language which didn't sound at all as smooth or liquid as Gaelic. But then everyone knew Gaelic was the mother tongue of the world, spoken most like in the Garden of Eden.

"You know, Nora," Sarah said, "sometimes I think it's all a dream, life is a grave, blank as a putting green. I know it's a banal idea. But I can't feel any reality most of the time, I seem to be floating a foot off the ground with just one toe trying to touch earth."

"Oh, my granny said there was once an old Chinaman chap that dreamed he was a butterfly, and woke up and wondered was he Chinaman who dreamed he was a butterfly, or a butterfly now dreaming he was a man? Makes one to think, doesn't it?"

"Wouldn't you want to be able to just sit around, Nora, and puzzle out things like that? Lot of time to waste, and no petulant thoughts. Just living the essentials?"

"I'm not a deep thinker. No head for it, we O'Haras."

"You think about God."

"It's me faith. It's part of me Omnipresent that's God. Without it, I'm naked as a worm—" Nora made a gesture that could mean anything; despair, doubt, some unthinkable disaster without faith.

"I'm getting to it, Nora. I'm getting closer."

"Without it the world is a nasty piece of work."

Nora enjoyed their talks. Sarah might be living in sin—for her no serious predicament—thank God it wasn't adultery —yet there was a kind of holiness about her. Maybe because she was a piano player of whom they said great things. Maybe she too was troubled. But not like what life did to me, trapped in calamity, drove me to strange habits. Not that Sarah read books like *Stripper's Weekend*, or *Swinging with Jack the Ripper*.

Nora kept her books hidden in a drawer that was stuck, was hard to open. Nights when Sarah couldn't sleep—"just tensions"—they would sit, the two of them, in their nightdresses, drinking hot milk and talking of religion and blind faith, and godheads, and even of saints. Including the wants of women saints who were fried and broiled, cut up most fearfully in their loyalty to Him. The Jews, now, were a hard lot, and were treated hard by Him, it seemed. All the revenging He took on them, and things He asked, like putting the shiv to your own son to test you. Punishing Sodom and Gomorrah, a regular olde London of orgies and vices. No show of pity or generosity as in gentle Jesus.

Mr. Beck would be snoring lightly in the bedroom while they talked. It did them a great good, a good talkout. Until the milk was cold and Sarah yawned. Time for shut-eye.

"Someday, Nora, we'll go off together, you and me, and live the proper life. Would you dare?"

"I suppose not. Let me put away the glasses and you go get some sleep."

"Night."

"God bless," said Nora, setting the glasses on a tray. In her room there was the temptation to open up *The Fancy Flogger and the Gypsy Virgin*. But instead, Nora said her prayers with some added asking of the protection of Mary for herself and for Sarah, and a bit added that Judith would not overeat, or mix up her pills. The housemaids at the Mandersons', where Herself was a houseguest, were a flighty lot. Scandinavian chippies with their blond ponytails and short skirts—arse wriggling, and long legs—horsing with the valet and the butler, giving the big eye to the chauffeur. A horny lot, those Swenskies with their nude sunbathing. A world of illegitimate baby birthings, like rabbit warrens, and porno shops in Copenhagen out in the open and those blue cinemas of detailed carryings-on. Nora added a prayer to have the strength to dispose of her reading matter down the incinerator in the morning. And write a critical letter to Bishop Callahan that that Irish book club needed looking into. It wasn't enough to keep scribblers like Joyce and Shaw and Henry Miller and Burroughs and Beckett out of the hands of innocent children, the young nuns and seminary lads. So, musing over the letter she planned to write—belching a bit from the milk—she fell into a dreamless sleep.

Sarah also slept, curled up against the sleep smell of

Gregory, nuzzling closer, wanting his warmth, his solidness; closer, *closer* so that he came half awake and muttered, "Huh, huh, what?" She said, "Nothing, nothing, darling, sleep." He put an arm around her and soon they both slept in that pleasant discomfort that lovers seem to enjoy. Several times in the night Sarah came awake and was not aware of where she was. Once even of *who* she was. But the closeness of Gregory reoriented her and she felt protected from the secrets of the dark corners of the room that suggested shapes of malice and spite. Lonely souls, Jacob said. It was reasonable to expect the universe was becoming overcrowded and souls would become curious about where they had been. Not—he added, his eyes twinkling—that there was any proof of this in the Kabala or the texts of the Hasidic seers he had studied so far. "But remember, souls don't take up much space—could be small as a mustard seed—so they'll never crowd you."

They usually had tea every afternoon, in what the Mandersons thought of as "The Chinese Room." Sir Aurel Manderson, an uncle of Morris', had been a famous Asian explorer, an archaeologist, who had charted the Cave of a Thousand Buddhas, and brought back woodcut blocks later dated as A.D. 868. He had also collected Han Bronzes and T'ang and Sung pottery. What was left of his collection was arranged on shelves in the room Judith preferred, as a houseguest, for taking tea. Actually, Jacob drank slivovitz, she brandy and they ate smoked salmon on slivers of dark bread, caviar on crackers, and certain knobby sausages from Eastern Europe, enhanced with a little garlic.

"I have sad news for you, Shana."

"Keep it then. I can exist without it."

"It's about Sarah."

"Sari?"

He flicked a crumb from his little beard, two fluttering fingers. "It's this. She is *not* inhabited by a dybbuk."

"Why is that bad?"

"If it were a dybbuk, an incubus that had taken up lodging in her, in a way of speaking, I would have driven it out. Israel ben Eliezer, who became the Baal Shem Tov, had the ritual for that worked out, the true path for *tzaddikim* to drive out the evil spirit."

"You're sure, Jacob? I mean, if not a dybbuk, what is the matter with her?"

"In the writing of the Germatric the premise is that the words of the holy text contain hidden truths, you could call them apocryphal messages. God, for reasons beyond me, works his way in calculated obscurity. *Tova toireh mikol sechoireh*—learning is the best merchandise. But after a certain point the heart, or rather our entrails, take over and learning isn't worth a pinch of snuff. With Sarah, after all my studying of her and talking with her, I see she is not cursed with a demon—no, she is sainted."

"Jews believe in saints? Come now, Jacob. Sari a saint?"

"You have to believe, and why? There is no other answer."

"Still, *why?*"

"Because the Lord has placed a few people of divine illumination here on earth. And only because of them does He permit the world to exist."

"Does she know it?"

"No, the saints do God's bidding without being aware of themselves. That is it, she is unaware, she is one of the *Lamed-vas Tzaddikim.*"

Judith patted Jacob on the closest cheek to her, leaned over and kissed it. "My darling *luftmensch,* we've been drinking too much. I'm beginning to believe you."

BOOK SEVEN

Limbo

The Book of the Lamed-vas Tzaddikim tells us there exists on earth thirty-six saints—but they are unaware of being saints. God permits the world to exist only because of these thirty-six saints. In times of crisis they do God's bidding— and of course the world thinks them mad . . .

JACOB ELLENBOGEN
Waiting for the Messiah

CHAPTER

40

Dr. Knott took Greg Beck to lunch. Voted thumbs down on the Cheshire Cheese, and went across the street from the *Daily Telegraph* to the Sam Weller. Ground floor full of boozing newspapermen, elbow to elbow with two or three birds or bints, as is the popular term. Second floor a buffet of cold meats. A waitress said, "Third floor ha-la-cart. 'Ave a nice bit of buffet in 'ere. Lager, wines, spirits." Agreed on that.

The waitress, a cheerful girl, sat them at a long table. "Lager or the 'arf barrel?"

Greg asked, "What's the best?"

"The 'arf barrel is very well spoken of."

It was good, only it was warm. The waitress explained, "That's 'cause it's from the big pot. Now, what will you eat? We're just out of the crab on the table. But there's 'am, roast beef, tongue, Surrey chicken."

"Do we go to the buffet table?"

"Ol' Nat will cut—I'll serve with a salad. Nat! the crab cum down yet?"

"Ain't down yet, love."

"Anchovies, Norwegian 'erring?"

Ol' Nat *was* old, half blind, pale eyes behind thick glasses. Parkinson's palsy had touched him. Watching him carve was a study in slow motion. They drank 'arf barrel wine (too sweet) and Danzig gold-flecked eau-de-vie (fine).

Dr. Knott asked, "Sarah? Ready for tomorrow?"

"Go and see her."

He said no, was just an observer.

Greg asked what conclusion he had formed about Sarah.

"There are no conclusions, Greg. There are only opinions, prejudices, moods created sour or sweet by habit, the weather, the electrochemical functioning of one's body and mind and nervous system. Some people thought of illness as an absolute. All this rubbing against what is accepted or rejected is something called the reality of the world."

"You're avoiding an answer, Doc."

"I long ago gave up the Aristotelian system of absolute where there *must* be an answer to everything, a reason for all action, a cause for every nuance of existence. Man has accepted that for much of his existence, but often today there is no answer—logic is rarely logic, and the greater cosmic mysteries will most likely never be answered."

"You're not much help, Doc."

He told him not to worry. Truth is, he added, he didn't know what would happen next. Perhaps only a great recital.

[From the journal of Edward Knott]

DECEMBER 14, LONDON:

My collection of press clippings grows. My favorite is an item of pure—the purest—British understatement in the staid London Times. *I copy it complete:*

MAN QUESTIONED AFTER STABBING

Detectives were called to Chelsea Manor Street, S.W., last night after a man, believed to be a postman, was stabbed to death. A man was being questioned.

No name of man suspected, no details or name of the postman.

But this is my favorite.

Anne Hugessen has a dispute raging with Britain's tax authorities for which no one can find a precedent. Miss Hugessen manufactures chastity belts, complete with padlock, and the tax men say they are subject to a 13.75 percent sales tax, like furniture and bookends . . . Miss Hugessen . . . insists they really constitute safety equipment and therefore are tax free.

DECEMBER 15, LONDON:
Have decided not to go to Sarah's concert. Am reading some reports of fertility rites practiced in backcountry America up to the time of WWI.

"In the ritual for planting flax, the farmer and his wife appeared in the field at sunup, both naked, the woman walking ahead, the man sowing. They chanted or sang a rhyme with the line, 'Up to my ass, an' higher too!' Every few steps the man threw some of the seeds against the woman's buttocks. Up and down the field they went, singing and scattering seed, until the planting was done. Then they just laid (sic) down on the ground and had a good time . . . A group of nude turnip growers, four mature girls and a boy, were observed by an old woman at sunrise. 'The boy throwed all the seed and the gals kep a-hollering "Pecker deep! Pecker deep!" And when they got done, the whole bunch would roll in the dust like some kind of wild animals. There ain't no sense to it, but them folks always raised the best turnips on the creek.' There was a perplexed girl who wondered why her neighbors, seemly church going people, insisted on wallowing in the dirt of their freshly plowed garden when they had beds inside their cabin . . ."

In the flat Sarah sat at the piano borrowed from Chalky . . .

Oh, sing unto the Lord a new song: sing unto the Lord all the earth . . . Yes, yes, and sitting at the piano her fingers busy with the Bach that would open her recital in six hours. No, a look at the Biedemeier clock on the fireplace made it five hours and forty minutes, her mind, memory and hands and piano strings carrying on the musical ideas of the long-dead composer. Over the inner tension of her mind were still the lines she had been reading with Jacob Ellenbogen that noon: "I will lift up mine eyes unto the hills, from whence cometh my help."

Cometh, cometh. The fingers pleaded with the keys and the keys brought forth as the hammers struck them, in no conflict and with cohesion, sounds like shrill cicada calling, mixed with the pervasive qualities that were hers when she was playing perfectly. No muscular twinges, no spasms of nausea or the fearful tearing of a headache that signaled an attack of the sadness on the complexity that is the rule of life. Yes, under the mercy and providence of God.

Dispense with technique, piety, Julian Salt had once told her early in their relationship. "Trust the raving of the blood." Oh, the fool and his Stone Age amateur psychiatry.

She sank into delicious languor and yet felt there was something hovering, forgotten, something pressing on her. *Oh, sing unto the Lord a new song.* No stupid advice. Good sound stuff just now. Stupidity is often selfishness. She was selfish. But was it so selfish to be in love, to have love. Life's mischances came, but the game of him, her, body to body was good. A corruption of the flesh? No, just what Aunt Judith would call to live *"comme il faut."* Had this been wrong? Had she offended the Great Master, the omnipotent, impatient God? Love is cunning, daring, and Jacob had told her some *tzaddik* had thought it also had a touch of madness. *Sing unto the Lord all the earth.* Still, a weight came down on her, and what was it, what threatening? Was it the concert just hours away? In this, in pride and in sinful ego, had she challenged God, had announced she would conquer herself, *play* again, *be* again. What now of the new hopes of knowing, feeling, being? *I will lift up mine eyes unto the hills.* (Oh, yeah?) *From whence cometh my help.* (Help, where are you?) I have been wrong. So wrong. Her eyes went to the clock, a foolish thing of green stone and gilt bronze topped by a winged figure in a chariot driving two rearing horses. As she watched, the winged figure swung its whip, the horses in pain reared up higher, the wheels spun, the legs of the horses were blurred. And a spasm of

(332)

apprehension shook her. The room was darker, but as in the negative of a filmstrip. The dark was light and the light dark, and she knew, she knew she must try to hide some place. But, Duty's Child, she shook her head and played on, great ringing chords of sound. She remembered what someone once read to her, or something she had once heard; read, or been told:

The way to innocence, to the uncreated and to God leads on, not back, not back to the wolf or to the child, but ever further into sin, ever deeper into human life.

A hell of a thing to remember now. She would do ten more minutes of practice and have Nora heat some milk, then she'd drink it and lie down. Rest—not think—until the car came for her. Greg was at the hall making sure the lights were right. The dark was gone and the light parts were in shadow again . . . She knew, *knew* for the third time He was coming. Why had she insisted to Greg she wanted to be alone? Why now this chaotic mixture; a concert and the moment of facing the final essentials of her quest? Still, she had greedy expectations, yet a doubt, was it any truer than the crimson oleographed Sacred Heart Nora had on the wall of her room?

The sickness, the puzzling incomprehensions, as Dr. Knott had politely called them, was on her. Her fingers fell away from the keys. No, not now, no dissociated schizoid thinking. Give me your confidence, God—cool, astringent doses of hope.

Lord, I see you, how large you are Lord? How much indeed in your image you made man. And all around me are sounds like famous tenor arias, as if floating on the thick rolling clouds on which God walks slowly toward me—a mile each step, the thousand-mile-high figure in a fluttering of drapes . . . You are not one to go naked, but the laughter is cruel and fortissimo as you thunder at me for my doubts.

He spoke in the ancient tongue of before Abraham and Moses, and in cruel tones that rebuked Job. But in His palm stands Jacob translating. God spoke with taste for essentials.

His eyes were huge purple pools—eyes I had seen one afternoon visiting the London Zoo with Gregory.

How direct His words, and Jacob whispered them to me. Words that whipped me—none of the Protestant *haute bourgeois* comforting patter, none of the Christmas coloration of the Bethlehem theogony.

Sarah wanted to cry out some absurdities of repentance, of asking for mercy, forgiveness for doubts. The world turned sideways and she was slipping, her fingernails clinging to a huge round map, a globe, its surface covered with spar varnish. The very globe of the world that used to stand in the corner of Daddy's study, a room where the calf-backed lawbooks stood in rows. She slid across Europe as she had across Pointer's Pond as a child in icy winter. The Alps were only printed; they raised no bumps to cling to. The Urals resisted her fingernails and Siberia was colored green with a crosshatched line of the trans-Siberian railroad that she and Dody Henderson had traced in the sixth-grade geography class. And in *Music, Third Period,* the voice of the teacher was heard over the howling of the wolves in the snow-covered forests: "Jews have a special musical sense." The sled ran on, the three maddened, frightened horses ready to drop as the driver whipped them up, and a dybbuk was present—came out from the furs that covered him, and the frost vapor that came from his mouth formed Hebrew letters: "We must throw out the passengers to the wolves or we shall not escape."

"No, no, throw me out." But the dybbuk only shook his head, the little moustache and Napoleon III goatee covered with frost rime. Out went Beethoven, the mighty head scowling, the shaggy brow broader than ever. Next out was Mozart, and followed by Debussy and Rachmaninoff. But spare Bach! The great J. S. Take the sons; the wolves' stomachs will never know the difference.

But God insisted that just as He told Abraham to sacrifice his son, so must she, Sarah, obey and prove her faith. It must be Bach. She saw the teeth of the panting wolves biting the wood from the back of the sled, their breath was foul and they were gnawing at their own tongues, blood spurted— blood the color for everything she dreaded. She cried out instead if He *was* God, take my life. Never in love with easeful death, but now *now* God read from a scroll, a pair of old-fashioned silver-rimmed glasses set low on a nose as big as Greenland.

"A time to be born, and a time to die; a time to plant, and a time to pluck up that which is planted. A time to kill, and a time to heal; a time to break down, and a time to build up. A time to weep, and a time to laugh; a time to mourn, and a time to dance. A time to cast away stones, and a time to gather stones together; a time to embrace, and a time to refrain from embracing."

Nora had been ironing a last crease out of the gown for Sarah's recital. You would think they would have caught the creasing along the hem line before they delivered it. But you couldn't get the help no more to give you a fair day's work for a fair day's pay anymore. And she, Nora, with such a headache she was cross-eyed with it, a cloth with vinegar soaked in it bound around her head. No time to groan— there was Sarah to dress and get ready; get one more glass of warm milk into her and assure her her stockings were in order and the hair done right.

The iron seemed to be too hot, a fine time to be scorching anything. She had tossed all the depraving books down the maw of the incinerator in the hall; it smelling of the *Times* burning, herring heads and grapefruit rinds. The filthy curse was all behind her now. She'd bring herself to reconciliation with grace. Oh, how one hungers for consolation. All that foul reading, and she and Sarah together would from now on be—

She, Sarah, falling from the piano stool, a wailing like the keening at a wake; that sound when a bad moment becomes all the problem of the universe rolled into one ball, the size they blow down the horse's throat when it's taken sick.

Nora pulled the iron's cord from the socket, stood the iron on its side—Mary, Mother of God!—and went into the living room, hurrying, pulling the vinegar rag from her head, dropping it any place at all along the way. Sarah was twisted on the floor, all of a lump, one side of her face pressed against the rug, legs loose as on a broken doll dropped down a stair well. But she was alive, all alive-o; mouth twitching and fingers flying about as if she were still on the piano stool, "tickling the ivories," as cousin Tim used to say.

It was Sarah's eyes, wide open, that made Nora cross herself. Kind with wonder, eyes full of understanding, you'd think you were looking at a saint.

CHAPTER

41

Manderson House, London
Oct. 22.

Dear Gertrude:

By this time I'm sure you know the whole grotesque *megillah* of what has gone on here. At least that part the frivolity of the world press has been reporting. The more sensational press has been running a travesty of headlines, like STRANGE DISAPPEARANCE OF PIANIST GENIUS and THOUSANDS RIOT AT HALL AT SUDDEN MYSTERY CANCELLATION OF CONCERT. But the facts that haven't come out are rather fascinating in their own *outré* details. First of all, good old Nora has gone off with Sari someplace. Run off at the moment we don't know where, even if we have told the press that we're well aware of where Sari has gone with a bad attack of shingles. I didn't expect *that* of Nora when I lent her to Sari. Nora is much more than a servant or a companion to me. We share the secret wealth of retrieved time. She's someone more than a person who takes care of the little amenities that, together, become the larger comfort for me. In our nearly thirty years together, we have become a kind of women's republic of two. I put this desertion of me to a glandular imbalance, or the change of life.

But you want to know, I'm sure, what really happened. I was dressing for the concert at around seven, aided by one of the Manderson maids. The Mandersons are in Scotland grouse shooting. Old Morris said to me before he left a week ago, "I'd rather be at the recital, being of Jewish descent. But I'm expected by the tenants and beaters, as a third generation Englishman, to be on the moors when the season opens." So concert night I was just wondering about a string of pearls to wear, or the ruby clips, when Gregory Beck came rushing in, looking as if someone had suggested he was ready for Extreme Unction. The most shocked human being I've ever seen. In real agony.

"She's gone. Gone off."

I said, "Who?" like a fool.

And he said, "Sari," and he added, "She, this afternoon, wanted to rest, be alone before the concert, take a nap. And I was at the hall making sure the lights and the sound shields were properly in place. When I went back to the flat to get her, she and Nora were gone."

Again, like a fool, all I could say was, "Nora gone? Whatever for?"

He handed me a note written on the back of a sheet of music. I have it here as I write. It's in Nora's nun's training elementary school script.

Darling Greg:
Nora is writing this for me. In some ways I'm all on ends, in other ways, fine and I'm packing to leave London at once. No concert of course. Don't worry, I'm sure, damn sure, I'm psychologi-

cally sound, I've just gone through an amazing experience, and am still shaking with the staggers, so much, I can't hold a pen. Have confidence, dear love, I am not mad, but I have come around to accepting God totally: Even if none of us are never meant to understand the whole design. I don't feel that I am psychic, but I have been chosen.

I can't give the concert now, perhaps never. Perhaps, perhaps [three words I can't make out] and so I'm sorry for all those people I disappoint, but I must go my own way, not self-indulgent but in awe. And, Greg, just now without you. Forgive the strange irrelevancies of this cockeyed note. While it may to you seem mixed up, for me and for Nora we've made a sort of pact, both feeling we're changing our lives in a most spiritual way. As for you, me, remember quoting Nietzsche, "what is done out of love takes place beyond good and evil."

Of course I love, substantially in essence as before, there is a new understanding, a vital one in myself. Don't try to find me just now, I must go along the new way . . . But some point in the future, you, me, we . . .

That's all to Sari's letter. But there is a footnote by Nora herself, as herself.

Dear J.P.

This above writing is not actually word for word what Miss Pedlock dictated, but not wanting to act shirty, just wrote what I made of her talking and dictating, and what I could make sense of with my own bit of education. After her words, *me, we* in the note, I couldn't make out head nor tail of her message. It was not at all plain, and with her talking lickety split, words running together. So I am sorry there is not more of her message from her. But you'll get the gist of

(339)

it, I'm most sure. You may think me all flummoxed myself to be going off like this with her, but I too have had a big change, and have seen my own way through a mean time and a hard horror it was. But I'll not bother you with its detail, not here. I regret after all the years to leave you like this, so sudden like, but the path I take is the one I shall follow and I will say a prayer for your well being. God take you under his wing.

Yours,
Nora Mary Margaret O'Hara.

Of course, Gertrude, I feel Nora she'll be back. She's a good soul, full of facile moralizing—Irish sentimentality. And knows I need her and she needs me. Our lives have been interwoven for too long a time. Meanwhile I have Gregory on my hands. He's taken it fairly well after the first mean shock. But is restless, calling airports, checking shipping lines, harassing Dr. Knott to alert clinics all over the world in case they hear from her. In other words, while he appears normal on the surface, he's badly unstrung inside. No doubt he deeply loves Sari. It has done something drastic, he claims, to his life. Set up a complexity of reflexes, drives, impulses. He confessed to me something of *his* past that I may tell you when I see you again. Meanwhile, we don't dare go outside—as the press and cameramen haunt us. It's all really a fantastic sensation here in England. The concert canceled at the last minute, Sari gone, and all kind of rumors spreading. None of them true (I hope).

I told Gregory there was no use checking ports or air flights. Nora, after all her years with me, in traveling and arranging passage and space for us, is an expert at these things, and has Irish IRA ways of doing things, getting special secret favors, with a folded $5.00 bill, and her knowledge of things. So I'm sure they both slipped away somehow unnoticed. I suspect they went

(340)

north to Scotland and from there went to Ireland, and from there no one knows. So far. It's all exciting, and yet painful—more than just *démodé*.

Dr. Knott has talked to Sari's parents by overseas phone, and they will most likely fly over tomorrow. Jacob Ellenbogen is very attentive and is making calls to the various Hasidic brotherhood around the world to watch out for her, in case she wants to continue the study of mystic Hebrew lore. The brotherhood of Baal Shem Tov are expert diamond cutters you know, and form a close knit Talmudic Mafia and know each other.

Dr. Knott keeps saying we should not have permitted the recital. And he alone should have attended to Sari, he being so aware all was not well—we didn't need a professor to tell us that. It's easy for him to say *now*. I think his damn professional pride was bruised by us having Jacob teach her Hebrew lore and the wisdom of the Jewish seers. Dr. Knott will come to a *messa meshina*.

I'm having Charles rush to London. He's in Switzerland on some rabbinical research mission, a bit let down, I fear, as he wasn't last time elected president of the world body. But they hung honors on him, enough decor to please a Congo tribal chief. Also coming here to confer, while on his way to Brussels, is Judge Woody Pedlock, Sari's father's brother, as I've radioed him to stop over for a family coffee-klatsch over this crisis. We shall have to take some drastic action now. We can't let Sari go roaming over the world in her condition, whatever it is. Being God-intoxicated is a fearful burden, Jacob claims.

I have been so involved, so busy warding off reporters, hiring an investigating agency to go out to hunt for Sari, that I feel nearly young again. Not as I have been myself around the last few years, just as the custodian of a ruin, myself.

Ignore press stories on all this. I'll keep you posted. Pinch the cheeks of the grandchildren for me and give regards to Saul. I don't like what you write in your last letter of your new diet; I've tried them *all*. The only one that works is a *jour maigre*—pushing yourself away from the table a half hour early, three times a day.

Love,
Judith.

Judge Woodrow Pedlock of San Francisco, and his wife, Nell, had been on their way to Brussels, where the judge was going to advise on some legal rights of enlisted men, American troops attached to NATO. Judith's cable had rerouted them to London where a family meeting was being held in the matter of the disappearance of his niece, Sarah Pedlock.

Judith had reserved a suite for the meeting at The Inn on the Park, and as the morning sun gave up its efforts, and a light London rain began to fall, the judge and Judith sat drinking coffee while waiting for Rabbi Charles Pedlock, Dr. Knott, Gregory Beck to join them. Nell was gone shopping, and Jacob Ellenbogen had begged off attending, on the phone.

"I am not a member of the family, and you have a rabbi coming, and a learned judge. Enough is enough, Shana."

"Jacob, you're like family to me—better than family at times—and you'll like Woody. He's a judge with sense."

"Which is better than mercy, say the sages. Later I'll meet him. And don't call it a crisis—say it's a situation—sounds better."

Judith had wanted Jacob present, but she knew the beautiful little man was stubborn. And while he was wise, perhaps to men like the judge and Rabbi Charles Pedlock, he spoke in a way they might feel unworldly.

Judge Pedlock put down his coffee cup. He was a strikingly handsome man in a florid Western manner: at his prime. She suspected he sometimes regretted leaving the law firm of Pedlock, Hayes, Macklin & Pedlock for the bench. But Nell, a rigid Episcopalian with social aspirations, wanted to see him some day of national reputation, seated as "the Jewish member" of the United States Supreme Court.

Judith held up the coffee pot. The judge waved it aside. "Before the rest get here, am I to understand you are seriously considering suggesting the girl should be committed? My brother Linc and Fran are flying in tomorrow and of course they would have the final say, but it will be a shock."

"I'm against a legal commitment. Before the wailing and the hand wringing, Woody, begins, I want to present the facts today to a kind of family hearing. We want Sarah to go back to America—so we need to use pressure."

"Even so, threatening to commit a person, Judith, needs a certificate from two doctors, and a signing of the commitment papers by a judge."

"I know that. Sari has had to have an examination by Lloyd's doctors to get insurance coverage for the concert. Leon Solly insisted he be protected in case the concert didn't go on. Well, it didn't."

The judge twirled his watch chain from which hung a Phi Beta Kappa key, a small gold nugget given him by a client—now, alas, in federal prison—and the seal of the Golden Union Club of San Francisco. It was not just a display of vanity; the judge used the dangling objects as a kind of worry beads, fingering them when faced with a serious problem, theories and hypotheses of human behavior.

"I gather, Judith, you've talked to the examining doctors?"

"Snotty types, very broad A. Their reports on her nervous condition, call it her general neurotic make-up, are enough. But these Harley Street clowns, they—"

"They will refuse to certify her as she's an American?"

"That's right, Woody; however, for a fee, I have a copy of their examination and if we can get Sari back to New York, that, and Doctor Zimmerman, our longtime family specialist, will go along with Linc and Fran if they—*not* we—decide on this thing."

"I'm sure he will," said the judge dryly.

"Woody, I'm not a Pedlock. You are. It's an irrational family matter." She sighed. "Maybe I went about it all wrong. Taking her on this trip, trusting her to Dr. Knott, saying he'll—oh, it seemed such a good ingenious idea."

"He'll also sign the certificate, Doctor Knott?"

"It's just to scare her to go home." She twisted a lock of her freshly set hair. "Doc, he's a little *meshuga* himself."

"Oh, fine, the mad leading the mad. Sounds like the UN," said the judge, rising and going to the large window overlooking Hyde Park. "Just dandy . . . These soldiers down there on horses, in the red coats and silver helmets, go by here every day?"

"The Royal Horse Guards, morning and evening. I think maybe you can convince Edward, Doctor Knott, that it's up to Linc and Fran."

There was a knock on the door and Judith called out, "Enter," and Gregory, unshaved, carrying his topcoat and hat, came in. "Anything? Any word?"

"No, Greg, nothing. This is Judge Woodrow Pedlock, Sari's uncle. Woody, Gregory Beck. I told you about him."

The two men shook hands. The judge with a cheerful look he didn't feel, and Gregory with a glum face. "Young man, your face is damn familiar. The name too."

"I've been in California courtrooms." He looked at Judith. "I've told Judith the whole story."

The judge alerted his eyebrows and they rose like shades. His mouth curled ironically at one corner. He tapped Gregory on the shoulder. "Of course, right as rain, I remember. Caused a sensation in our neck of the bay, Judith. My boy, you had rotten legal advice and namby-pamby experts. If it had been in front of me, I'd have asked the state to get firmer evidence over a rifled grant, or I'd toss it out of court on its ass. However, we're not here to cut up old legal touches."

"No, we're not. I want to find Sarah. This is all a case of nerves. She shouldn't have planned a concert. Maybe never play one again."

"Easy for us non-artists to say. But they feel, I gather, the chosen to be the intermediate between the universe and man."

"In a way, judge, yes."

Rabbi Charles Pedlock arrived, carrying a furled umbrella and a wet bowler hat. He had not unfurled the umbrella, fearing it would look awkward when raised and ungraceful when rerolled.

"Just got in from Heathrow. Plane an hour late. Judith, how are you—Woody—Gregory?"

They both nodded, as if to admit that they were fine would be out of place at such a family gathering, under present conditions. Dr. Knott came in just behind him, to be introduced.

Charles Pedlock was a bit put out at being called to London by his stepmother, but he only kissed her cheek and gave her an affectionate look. He had been in Zurich with Netta Rosegold, the publicity girl for the rabbinical groups, looking over a collection of old Torah covers going back to the ninth century that were for sale. He had been thinking of sticking Dov Ganzler, the sourpuss art collector/millionaire on the coast, with the cost of buying them for the temple. What a depraved species art collectors were.

He addressed Judith. "I know something has to be done with Sarah. I'm sorry it has come to a head. A bad moment, yes?"

"As long as you don't see it, rabbi," said Dr. Knott, "as a wrestling match between science and faith."

"Eh?" Charles hadn't been listening. Netta Rosegold had proved to be a most delightful handmaiden, and away from her duties a more simple girl than one would imagine, once the veneer of Madison Avenue and Hollywood had been dropped, like a dressing gown. He smiled as he thought of the evening before, when—Judith broke his images of the hour in his room examining the catalog of the Torah covers, and he asking Netta for her advice on which she liked best.

Judith said: "It's rally round the family flag, gentlemen."

Judith filled Charles and Dr. Knott in with what they had been talking about. Charles said, as if discovering a new facet about Sarah, "She perhaps should not have planned to give a concert again."

The judge seemed to be brooding: "Wisdom after the facts. Let's see that medical examination report, Judith. You've read it, Beck?"

"No."

Judith produced a batch of papers in a blue cover tied with a red ribbon. "Very British," said the judge, taking it. He read it, Gregory read it. They talked about it. Quoted from it.

Dr. Knott stood in his hairy tweed jacket dewed with raindrops. He shook out his cloth hat as he waved off the report.

"Hogwash, besides I've read it. Insurance company hoopla. As scientific as the ancient Greeks reading the entrails of a chicken for omens from the gods."

Judge Pedlock cocked his head to one side, studied Dr. Knott's face as the doctor poured himself a brandy from a bottle on a tray.

"You wouldn't sign a certificate of restraint for Sarah Pedlock on this kind of a report?"

"I didn't say that." The doctor sipped the brandy, sniffed it, took another tot. "If all parties want her put away"—he shrugged his shoulders—"I might, just *might*."

Gregory shouted, "On just two insurance doctors' hasty opinions?"

"Please," said Judith, "this is a human being—not medical tests."

The judge said, "Two medical opinions—that's all it needs. Of course, the girl could ask for a hearing."

Judith pursed her lips. "It is a difficult thing to talk about. It's easy to say damn the Pedlock family name . . . But I will never permit her being locked up here in England."

The judge held up a hand, Gregory caught the glint of light reflected on a blue stone cuff-link. "Just what truly is her condition at this moment, Doctor? To the best of your knowledge?"

"Am I on the stand, your honor? To know all that, at this moment, judge, I'd have to put salt on her tail to catch her first. But from the time I've spent with her professionally, studied her in detail, I'd say to the world she'd appear mad. Insanity, as you know, your honor, is only a legal term, *not* a medical one. Madness? I'm not going to smoke up the air here with medical and physiological terms; simply that madness comes in various degrees. And what is mad to you, is not mad to me, and what I think a bit paranoiac, you may think just cute and—well, never mind."

"God," said Charles, "seemed mad to some."

"In a nutshell, Doctor Knott," said the judge. "I will absolve you from being committed to what you say now. Christ, you're making me sound stuffy—pass the brandy."

"Thank you; absolved? very legal. It's like this. Creative people are often strung so tight they give off strange tunes. They could be borderline cases, say whacked pious, saints, monsters, painters, composers, fanatical leaders. They live on a level where their nerves scream like a steam siren—for them. Sometimes they take drugs or to drink, or to strange relationships with the universe, rocks live."

Judith said, "These commitment papers are only to scare Sari to get back to America for treatment."

"Yes," said Dr. Knott. "What she needs and must have is intensive psychiatric care. The sooner we get her back to the United States and into a good sanitarium for some particularly sophisticated treatment the better."

"What hope is there?" asked Gregory.

Dr. Knott shrugged. "There is a Doctor Millheim, a former *Mitarbeiter* of Karl Jung's, who has done well with a congeries of neuroses. Let's face it, if we threaten to commit her here, it should make her prefer to go back to the United States and a sanitarium. I know that the threat of commitment is mean, but isn't there a saying you laymen use, 'for her own good'?"

Judith frowned. "Please, no mockery, Doctor Knott. Clearly you've made a decision about just how far she has gone into—*what?*"

"If you all want clinical words, very well. Sarah is often hallucinating; she is in an advanced form of delusional psychoneurosis. It requires particularly prolonged treatment at this stage, a condition which has gone much beyond what existed when we got on that ship. But intensive psychiatric care which can only be given her in some kind of confinement. It doesn't have to be legal commitment."

Gregory said, "Damn. All those clinical terms—love and care are what she needs. Understanding!"

"What kind of hallucinating?" asked Judith.

"Angels can help do the dishes. One can hold special conversation with the godhead; Joan of Arc, De Gaulle, Mary Baker Eddy, Dostoevsky, Kafka. We square folk could, in the right to protect society, and if the wind is right, certify any of them if we dared."

"And the girl," asked Charles.

"She's certifiable," said the judge. "Legally."

"You sonofabitch!" It was Gregory up on his feet, charging the judge. The judge, moving quickly, skillfully side-stepped the blow Gregory swung at him and, as he did, the judge took a swift chop at the side of Gregory's neck with the side of his right hand. The body fell to the rug with no thud, just a thump. The judge smiled sadly. "I've been lunged at by Mafia hoods and switchbladed by Black Panthers, and crooked cops had some ideas to do me in. So I work out three times a week, Judith, in a gym and take karate lessons."

Judith looked down at Gregory risen to his knees, shaking his head and moaning.

"You a black belt, Woody?"

"No, but nearly. I'm sorry, young fella, but I have a glass jaw, can't take a chance."

Charles Pedlock abhorred violence but kept quiet.

Dr. Knott was laughing as he handed Gregory a half glass of brandy. "Here, clear your head, Greg."

Gregory refused the drink and stood up, brushing his disordered hair out of his eyes. "I'm going to find her. We're getting married. We'll go live where you damn busybodies can't touch us."

"Very gallant," said Dr. Knott. "Nothing like unrationed optimism."

"Greg," said Judith, "oh, how I feel for you."

Gregory turned, wobbly somewhat, and started for the door. The judge flexed his fingers. "You'll be all right. I didn't lay it on to kill."

Gregory and the judge looked at each other, standing four feet apart. Gregory went out quickly, carefully closing the door behind him so it didn't slam.

Dr. Knott examined his wet hat. "Hopeless romantic gesture. You don't see many of them anymore."

"Hopeless?" asked Charles. "It's a point of view."

"There is always a way, isn't there, rabbi?" Dr. Knott said. "To prove us all fools in our judgments."

"You believe that?" asked the judge.

"Not positively, just firmly."

Judith slapped her thighs with her ringed fingers. "Linc and Fran must decide—she's their child that's lost."

"Lost?" said Dr. Knott, putting down his glass. "In some silly way I wish I were Gregory going on his hunt. But then I've always been a romantic horse's ass. The bittersweet of that failing has kept me from the dreadful reality of this bucket of ashes we live on."

Rabbi Pedlock, to counteract this idea, began to think of some splendid quote from the *Reader's Digest* or Old Testament, to show man's great debt to the Creator. All he could think of was "The thorn outlives the rose."

No good at all.

CHAPTER

42

Gregory felt again that he had become the locked-away-man. A prisoner contained only in himself. It was as it had been at San Q, and even later, before meeting Sarah; that he existed unto himself with himself. What was the world seemed again outside of his range of feeling and being. That had changed with Sarah, there had been a blossoming (if, he thought, one could think in those old-fashioned terms), yes, a blossoming, a blooming. A feeling of being part of the whole. There had been a relentless thrust accelerating love for another human being. Being needed and doing.

He had in no way resented the change caused by loving, serving Sarah. The widening of interests and sensation had been a rebirth, a going forth. Now, as he sat in the empty flat, alone, again he was the locked-away-man. All the sad, gloomy emotions of existing in a dark corner, and the darkness inside him matched the dank blackness, the gloom of the bad London weather. He had always suspected that the weather in Dickens' novels, in the Sherlock Holmes stories, were cunning inventions of their authors to thicken the atmosphere of their plots, the heightening atmosphere of their dramas. But it was *all* true, damn it; this tacky, unpleasant pea soup color, the greasy drizzle on the stone walks. The pockets of fog were actually there, not made for literature, but because it was the nature of this island, the wet, imbecile façade of a strange city.

He wanted to go away at once to find Sarah. But where to begin? He had never felt so alone, so much in need of the one person who had liberated him once before from the locked-in cell of himself. Upstairs someone was playing a recording of *Carmen.* *"Là-bas, là-bas, dans la montagne!"*
The reality, the exalting reality he had known on the ship and in Italy, the days of preparing for the concert, were lost. Now it was the dismal fantasy that locked around him, the kind he had sunk into in his prison cell. Where the shared smell of men and their foul leavings, the harsh lights, the clang of iron on iron, *jong jong* on *jong* had been mixed with bad dreams, idle hopes. And wondering just *what* had actually happened. There were times then when he was sure he had murdered Agnes. Could recall in the dark cold nights the intense voices of their final bickering, the lifting of what was it? The bronze reproduction of the Winged Victory, or Grandpa's old blackthorn cane with the lethal lead inserted under the brass tip; the old man had bought it in Singapore? A stick Gregory had cherished since boyhood and claimed as his own. Both items, statue and cane, didn't seem to be on the inventory—if he remembered—when they came to sell his assets to pay the legal fees for his defense. Were they on the bottom of San Francisco Bay? Or had he imagined melodrama? *("Là-bas, là-bas.")*
There were times, of course, when he was not sure he had not killed her. And if he had, was it an accident? A shove, a blow, her head fallen hard against the old blacksmith's irons they used as andirons in the boulder fireplace? It was never too clear in court, or out, if his lawyers actually felt him innocent. It was at those times that his conviction of the crime was clearly in the cards, that he felt strongest he had

not done it. When Agnes' face was not before him. When he couldn't remember what she looked like, then he wondered, yes or no?

Now with Sarah gone, sitting alone in this stormy city, he again had a sense, a feeling of crime behind him. He must not think of it. No. He had *not* killed his wife. Someday a tramp, a madman would confess. In novels he read as a boy, they usually did tell the truth on their deathbeds. If the murderer was a young man, Gregory felt he would have a long time to wait for that confession.

So he didn't want to sink again into the living nightmare of a wife killer. He would have to find Sarah. He looked out at what was left of the day, a period never really daylight, now smothering itself in a deeper darkness in which street lights, reflections from signs, reds and greens, were visible in an aspic just before more fog blotted them out. He began to pack a bag. It was Sarah he had to find. First of all for herself—those Pedlock bastards and bitches—they must never lock her away. They did not know her, understand her as he did. All the times—he, she, they had been locked together in love, skin to skin. All the strange personal dialogues they had poured into each other's ears in serious or amused whispers. The days and the nights they had woven together intimate, decent, indecent, the close living —into making two lives one. How explain that to doctors, to a Karaitic crazy judge? All would end with certification— end in a walled institution, hard-faced nurses with needles loaded full of vegetable existence to shoot into warm living flesh.

He retched, tasted bile, packed shirts, slacks, some underwear, a ball of socks. He examined a small royalty check from the textbook publisher and the six hundred dollars that Sarah in her rush to leave had left between the pages of a Mozart score; one more of her odd hiding places. But where was he to go? To begin the hunt? (*"Dans la montagne . . . là-bas."*)

He put on the damp topcoat and hat, pushed the hat onto the back of his head, sat in a deep chair, legs spread-eagled on the worn rug. Thinking. Where? where? would she and Nora O'Hara head for the Greek Islands? Spain? South America?

He picked up a phone directory and turned pages to hunt up the phone numbers of American Express, Air France, Thomas Cook, others. Sarah was crafty, imaginative. She would find some way to cover her tracks, circle back, or hide her identity. He would call American Express first. He tried out an opening line of inquiry in his mind. ("Pardon me, I'm trying to trace, for personal reasons"—No. "On a vital business matter"—No. "A tragedy in the family"—yes, better—"a Sarah Pedlock who in the last two days may have—")

He put his hand down on the phone to lift it from its cradle, and it rang. Sarah, of course . . . calling, informing him in that whisper of hers whereabouts he could join her. He lifted the phone feeling the adrenaline doing its booster work in his system.

"Hello, Sa—"

"Hello, Greg, old man, that you?"

"Chalky?"

"Right as rain. You all right? You sound in a flap of some sort."

"Sarah's gone and—"

"Damn well she is—the whole town knows that. Big dust-up in the press and musical circles. Oh, it's just not done, you know, I mean waltzing off like that leaving the rest of us holding the baby."

"Have you any idea, Chalky, where she could have gone to?"

"Was just going to ask you about something she called me for. Oh . . . about three hours before the concert. Been up to my arse with some musical festival in Manchester till now."

"What, damn it, man, what? I'm off my nut with worry."

"She asked me to ship her a piano, a little Knabe she liked, crate it and ship it to . . . damn it, hold on while I find the blazing bloody memo."

Gregory grasped the phone hard. He heard Chalky

Charters breathing that special British breathing he seemed to cultivate, almost an accent to it, a languidly polite complaint.

"Chalky."

"Hold your water . . . Ah, yes. Salzburg, that's Austria, you know." There were queer dissonances on the phone. "Yes, sure it's Austria."

"Any address?"

"The Bad Ruchenhall Hof. Can hardly read my own writing. Yes, Salzburg."

"Thanks, Chalky. Look, don't give that address to anyone . . . I mean the family. They want to put her away and—"

"Understand you perfectly . . . Oh, bad show. Called you, as it's going to cost sixty pounds to crate and ship that piano—and that has to be paid in advance. Sorry."

"Hold the piano until you hear from me. I'll be there in a day or so. Salzburg."

"Don't know if you'll catch her there. Said she was going to be there in the spring—wanted the piano there when she turned up, and to mark it for storage."

"I'm flying out tonight. If you hear anymore, anything, from this end, let me know at the Bad Ruchenhall. I'll keep in touch. I'll find her.

Chalky made a deep throat noise and Gregory could picture him standing there among his gilt and polished antique musical instruments, dressed for business, eying the passing birds; gray waistcoat, thin gold chain across it, a Players smoldering between his fingers. Chalky's voice was full of warmth.

"Bound to find her, I'm sure. Luck and all that. You crazy Americans."

Gregory hung up and spun around, not inspecting the room but rather in his mind's eye seeing the green-bordered road between Innsbruck and Salzburg, the village of Lofer—the sough of oak boughs in a breeze—and beyond. Maybe she was in Vienna? She had spoken of the Imperial Palace, the Gumppoldskichen. But she had also mentioned the Convent of Las Descalzas Reales in Madrid, and, goddamn it, they had talked of *too* many places.

He called British Overseas Airways and asked about a plane for Austria, Salzburg. A voice told him there was a plane at 10:15 that night—if fog permitted takeoff—with stops at Heidelberg and Lucerne. He made a reservation. Adding a few items to his bag, he wrote a note for the daily—a nice old number—who did the flat. He thought of a letter to Judith, but decided against it. What could she or any of the family feel, know—truly know—about himself and Sarah? As his grandfather had once expressed the personal injuries we take in this world, quoting someone he'd read. "What does it matter, as long as the wounds fit the arrows?"

The Manderson Silver Cloud Rolls-Royce moved with the respect its driver felt it deserved, through the traffic on its way to Heathrow Airport. The Mandersons were still residing in Scotland, but the car and its London chauffeur were for Judith's use and her guests. She was not one of the four passengers, having felt, she had told Judge Pedlock, "No use making a mob scene of it when you meet Linc and Fran. Besides, they might resent what has happened with me having been in charge of Sari."

"Nonsense," said Nell Pedlock, wife of the judge. "But you may be right about too much of a crowd of us." So it was the judge and Nell, Rabbi Charles Pedlock and Dr. Knott who were on their way to Sarah's parents at the end of a flight to England from Washington's Dulles Airport.

The judge was wondering how Linc and Fran would take the news that there was yet no sign of their daughter's whereabouts. They would play it, the judge thought, by ear. There was a solid hardness about Linc, as there had to be to remain the District Attorney of Hawley County, Maryland, on the Eastern Shore. The judge remembered splendid shore dinners, the terrapin stews, the great scarlet lobsters in their armor, and he recalled to the times of their youth together, two lean overearnest brothers and a widowed mother, the hard years plugging away to get through law school on slender means. And how, since then, the law had swallowed them both up, giving them little time in their

(355)

youth for their wives and families. Now . . . he smiled at Nell and pressed her hand.

"We'll take off for Brussels," she said. "Be firm, Woody, don't get fly-papered into staying on here."

"We'll see."

"There is nothing to be done until she's found."

"We'll see."

Dr. Knott, his cane between his legs, winced. "Perhaps it's better if she is not found. It could be she'll be better off trying to find herself."

"Is that possible, Doctor?" asked Charles. "I mean, after all, if in her condition."

"Hell, rabbi, her—what you call?—the problem of her condition, isn't going to change if we do find her. There is a key in her back being turned tighter, tighter, and if the spring breaks, flies loose . . ."

"It could get worse I mean, after all."

"It's at its worst right now," said Dr. Knott, and turned away to look at the green countryside rapidly being darkened like a stage set's lighting, shifting the mood of a drama. No use trying to explain to these laymen that whatever Sarah's state of mind, it wasn't something you could chart like a fever or steam pressure. Anything could happen. Not for the best, very likely. Dr. Knott was in a bad mood, was surly like a dog. He hadn't written up his journals in three days and he felt now they—the texts of his journals—would be his major work. Someday, perhaps, they would be printed (what had survived of them). He grimaced at the thought of the loss of the first forty years of them—over fifty huge volumes left in his boarded up Berkshire cottage, and finding them ten years ago, practically all chewed up, eaten by mice and silverfish. Mere piles of pulp and droppings, not aided by a leaking roof.

Gone, gone, all the prancing years of his prime, all the seemingly valid ideas and adventures, foolish, prolonged, yet hardly regretted. All the details of one man's journey through time and space. Still, about a dozen volumes would remain—the tail end of a life—with tin cans tied on it? All passion spent, (nearly) all ideals warped, all hope, if not abandoned, at the best embalmed in doubts, rimmed in ironic comment. Still, still enough left to amuse posterity. Not that he was a Pepys or a Gibbon. Just *what* was he? He didn't feel able to try to answer that one now, riding in this luxury jitney.

"I would suggest," he said, "we don't all overwhelm her parents with all of us talking at once. I feel the judge or the rabbi should take over. I'll add a few well-chosen heart-warming nothings, if you feel I should."

Charles Pedlock pulled down his yellow waistcoat, cleared his throat. "I suppose some spiritual condoling would be in order. Woody, are they practicing Jews?"

"What the hell does that matter?"

"A great deal. I wouldn't want to impose myself on them if they would be offended, or put them out of countenance by what I would say. But if I had a clue—"

"Agnostics," said Nell, crossing her fine legs and wondering if she could get the judge out of this family hassle. She was Episcopalian—and the judge sardonically went along with that—but wasn't really a church member, although she had tried, Lord knows, yes, she had tried. Now when it seemed there was gossip, only gossip, mind you, that Judge Pedlock might get "the Jewish seat," in the next vacancy on the Supreme Court, it was a good thing he hadn't fully affiliated. She remembered from her college class in History Four the remarks of a French Protestant prince when offered the throne if he converted: "Paris is worth a Mass." But better not say that to her husband. Woody was still Jewish enough, even with, was it a Baptist mother? to have that damn Jewish sense of honor, pride in moral integrity you found in certain of the race; not that all had it. Not the screenwriters, the sharp wheeler-dealers, the anteater-nosed tax lawyers of Los Angeles. She had tried to steer Woody properly into the nonlegal world demanding changing approaches. But he was stubborn, and Nell took pride in that too, she supposed, when it didn't rile her when first married. The hunt club set, and the yachting crowd and the real Native Sons (Woody had promised not to quote the old San Francisco lines "The 49ers married the Barbary Coast whores and sired the Native Sons"). The best people had

(357)

been standoffish about the Pedlocks at first, but accepted them in the end and their son Rufus (named after Woody's great teacher, Rufus Martindale, law professor). And in the last ten years, face it, her friends told her, being Jewish had become almost an IN thing, fashionable, with Lennie Bernstein, that cutie-pie, Woody Allen, Barry Goldwater (well, wait, could you count him in *or* out?). Nell yawned. It had been a good life, and would be better, and she focused in on her Washington hopes, then felt ashamed of herself, just a bit. She knew the judge's rigid values, codes; it wasn't going to be too easy to get him to go along with the ragtail doers and movers, the sharks, the ass-kissers in the national capital.

She said, "The truth is, rabbi, Fran has always considered herself Christian, as did her parents."

"Ormsbee *used* to be Ornstein, wasn't it?"

"Oh, I suppose that's just country club gossip." Nell settled back. What the hell was wrong with being Christian, what was wrong with being Jewish? What the hell was wrong with being human? Nice people in both groups, and a lot of shitheels too.

The rabbi gave her a tolerant look, and patted her well-formed golf tanned hands clasped in front of her. "I suppose just us being there, a family, will be enough to buck them up. You're so right, Nell."

A beautiful woman, this Nell Pedlock, a little past her prime, the rabbi decided. But still that look of a sensual woman, *chic* too, if chic meant what it had meant once. *Saftig* was too vulgar. He wasn't one of those rabbis who merely recited the wisdom of the Torah and the comments of the Talmud, and was firm about ritual and points of dogma. He hoped not. Modern Judaism was for him a living, vital force, in good taste, in step with the times. A transmission belt, as he saw it, between an older view of a hairy godhead and a more up-to-date version. Human, not computerized—but with it, as the teen-agers put it. He hoped he was a man of understanding. He knew his weaknesses, his failing at times; he was human, all too human. But perhaps that only helped him understand the catastrophic problems of others. It's not self-satisfaction in my position, my community duties. No, no, thought it almost self-pity at the best I can do. Not that it's a record to shame one. He refused to think of Netta Rosegold waiting for him in Zurich with the lists of ancient schul relics he wanted for his temple collection. And he always almost succeeded in not thinking of her, her grace, her Fifth Avenue charm, pert city-wise face as she listened to him explain some point in Reform Judaism. She a new version of a proper handmaiden out of the Old Testament.

The Rolls Royce was approaching the airport in the fast-gathering dark. The weather had cleared, the fog was mostly gone, just ghost wrappings in far corners. The traffic had thickened under the blue-purple sky, a sky, Nell thought, the color of the inner skin of a Concord grape. There were a rash of green and red lights, some revolving. Two planes were landing and one taking off with a *swoosh*, quite close, the jet pods sending out trails, gray-green, in the night lights, and the probing headlights of cars seeking entrance to the airport platforms.

Dr. Knott, feeling a stiffness in his knees, felt alien to this Rolls Royce of Jews—Nell seemed to have acquired a protective coloration like a captive princess in the House of David. He wondered what his Prince would have thought of them all. The Prince had never believed that any but Italian Jews had any claims to the true faith of those who made the Exodus and hadn't settled in Spain or Italy. "The rest are camp followers, beyond the fringe. Mongrels, Eduardo, they are merely retaining the outer forms, but the true core of the Temple's fire no longer warms them. The Jews of the next centuries will become something else; what, I don't know. Even if still called Jews by the rest of the world, but not *Jews*, if you follow my thinking, Eduardo."

Dr. Knott decided that the Jews were the most perfectly adjusted snobs and moralists in the world. As the Rolls came to a stop and a porter opened the car door, he decided to hang back a bit and merely observe. Nothing can be decided, nothing to be judged. He felt alone and melancholy and among total strangers.

(359)

Judith and Jacob were taking a late-night walk, arm in arm, down St. James Street.

"I'm so upset about everything."

"A *Kiddush* and *broche* on a Friday night it isn't."

"Where will she go, what will she do?"

"Shana, who knows on what sea we drift, what tide moves us?"

"Is there something that directs us, gives us comfort in our needs?"

"No matter what we get, it isn't enough. We're greedy. Let me tell you a story. They say it happened to a Jewish grandmother and her little grandson. On a fine afternoon they were walking on the shore by the sea, all dressed in their sabbath best. A happy scene—the old woman, the young innocent child. Then out of the waters came a huge wave. What can I tell you, it swept up the little boy and, before you could say Moise Rebeinoo, took him away with it into the sea. Quick like that. The grandmother, in horror, could only look up towards God someplace, all seeing, above the blue sky. 'Why him, God!' she cried out. 'Why a young child who has his whole life ahead of him. In your wisdom, why him? when you could have me. I've lived enough. I beg of you, me a pious old woman, don't let this happen.' And with that plea there was a blast of thunder like a thousand ram horns, and the wave was back and the little boy with it, and spat him out. Wet, yes, but left on the shore. With a few slaps by the grandmother, she had all the water out of him."

"If one had faith, Jacob, like her, a very pious old grandmother, to get what she wanted from God."

"But like all of us, was she satisfied? With the grandson safe in her arms, and him breathing again, a little pale, but brought back from the sea, she looked up again towards God and she said, sternly, 'There was a hat, too.'"

AN
AFTERWORD

Twice a month the Aegean Sea steamer *Leonidas* leaves Athenai (which the tourists call Athens), sails out of Piraeus for a leisurely trip—the boilers are old, the captain one-eyed—sails for its voyage among the group of Cyclades Islands to the east. The *Leonidas* is not a tourist ship, but an old hulk bleeding red rust, with roaches sharing the *soupa avgolemono* served during its greasy meals. Beyond Mykonis it services a smaller island, Peneios; here tourists never come. The few ancient ruins were knocked down by earthquakes centuries ago and covered up by farmlands. The Byzantine ikons it offers are modern fakes made during the stormy season by the natives to sell in Icaros by Madame Vlakhos, the island's business-woman.

The farmers raise almonds, olives, goats, make an over-sharp *feta* cheese out of the goat's milk, and brew *mesucha* brandy from their small black grapes.

There are only three non-Greek residents on the island; a small land mass of steep yellow rocky spurs rising from the fruit-green sea, with hard-worked land in its valleys. Olive trees as ancient as Plato, some claim, and fishermen who bring in octopi and gold-scaled sea bass, and a fish that produces the red Tarana caviarlike roe. The Tarana is all shipped to the mainland for sale except for some small amount that one of the non-Greeks buys, an old man who lives alone with two large sheep dogs and is supposed to be either a professor studying ancient inscriptions on island rocks that were once a temple, or, as Madame Vlakhos suspects, a Mafia chief hiding out.

The other two non-Greeks, "The Americans," are a young man and a young woman who live in an old stone house rented from Soutsos the Innkeeper, a house overlooking Valona Harbor (and the only harbor), where you have to come ashore through the hissing surf, carried on terra-cotta-colored Greek shoulders.

The Americans are a very happy couple, at least there is a great deal of laughter, shouting and rushing around before the day is heated up by that lime-white Greek sun. They walk along the goat paths through the deformed oaks and the vineyards where lizards with jeweled eyelids bask. At the Delphi Inn the Americans drink several glasses of ouzo. Then at the stone house for hours in the afternoon there is heard piano playing, often late into the night, even sometimes before dawn. The mayor of the island, old Basil Pappas, who has been to Jersey City and Copenhagen as a sailor, says "It is very classical music. No one in the big cities goes to hear it without the men in hard shirts and little black ties, the women, all whores, half naked."

The bringing of the piano from Athens by the old steamer *Leonidas* was a great event to the islanders. No such excitement since they killed six German paratroopers who were dropped on the wrong island, threw them down an old abandoned well after they were beaten to death with farm tools while they slept off the native brandy.

It was a huge grand piano and was lifted from the hold with care, hoisted up on deck while the Americans, the young woman and man, went dancing around giving orders and threatening death to anyone who scratched the instrument.

It was brought ashore straddling the largest fishing boat and carried to land by part of the male population, up through the surf. A wall had to be taken down, in part, to get the piano into the stone house.

That night everyone except those dying or giving birth (among the human population) sat in the uncut grass before the stone house while the male American passed out glasses of *mesucha* and inside the American woman played. It was marvelous playing, they all agreed. Sometimes low and painful yet good to hear, sometimes very loud and wild like those whom the gods touch in a special way. It sounded then, too, like weeping. Amazing what one could get out of this instrument, said the mayor. "A tool of wood and strings and ivory teeth."

The two Americans were well liked. They didn't have much money, but it was soon clear they paid for everything. Once a month during the cooler season they would leave the island for a week or so, on the *Leonidas*, and come back with enough to pay their bills. Madame Vlakhos, the agent of the fake ikons—who handled hashish as a sideline—once reported that she had come across the American woman giving piano lessons at a school for girls in Argos. So that must be where the money came from to pay the modest rent on the stone house, and to buy the brandy they drank a lot of, and the cheese, a leg of lamb, the meat and potatoes for the *musaes patates* they lived on.

No one asked just where in the Ou-Ess-Aye they came from. The Americans received no real mail, just some magazines, not even news magazines whose pages the islanders liked to paste up as wallpaper. But no, these were publications about music, about art, about the designing of buildings of glass houses with too many stories and windows.

The Americans were not standoffish, not like the professor (the Mafia chief?) who set his dogs on you and put up a stone wall set with broken glass around his place. No, the Americans—no one called them anything else but the She American and the He American—mixed with the people, tasted the Greek dishes, even once at the August Feast to the Virgin danced in the courtyard of the inn and smashed the dishes on the floor as ritual called for.

Sometimes they would stand arm in arm looking out at the sunsets of the Aegean, a sky colored like gypsy rags, and then go home to the stone house, arms around each other. Perhaps that was their sad hour. There were times when she leaned very heavy against him and he seemed to be whispering in her ear. A very loving couple, said Madame Vlakhos, the ikon agent. "Like Garbo and John Gilbert," she said, remembering the cinemas of her far-distant youth in Istanbul.

Sometimes the Americans stayed in the stone house for days. Not often, but usually when the cold blue winds came down like damn Albanians in the bad months and the clouds were pregnant with darkness. A time when the goats were brought into the kitchens to keep them from being blown away down the cliffs. When the weather cleared the Americans would come outdoors, blinking their eyes, looking pale, and standing very close and affectionate. They would grip each other's hands as if handcuffed together, and at the inn they would have a few glasses of ouzo and go back to the stone house and she would play the piano long into the night. At first only a few people would come and sit on the grass in front of the house to listen. Then a late fisherman, picking at his salt-sore hands, was joined by his wife and growing daughter, the two waiters (and lovers) from the inn, the three men from the coastal station, the fish buyer if on the island. And youths whom it was better not to ask what they were smuggling into Turkey, or bringing back after bribing the coastal station watch. The piano playing would go on and on as the sky sugared over with heavy stars.

Near dawn the whistle of the *Leonidas* might be heard if it was that time of the month. Bringing the news of the world that had not been strained through the static-mumbling radio at the inn. At the stone house the shutters would be closed, the piano silent. The Americans, most likely the two of them were asleep in the big golden oak bed with leaping dolphins carved on the bedposts.

Madame Vlakhos, the ikon agent, who had traveled a

great deal in her youth, would nod her head. "There are three things that can't be hidden: the deep love of two people, a mountain, and someone riding a camel."